Advance Praise for *A Small State's Guide to Influence in World Politics*

"Tom Long has written an invaluable primer for policymakers and diplomats in small states and scholars of International Relations. He offers a new methodological approach to navigating the asymmetries of inter-state relations, based on exhaustive research, a fairly comprehensive bibliography, and a wide-ranging examination of relevant case studies. From a Caribbean perspective, I would have preferred that he had referenced the writings of Shridath Ramphal and Ronald Sanders, but this should not detract from the quality of his research, which is a major contribution to small state diplomacy and IR theory."

Riyad Insanally,
Former Ambassador of Guyana to the USA and
the Organization of American States

"Most books on small states tend to detail a particular issue or the external behavior of states in one region. This book is a remarkable attempt to go beyond this by analyzing the entire spectrum of small states—European as well as in the developing world. Long does this by formulating a detailed pre-theoretical framework through which small state influence attempts can be impartially assessed. The book is notable for both its attention to careful theorizing, as well as the breadth of cases drawn on in support of the author's thesis. Anyone interested in the security and economic behavior of small states will find much to ponder theoretically, and much to draw on descriptively. This book is an important addition to the small state literature, and it deserves to be widely read."

—Jacqueline-Braveboy-Wagner,
City University of New York

BRIDGING THE GAP

Series Editors
James Goldgeier
Bruce Jentleson
Steven Weber

A Small State's Guide to Influence in World Politics

TOM LONG

OXFORD
UNIVERSITY PRESS

OXFORD
UNIVERSITY PRESS

Oxford University Press is a department of the University of Oxford. It furthers
the University's objective of excellence in research, scholarship, and education
by publishing worldwide. Oxford is a registered trade mark of Oxford University
Press in the UK and certain other countries.

Published in the United States of America by Oxford University Press
198 Madison Avenue, New York, NY 10016, United States of America.

Library of Congress Control Number: 2021950184

ISBN 978-0-19-092621-2 (pbk.)
ISBN 978-0-19-092620-5 (hbk.)

DOI: 10.1093/oso/9780190926205.001.0001

Contents

Acknowledgments

In autumn 2015, brimming with enthusiasm after the publication of my first book and the submission of several articles on small states, I suggested this book for the newly created Bridging the Gap series at Oxford University Press. The pitch was for a book of somewhat outlandish breadth, with the aim of saying something meaningful about the international relations of the majority of the world's states. Even more audaciously, I suggested that a book on the often-marginalized topic of small states would offer something for students and scholars of International Relations as well as to policymakers in those many, and diverse, countries. I was fortunate that the audience for that first pitch was Jim Goldgeier, professor, dean, and series editor. Without Jim's encouragement, interest, and questions, this book probably would not have been written—and certainly not in its current form. More generally, Jim deserves recognition and appreciation for his dedication to helping early career scholars, myself included, find paths in academia and beyond.

This book aims to cover an immense topic: the international relations of small states across the world, through several decades, and across multiple issue-areas. To try to grasp such a broad subject matter, I have benefited from—and thoroughly enjoyed—the work of hundreds of scholars who have written about small states, regional dynamics, and the politics and foreign policies of countries that are often overlooked in the so-called "mainstream" of International Relations. Delving into this disparate and diverse literature has been a reminder of the quality, breadth, and vibrancy of research that began quietly constituting "Global International Relations" well before the term was en vogue.

I owe a particular debt of gratitude to several scholars who shared insights and read substantial portions of this early manuscript. For thoughtful comments on early draft chapters, I thank Godfrey Baldacchino, Jacqueline Braveboy-Wagner, Alan Chong, Jack Corbett, Kristin Haugevik, Neal Jesse, Sverrir Steinsson, and Anders Wivel. Several scholars generously responded to my out-of-the-blue emails to share their thoughts and expertise, including Sebastián Bitar, Mahima Duggal, Harsh Pant, David Styan, Haley Swedlund, Christos Vrakopoulos, and Susan Wing. Conversations and correspondence with Brantly Womack were tremendously helpful and encouraging; my own approach to small states and International Relations (IR) owes him a considerable intellectual debt. Parts of this book have been presented in a multitude of venues, including the annual conferences of the International Studies Association, during my time at the University of Reading, and in my visits to the Centro de Investigación y Docencia Económicas (CIDE), in Mexico City. I am honored to have maintained an affiliation with CIDE through the period in which I have worked on this book.

I am also grateful to my managing editor at Oxford University Press, David McBride, and to project editor Emily Benítez for their support and for guiding the initial proposal and, later, the book manuscript through review and production. My thanks to the anonymous reviewers of the proposal and the manuscript for their incisive comments, as well as to other members of Oxford's editorial and production team for their careful attention. My thanks to Lisa Scholey for expert assistance with the preparation of the index and proofing. I also want to express my gratitude to the entire team behind the Bridging the Gap initiative, from which I learned a great deal as a doctoral student and early career researcher, and to the support that worthy initiative has received from the Carnegie Endowment.

This book has largely been written since I joined the Department of Politics and International Studies (PAIS) at the University of Warwick. The department has provided a supportive environment for research and writing since I joined in 2017. A big thank you to my students, especially in my MA modules on rising powers, who have engaged with elements of the arguments and cases of this book in our shared attention to asymmetrical relationships and regional dynamics. In addition, my thanks to my colleagues at Warwick, and in particular to Christopher Browning, whose work on small states and IR is always smart and salient. My colleague and friend Benjamin Smith was a sounding board during the development of many pieces of this book, in frequent conversations as we slowly traversed the canal paths of Warwickshire. I received research assistance for Chapter 5 and comments on early chapters from Brenda Vázquez Uribe, with support from PAIS at the University of Warwick.

It has been a winding road from my first, optimistic proposal of this book on a sunny Washington, DC, day in 2015. That road included a move to England, professional changes, a beautiful new daughter, and (less happily) a global pandemic, during which this book was completed, with some delay. My greatest debt is to my companion on that journey, my wife, Marta Sainz, for her patience, forbearance, and support through it all. Finally, I'd like to dedicate this book to my daughter, Sophie.

1

Introduction

I teach graduate seminars on rising powers in International Relations (IR). In the first class of the year, I ask students which countries they consider "rising powers." China, India, and Brazil are always the most mentioned. But almost every year, a couple students will propose Singapore as a member of the rising powers category. That Singapore—a city-state with a population of 5.6 million—has placed itself, in the minds of some, in a category more commonly associated with the giant BRICS (Brazil, Russia, India, China, and South Africa) is suggestive of its success transcending the role of a "small state." Certainly, counting Singapore as a rising power is a minority position. But the view that it is dynamic and influential is widespread.[1]

Singapore is perhaps an extreme case, but it is hardly the only "small state" that surpasses the limited expectations typically associated with the category. Students sometimes mention Qatar (population 2.8 million) because of its long reach in communications, culture, travel, and finance.[2] Norway, Finland, and Sweden are treated as international paragons for their social democracy, high living standards, and influence in matters of peace and conflict with minimal attention to their size.[3] Switzerland has stayed at the margins of destructive conflicts on its doorstep and emerged as a wealthy global hub. In 2020, Uruguay was feted for its relative success controlling the COVID-19 pandemic despite the catastrophe next door in Brazil.[4] After decades as a sort of U.S. protectorate, Panama has managed, expanded, and benefited from one of the world's most important waterways.[5] Cuba has been a global icon (or villain) since 1959, projecting power through its example, its military, and its medical and sports programs.[6] A frequent development success story, Botswana uses its successes to recast relations with international donors.[7] Though criticized for its authoritarian slide, for decades, Rwanda shaped international narratives about its past

---

[1] One analyst aptly writes of Singapore's "virtual enlargement." Chong, "Small State Soft Power Strategies."
[2] Kamrava, *Qatar: Small State, Big Politics*.
[3] Ingebritsen, *Scandinavia in World Politics*; Pedersen, "Bandwagon for Status."
[4] Taylor, "Uruguay Is Winning against Covid-19. This Is How."
[5] Long, "Putting the Canal on the Map"; Conniff and Bigler, *Modern Panama*.
[6] Brenner and Eisner, *Cuba Libre: A 500-Year Quest for Independence*.
[7] Maipose, "Botswana: The African Success Story."

A Small State's Guide to Influence in World Politics. Tom Long, Oxford University Press. © Oxford University Press 2022. DOI: 10.1093/oso/9780190926205.003.0001

to pursue its own goals, deflect scrutiny, and maintain access to donors and investment.[8]

This book argues that small states can achieve important international goals and exercise influence, but not without overcoming significant constraints. Recognizing such challenges is nothing new, but here we argue that the pattern of opportunities and limitations that small states face does not result from an immutable, distant, and unforgiving international system. Nor can such constraints be understood solely as the result of small states' limited domestic capabilities. Instead, we must understand small states in the context of their relationships with other states, especially their most salient, asymmetrical relationships. These ties exercise the greatest effects on small states' international identities, the definition of their interests, and the options available in pursuit of their goals. The book provides a framework that scholars can use to analyze the international relations of small states. Likewise, policymakers can use this book's approach to assess their state's challenges and identify situations most amenable to change. Small-state policymakers must then match their unique resources with the strategies best suited to achieve influence in asymmetrical relationships.

By all but the narrowest definitions, most of the world's states are small states. Driven by decolonization, imperial dissolution, and secession, the number of small states has increased steadily since World War II. Once created, they are rarely eliminated. Small states constitute majorities in most global and regional international organizations. Dozens have gotten rich in the globalized economy. Conversely, being big is no guarantee of success. Economically, many of the great have been humbled, as a glance at erstwhile members of the 2000s rising power club attests.[9] Nor does heft ensure capability or political competence, as the failures of several large states in confronting the COVID-19 pandemic indicates. Through the end of 2020, there were indications that small states outperformed their larger peers in containing the virus—though wealth offered undeniable advantages in medical capacity, vaccine procurement, and economic recovery.[10]

Despite their often-impressive performance, small states remain overlooked in international affairs, almost by definition. Likewise, they occupy a second-tier status in the study of IR. When small states are addressed, they are often seen through the lens of great-power geopolitics: they become victims, proxies, or pawns. On their own, they appear insignificant. Do small states matter for international relations? This book answers, robustly, in the affirmative. But small states' importance is not well captured by their numbers or their collective UN General Assembly voting weight. More profoundly, small states matter because

---

[8] Swedlund, "Narratives and Negotiations in Foreign Aid."

[9] Zarakol, "'Rise of the Rest.'"

[10] Pedi and Wivel, "Small State Diplomacy after the Corona Crisis"; Briguglio and Azzopardi-Muscat, "Small States and COVID-19."

they constitute, shape, and influence myriad relationships with other states, both large and small. IR's disciplinary fixation on "the" international system, and its related bias toward studying great powers, has distorted our field's ability to appreciate the situations of small states. Within the study of small states, one of the oldest questions has been whether polarity—the number of great powers in the international system—affects small states' prospects.[11] Instead, our relational perspective suggests that whether the international system is unipolar, bipolar, or multipolar at a global level matters less to a small state than the nature of its relationships with a handful of much larger states. If a small state is tightly bound to a much larger one—say, Moldova to Russia in the early 1990s—it is the nature of that asymmetrical relationship that matters, and not whether the large state remains a "pole" in the international system. In short, the satellite view of world politics makes the great powers visible but hides the multitude of states. It does not get us very far in terms of understanding small states' roles in international affairs. This satellite view even obscures most of the *great powers'* international relationships! Yes, great powers care about their relationships with other large states. But they also spend inordinate amounts of time concerned about much smaller locales. Without considering small states, we miss most of the "stuff" that makes up international relations. This gap limits the utility of IR to policymakers and students in much of the world.

In response, many studies of small states have taken a more microscopic approach. They stress the particularities of individual small states, attentive to the domestic and foreign policy characteristics of the world's bantamweights. These studies show how the diversity of small states—and other polities that may not be universally considered states—contributes to the texture of international politics.[12] That is no small thing: some of the most effective challenges to the exaggerated centrality of "anarchy" in IR emerged from closer looks at small states.[13] Individual studies often suggest the difficulties of comparing or drawing lessons across the ambiguous category of "small state." However, studying small states' domestic characteristics and foreign policy concerns in isolation can create an inverse set of blind spots to the satellite view. A microscopic focus on individual small states allows us to perceive their marvels, but proximity blocks out shared issues and constraints.

---

[11] Rothstein, *Alliances and Small Powers*; Keohane, "Lilliputians' Dilemmas"; Handel, *Weak States in the International System*; Maass, *Small States in World Politics*; Jesse and Dreyer, *Small States in the International System*, 21–25. For an early contrary perspective, Elman, "The Foreign Policies of Small States."

[12] There is an extensive literature of this nature, often published in very diverse outlets. But one may get a sense of it in some more prominent volumes that collect such single-country studies: Archer, Bailes, and Wivel, *Small States and International Security*; Hey, *Small States in World Politics*; Goetschel, *Small States inside and outside the European Union*.

[13] Hobson and Sharman, "The Enduring Place of Hierarchy in World Politics."

Instead, this book adopts a relational approach to small states. That focus brings the analysis closer to the concerns of small states' diplomats, who engage less in generalizable grand strategies and more in discrete issues and interactions. We define, theorize, and investigate small states in the context of their salient asymmetrical relationships. In the most prosaic terms, these are the relationships between a small state and a great power. The patterns and dynamics of asymmetry—a significant disparity in material capabilities—shape the international environment that small states face. But not all asymmetrical relationships carry equal weight. For each small state, the importance of a few relationships rises above the rest for reasons of size, proximity, and interdependence. Historical and cultural ties also contribute to salience. These salient asymmetrical relationships shape a small state's international outlook. The very category of the "small state" needs to be understood as relative and relational. Small states are "small" only when juxtaposed to much larger states. Just as asymmetrical relationships constitute small states as "small," they constitute great powers as "great."

States' positions in networks of international relationships affect their identities and interests. Deriving identities and goals from domestic politics alone is inadequate. Relational position affects how states perceive their own goals, as well as the opportunities and constraints they face. From a satellite view, the broad network of relationships is similar in appearance to the "international system." While the "system" constitutes the context for all states' actions, its relational underpinnings matter.[14] A few relationships within the system are salient for given actors, while most blur into the background. A small state's ability to achieve influence—to affect the behavior of other actors to achieve its goals—is conditioned by the dynamics of its salient asymmetrical relationships, not an immutable structure.

For that reason, the idea of asymmetry runs throughout this book. Asymmetry imposes constraints, but the distribution of material resources does not translate neatly into political outcomes in conflict, economic bargaining, international organizations, or the management of transnational challenges.[15] Despite macro-level asymmetries of population, gross domestic product (GDP), or military budgets, small states can develop their own material, social, and ideational resources to pursue their goals. Employing multiple models of might, which we describe as particular-intrinsic, derivative, and collective power, small states retain varied abilities to respond to the opportunities and constraints produced by relational conditions, and to shape those conditions over time.[16]

[14] Here, our treatment of relationships and the "systemic" level follows Jackson and Nexon, "Reclaiming the Social"; Nexon, "Relationalism and New Systems Theory."
[15] Womack, *Asymmetry and International Relationships*; Long, *Latin America Confronts the United States*.
[16] Long, "Small States, Great Power?"

Despite material disadvantages in their salient asymmetrical relationships, many small states have achieved security and economic success. But have they achieved influence? Or does their wellbeing remain dependent on the whims of great powers? Can small states define and pursue their own goals successfully, even when great powers are involved (and perhaps opposed)? To achieve influence in bilateral relationships and beyond, small states must diagnose relational conditions and adapt their strategies. One effect of asymmetry is that a small state's ability to achieve influence will depend heavily on political conditions within large states and on the nature of relationships with those large states. When seeking a particular goal vis-à-vis a great power, a small state should assess the combination of three conditions. First, what is the degree of *divergence* between the small state's preferences and the great power's status quo policy? Second, how *salient* is that issue in the relationship and to the policymakers in the great power? Third, to what extent do the great power's policymakers have *cohesive preferences* about the issue? By systematizing the interaction of these three questions, we present a typological theory in Chapter 3 and highlight relevant strategies for each type of case in Chapter 4.

Who are you calling small?

Before going further, we should clarify the object of our study: the small state. While polities of different sizes have existed throughout history, the idea of the "small state" dates back about two centuries in European diplomatic practice. The emergence of the idea was linked to the practice of great-power diplomacy among the Concert of Europe. States who were excluded from the Concert of Europe's diplomatic deliberations were considered small.[17] Outside of Europe, and in a context where state forms were (re)created through colonization and decolonization, the historical origins of the idea of the "small state" are complex and varied. In Asia, small states are artificial and relatively recent constructions, absent from the historical record before European colonization, Alan Chong argues.[18] With reference to the Middle East, Máté Szalai makes reference to "small regimes" that are "dressed as 'states.'"[19] Even in Europe, one has to accept considerable stretching to designate "small states" through the centuries. Long-run studies often include polities whose statehood would be dubious under today's conceptions.[20] If the idea of the European small state coalesced in the

---

[17] Neumann and Gstöhl, "Lilliputians in Gulliver's World?"
[18] Chong, "Small State Security in Asia."
[19] Szalai, "Small Regimes in the Middle East," 8.
[20] Maass, *Small States in World Politics*. For a discussion of the variety of political forms and their relationships, see Sharman, *Empires of the Weak*.

great-power summit of 1815, it was formalized and globalized over the next century. It remained linked to exclusion from the halls of power. Within Europe,
smallness in population and territory was often linked to omission from key diplomatic councils.[21] Outside of Europe, however, exclusion was justified with reference to civilizational and racial hierarchies instead of by size.[22] These practices
left both large and small non-European states at the margins—even when their
independence and "state-ness" was not in doubt.[23]

The small state is no longer defined by exclusion from international bodies.
Instead of small states being defined by their exclusion, *inclusion* in these international organizations is an important marker in being accepted as a *state*, large or
small. In that context, some states embrace the identity of smallness as a shared
marker in international society.[24] But size—often related to GDP rather than population—remains a criterion for invitations to international affairs. Great-power
clubs, like the G7 and G20, exist and still function as a sort of political and economic
concert. Small groupings of large states—whether the "G2" of China and the United
States, the UN Security Council's (UNSC) Permanent Five (P5), or "the Quad" of
the United States, the European Union, Japan, and Canada—seek an oligopolistic
control of the international agenda. Small states have gained greater access to global
debates than they had in Vienna in 1815 or in the Paris Peace Conference of 1919,
though their formal influence in international councils varies. Some regional and
global organizations grant even the smallest states formal equal weight under one-
state, one-vote rules or consensus-based decision-making. Elsewhere, small states
have membership but infinitesimal voting power; such is the case in the World Bank
and International Monetary Fund. This bifurcation is encapsulated at the core of the
international system: the United Nations reserves special rights and duties to the P5
while giving small states equal rights only in the less powerful General Assembly.

Small states in history

As this picture suggests, defining who counts as a small state is not a simple
matter, and there is no universal approach. The question of definition remains
an area of contention among small-state scholars. In diplomatic practice too,

---

[21] Neumann and Gstöhl, "Lilliputians in Gulliver's World?"; Maass, *Small States in World Politics*.
[22] Keene, "The Standard of 'Civilisation,' the Expansion Thesis and the 19th-Century International Social Space."
[23] Schulz, "Civilisation, Barbarism and the Making of Latin America's Place in 19th-Century International Society."
[24] Browning, "Small, Smart and Salient?"; Corbett, Xu, and Weller, "Norm Entrepreneurship and Diffusion 'from below' in International Organisations."

multiple definitions abound.[25] Before considering modern definitional debates, we consider small states in historical perspective. This helps set the chronological scope for the book's theory and cases. Historical examinations of small states run into several conceptual problems and empirical challenges. First, small polities in earlier eras did not necessarily constitute *states* as we typically conceive them—even in contexts where IR theory long suggested that the units of the international system were fundamentally alike. At the extreme, small states' plight is often described with reference to ancient Greece. Thucydides (c. 400 BCE) depicted how the inhabitants of the small island of Melos insisted on their independence against the mighty Athenians, only to be crushed, killed, and forced into slavery.[26] This became one of IR's favorite morality plays. The lesson? The vulnerability of small states is an eternal element of world politics. But how comparable was Melos to the small states of today?

Much more recently, IR scholar Matthias Maass built a dataset to examine rates of small-state survival from the 1648 Peace of Westphalia—an oft-used marker for the European sovereign state system—until 2016.[27] Explicitly adopting a systemic level of analysis, Maass argues that small states' survival was overwhelmingly affected by several characteristics of international society, and especially by the nature of relations among great powers. Waves of small-state "extinction" accompanied the Napoleonic Wars and German and Italian unifications. Great-power cooperation in the Concert of Europe preserved more small states, but at the price of their autonomy. Remnants of that concert coordinated the dramatic expansion of colonialism in the late nineteenth century, blocking the creation of non-European small states. It was only the eventual great-power embrace of collective security and the U.S.-led expansion of norms against territorial conquest and in favor of self-determination (albeit selectively) that reversed the decline. Then, decolonization boosted the number of small states.[28]

While fascinating, this satellite view gives a skewed picture in several respects. Despite Maass's attempts to delimit his category to units possessing a sufficient degree of "stateness" and autonomy, the roughly 400 European units included at the beginning of the study are a poor fit for the assumption that polities in the international system are functionally "like units." This much has been made clear in IR's deconstruction of the "Westphalian myth" that sovereignty and an anarchic international states system emerged, reasonably complete, in 1648.[29]

[25] For recent extensive review of these definition debates, see Maass, "The Elusive Definition of the Small State"; Archer, Bailes, and Wivel, *Small States and International Security*, chap. 1.
[26] Baldacchino, "Thucydides or Kissinger?"; Hanson, *The Landmark Thucydides*.
[27] Maass, *Small States in World Politics*.
[28] Maass, *Small States in World Politics*. On great powers and the emergence of new states, see Coggins, *Power Politics and State Formation in the Twentieth Century*.
[29] Osiander, "Sovereignty, International Relations, and the Westphalian Myth"; Krasner, *Sovereignty: Organized Hypocrisy*.

The units included during these early centuries exhibited great variations in internal structure and external relations. The very notion of states as rulers over particular territories, for example, developed later.[30] The ideal of statehood as linked to a particular territory "originated in the actions of European polities and rulers outside of Europe rather than within it," especially in the conquest of the Americas. The diffusion and implementation of the state, large or small, was gradual and uneven.[31] Even "throughout the nineteenth century sovereign equality was available only to a minority."[32] Despite medieval European roots, the state as IR knows it today is part and parcel of modernity. Before that, there was a world of disparate polities.[33]

That diversity existed within Europe, with higher levels of interaction and elements of shared culture and religion. Variation in political forms was even greater elsewhere in the world, but these accounts render those polities invisible. This signals a second problem. Most accounts of small states in history are largely populated by European states. The Americas make a gradual entry, while the rest of the world is largely absent until after World War II. The historical definition of "small states" as those excluded from European great powers' discussions means that the entirety of the "non-West" would have been "small" from the perspective of European diplomacy.[34] It implicitly accepts a jaundiced historical perspective as empirical fact. Doing so misses the variety of political forms and the complexities of relations among them. Recent studies of colonialism have illustrated how often it was built on fragmentary and negotiated relations with ensconced political leaders. It was shaped by private and parastatal actors, not just states. At the same time, state-like polities existed before and during European colonialism, but these are overlooked by standard Eurocentric accounts.[35] These polities had complex relations to territory and imperial and other authorities—but so did many European and American polities into the nineteenth century.[36] When tracing the survival, influence, and status of small states across history, one can easily fall into anachronistic treatments of the "small state" by overstating the "stateness" of European polities while overlooking cohesive political

[30] Branch, *The Cartographic State*.
[31] Branch, "'Colonial Reflection' and Territoriality."
[32] Buzan, "Universal Sovereignty," 236.
[33] Onuf, *The Republican Legacy in International Thought*; Harding, "The Origins of the Concept of the State."
[34] Neumann et al., *Small States in International Relations*.
[35] Sharman, *Empires of the Weak*; Dunne and Reus-Smit, *The Globalization of International Society*; Schulz, "Territorial Sovereignty and the End of Inter-Cultural Diplomacy along the 'Southern Frontier.'"
[36] In a more nuanced restatement of this process, Buzan argues that modern sovereignty was "imposed on the rest of the planet" by Europe during the nineteenth century (236). However, this picture looked much different in Latin America, for example, where debates about popular sovereignty, republicanism, and democracy raged during this period. Sanders, *The Vanguard of the Atlantic World*; Sabato, *Republics of the New World*.

organization elsewhere. And if the unit of analysis, the small state, is hardly comparable, then the lessons drawn about how great powers and the international system threaten small states may be the wrong ones.[37]

Ultimately, a more moderate historical frame of reference is better suited to the purposes of understanding small states' international positions and possibilities for influence. The contours of today's system as they concern small states did not really emerge until after World War II. Then, the status of international legal sovereignty, conveyed through recognition by the community of states, began to offer many of the benefits it conveys today.[38] Those include membership in an expanding roster of international organizations, a high degree of existential security through norms against territorial conquest, the erosion of formal empires, access to international development finance, readier participation in international commerce, participation in cooperative security alliances, and more.

We now turn to definitional debates about modern small states. Instead of recapitulating these scholarly disagreements, we summarize three different approaches to the question of "who are you calling small?" The first emphasizes material indicators of size, especially territory, population, and GDP. The second emphasizes perceptions, ideas, and social construction. The third is relational and relative, allowing that a state might be small in one context but not in another. It is from this final approach that this book departs.

Material views

Early attempts to formalize the definition and construct a category of small states often drew on great-power-centric IR theory—but in reverse. If great powers were defined by the preponderance of their populations, territories, militaries, and economies, then small states were defined by the absence of those qualities. Material approaches usually suggest a quantifiable indicator for small states—such as a maximum population or economic size.

Simple, population-based approaches retain sway in international organizations today. The World Bank's Small States Forum references an upper-bound population of 1.5 million, though its fifty members include somewhat larger states like Jamaica (population 2.9 million). This approach closely follows the Commonwealth's small-state definition, which uses a limit of 1.5 million, but also includes "countries with a bigger population but which share many of the

---

[37] Many of these lessons that Maass draws bear similarities to those of the realism-inflected classics on small states. See, especially, Handel, *Weak States in the International System*; Rothstein, *Alliances and Small Powers*.

[38] Archer, Bailes, and Wivel, *Small States and International Security*, chap. 1; Thorhallsson, *Small States and Shelter Theory*, 46–47.

same characteristics."[39] The UN Forum on Small States includes more than 100 states, with populations ranging from tens of thousands to roughly ten million. Population-based definitions and categorizations are common in studies too. David Vital offered the most influential early numerical definition of small states: a population-based limit of 10 million residents for developed states and 20 million for developing states.[40]

These definitions have two lasting attractions, but also two serious limitations.[41] The first attraction is that the focus on material capabilities lends itself to quantification. Quantification, in turn, allows for the creation of clear-cut categories (e.g., a small state has a population of less than ten million people). With a bit greater complexity, one can include and blend different elements of material power by combining quantitative indicators into an index (such as IR's longstanding Composite Index of National Capabilities [CINC]).[42] The second attraction, related to the first, is that the focus on material capabilities appears to offer a more "objective" approach to defining small states.

But a focus on material criteria suffers from drawbacks. Clear-cut indicators allow for categorization, but some arbitrary distinctions are unavoidable. Moving from ten million to ten million plus one has no meaningful effect, but it would lead to a category shift. "The cut-off point between big and small states is rarely self-evident, and, accordingly, there is no consensus on what constitutes a small state in term of power possession . . . leading to confusion over how to recognize a small state when we see one."[43] Of course, one may be more nuanced and think of size as a continuum while still adopting a material and quantifiable approach. Treating size as a continuous variable, with attention to various elements of power, is surely a stronger quantitative approach than neat categorization—though it avoids a clear answer to the question of "who is a small state?"

A second concern is that material indicators tend to have a static quality; if the goal is to use them for time-series analysis, they need to be contextualized for the growth in world population and economy, the number of states, etc. That is a surmountable problem, but the bigger challenge is to account for how shifts in the international environment and more specific contexts change the salience of certain types of capabilities—for example, the growing importance of possessing a sophisticated and diversified economy as compared to controlling a large territory and/or population.

[39] The Commonwealth, "Small States," n.d., accessed November 19, 2020, https://thecommonwealth.org/our-work/small-states.

[40] Vital, *The Inequality of States*.

[41] These are discussed at length in Archer, Bailes, and Wivel, *Small States and International Security*, 5–10.

[42] The CINC is part of the Correlates of War project, and the underlying data are available here: https://correlatesofwar.org/data-sets/national-material-capabilities.

[43] Archer, Bailes, and Wivel, *Small States and International Security*, 8.

A different, materially focused approach departs from the structural realist emphasis on the distribution of capabilities. According to this view, most associated with Kenneth Waltz, the nature of the international system is determined by the distribution of capabilities across states.[44] While Waltz was concerned with large states, other scholars noted that small states' position in the international system can also be understood through that distribution, again, as the inverse of the great powers. Whereas the influence of great powers is "system-determining" in Keohane's words, small states are "system ineffectual."[45] This systemic position also creates different interests. Great powers have wide-ranging or even global concerns; their scope of action is likewise geographically and thematically extensive. Conversely, small states are characterized by a focus on local and subsystemic issues, with little capacity for action beyond their borders or immediate neighbors.

However, this interpretation of small states' interests is anachronistic, to the extent it ever applied generally. Many of small states' salient interests will be local in scope—but that is also the case for medium and large states. Witness India's fixation on Pakistan, or Russia's attention to its "near abroad." Small states' interests and actions can also be global in scope, and perhaps increasingly so. Climate change is an existential, global-level threat for some small island states, and they respond accordingly at the global level. Small states are deeply engaged in global finance, sometimes as tax havens, offshore banking centers, or hubs for money laundering. Small states may have large and transnational diaspora communities. Today, many small states cannot afford to have only local interests.

Ideational views

The limitations of material approaches to small states, as well as divergent theoretical concerns, have led scholars to emphasize ideas, perceptions, and social dynamics.[46] Diverse ideational approaches to definition emphasize how states perceive their own size and socially construct "smallness." Others have noted the importance of self-perception, defining small states as those whose leaders understand themselves as small. Rothstein linked smallness to leaders' perceptions that their own state's security depended on the assistance of others.[47] Goetschel emphasized "the self-perception of the state in respect to its international environment."[48]

---

[44] Waltz, *Theory of International Politics*.

[45] Keohane, "Lilliputians' Dilemmas."

[46] Browning, "Small, Smart and Salient?"; Baldacchino and Wivel, "Small States: Concepts and Theories."

[47] Rothstein, *Alliances and Small Powers*.

[48] Goetschel, "The Foreign and Security Policy Interests of Small States in Today's Europe," 28.

Following this logic, some scholars allow states to define themselves as small (or not) by using the membership of the UN Forum on Small States. Because states opt into the forum, it offers a simple indicator of whether states self-identify as small. Compared to a history in which the term "small state" or "small power" was often a derogatory classification,[49] the trend to positively embrace smallness is intriguing.[50] Since its establishment by Singapore in 1992, the UN Forum on Small States has grown to include 108 states.[51] Under its own Small States Forum, the World Bank convenes some fifty small states to discuss economic and development challenges. In global climate change negotiations, the caucus of self-denominated small island developing states (SIDSs) links members' interests to smallness and environmental vulnerability. Even at the great-power-driven UNSC, the self-identified "Small Five" have called for reform.[52] Such groupings have often tried to contrast "small size" with "big ideas." In doing so, they embrace an international identity that is innately at odds with material power- and size-centric approaches to international hierarchies and pecking orders.

However, as we discuss later, small states' leaders may identify as small in some international environments (e.g., a global forum) but not in others (e.g., a subregional meeting). Another approach goes beyond those mentioned earlier and looks at smallness as a positive element of state identity connected to discursive practices or even performative strategy.[53] Rather than seeing smallness as the perception of limitations, Browning argues that "states may in fact 'choose' to define themselves as small precisely as a strategy of gaining more influence over their environment."[54] These small states seek to be perceived as "small, smart, and salient." In the case of Finland, the identity of smallness has been articulated as allowing certain possibilities for action that diverge from an assumed absence of power.[55] As a definitional approach, this has limited generalizability, but it suggests an important turn in a different respect. Connecting state identities and discourses with state size opens an analysis of how smallness can constitute an ideational base for state action.

---

[49] Maass makes the same point about the German term "Kleinstaaterei," often used to question small states right to exist in the nineteenth century. Maass, *Small States in World Politics*, 72, 123.

[50] Wohlforth et al., "Moral Authority and Status in International Relations"; Corbett, Xu, and Weller, "Norm Entrepreneurship and Diffusion 'from below' in International Organisations."

[51] Chew, "A History of the Forum of Small States"; Ministry of Foreign Affairs, Singapore, "Small states," https://www.mfa.gov.sg/SINGAPORES-FOREIGN-POLICY/International-Issues/Small-States.

[52] The Small Five include Costa Rica, Jordan, Liechtenstein, Singapore, and Switzerland.

[53] Browning, "Small, Smart and Salient?"; de Carvalho and Neumann, *Small State Status Seeking*; Corbett, Xu, and Weller, "Norm Entrepreneurship and Diffusion 'from below' in International Organisations."

[54] Browning, "Small, Smart and Salient?," 673.

[55] Browning, "Small, Smart and Salient?"

Role theory offers another approach that builds on constructivist insights to connect state identity with international position. Scholars in this tradition connect being a "small state" with a specific international role that emerges from the conjunction of domestic factors, like identity and leadership perceptions, and external considerations generated by interactions with other states. Proponents argue that role conceptions better explain the diversity of small states' foreign policies.[56] When domestic factors received greater emphasis than international constraints, small states may resist great powers' expectations for compliance.[57] Guimarães sees the small-state role as constrained by hegemonic discourses, though small states may respond creatively and attempt to reject or subvert such imposed roles.[58] Conceptualizing the "small state" as a role is one way of trying to escape the limitations of purely material categories and systemic determinism, on the one hand, and the difficulties of comparing or accumulating insights from narrative and self-identification, on the other.

Relational views

This book adopts a different approach, though it recognizes the importance of material capabilities, perceptions, and positionality. When we consider who is a small state—and to conceptualize what a small state *is*—we need to think relationally. Relational approaches to conceptualizing the small state permit different theoretical perspectives and research aims. For example, in a largely realist account, Jesse and Dryer develop a relational treatment of state size based on regional hierarchies; those hierarchies are defined by state leaders' perceptions of capabilities. Following this approach, they create a five-part typology: superpowers, great powers, middle powers, small states, and microstates. A small state is "always weak at the global and regional levels, but strong at the sub-regional level."[59]

Asymmetrical relationships constitute small states, and the perceptions and dynamics of asymmetry shape the nature of a small state's international relations. Along these lines, we build on Archer et al., who "define a small state as the weaker part in an asymmetric relationship," while advocating a "qualitative and relational" approach. This is an important step, though they did not develop theoretically the implications of this reconceptualization.[60] More recently,

[56] Gigleux, "Explaining the Diversity of Small States' Foreign Policies through Role Theory."
[57] Simon, "When David Fights Goliath."
[58] Guimarães, A Theory of Master Role Transition.
[59] Jesse and Dreyer, Small States in the International System, 10.
[60] Archer, Bailes, and Wivel, Small States and International Security, 9. The implications of that definition were not always clear in the ensuing case study chapters, written by a variety of contributors.

Baldacchino and Wivel have expanded on this relational approach, arguing that for small states, "the consequences of limited capacity are exacerbated by power asymmetry, leaving small states to struggle with being price and policy takers overall."[61] We connect their relational and contextual emphasis with greater theoretical engagement with the dynamics of asymmetry.[62]

There is a legacy for such relational approaches in the study of small states, though deeper theorization of asymmetry is a more recent development. Asymmetry theory aligns with earlier arguments by Robert Rothstein and Maurice East that small states' perspectives on world politics differed in fundamental respects from those of great powers.[63] While this point of difference has been validated by much ensuing scholarship on small states, it assumes a mutually exclusive categorization of great and small. As elaborated by Brantly Womack, asymmetry theory does not turn on defining any given state as large or small; instead, its starting point is to treat size as a continuum of relations among states. Womack argues that material capabilities matter but must be understood within a social and relational context. Differences in material capabilities shape how small and large states perceive one another. Because of these differences, small and large states understand their relationships with one another in fundamentally different ways. Where states' relationships are characterized by unmistakable disparities in material capabilities, patterns of asymmetry will emerge. Asymmetry creates disparate perceptions, interests, and possibilities for actions, Womack argues. It is the *relational position* of the relatively weaker state that distinguishes it from the stronger state; this suggests something beyond Rothstein's point that small states are not simply "great powers writ small." When one considers positionality in this way, it makes sense that New Zealand, for example, may be a small state on the global stage while seeming quite large to its Pacific Island neighbors.[64]

Initially, it may seem that such a contextual and relational approach is no more amenable to comparison and cumulation than one based in self-identification. In a sense, that is correct—our approach does not sort states into fixed categories, as the example of New Zealand suggests. However, it does allow for the comparison of *relationships* and of how small states respond to similar combinations of relational positions and conditions. Explaining and illustrating how this works will be the major task of this book.

---

[61] Baldacchino and Wivel, "Small States: Concepts and Theories," 7.

[62] Womack, *Asymmetry and International Relationships*; Musgrave, "Asymmetry, Hierarchy, and the Ecclesiastes Trap"; Long, *Latin America Confronts the United States*; Oh, "Power Asymmetry and Threat Points."

[63] Womack, *Asymmetry and International Relationships*; Rothstein, *Alliances and Small Powers*; East, "Size and Foreign Policy Behavior."

[64] Brady, *Small States and the Changing Global Order: New Zealand Faces the Future.*

Organization and conclusions

The following chapters will build on asymmetrical and relational theories of IR to explore the situation of small states in international politics, propose a theory that integrates the constraints and possibilities small states face, describe possible strategies that respond to those conditions, and assess that theory in the light of some twenty short case studies.

Chapter 2 places small states within the broadest international context. Instead of characterizing the international system by the number of great powers and the ties among them, we explain world politics as a composite of myriad relationships. For any given small state, a handful of those relationships will be especially salient; usually, the most salient relationships will be asymmetrical. Great-power politics, institutionalization, economic governance, and the normative environment also shape the international background in which these relationships develop, from the perspectives of small states. Chapter 3 focuses on how small states' positions in international relationships impose certain constraints, while also creating opportunities to achieve goals. Small states are not all the same, of course, nor are they defined only by their positionalities. For that reason, we discuss the internal conditions and our assumptions about small states' domestic characteristics as they relate to the international sphere. Upon that foundation, we develop our typological theory about how small states' relationships affect their abilities to pursue goals. This framework should help policymakers diagnose their own states' relationships and opportunities. In the final theoretical chapter, Chapter 4, we build on asymmetry theory and our typological theory to detail certain foreign policy strategies for the pursuit of international goals by small states. These strategies emerge from sources of power that, while not exclusive to small states, are of greater relative importance to the weaker party in asymmetrical relationships. Again, our hope is that this provides tools for policymakers to match their diagnosis with a response.

Asymmetry stands at the core of our analysis and at the heart of our conceptualization of the small state. It also forms the core of our case studies in Chapters 5 and 6, which examine how small states in Africa, the Americas, Asia, and Europe pursue their security and economic policy goals in the context of asymmetrical relationships. Both the number and organization of the case studies are somewhat unusual within IR, so it merits a word of explanation. Each case-study chapter is thematic. Chapter 5 explores issues of international security; Chapter 6, international political economy; and Chapter 7, international institutions, law, and norms. Within Chapters 5 and 6, there is a nested organization, with a pair of case studies from each of the four regions mentioned previously. Each pair includes one case study of a specific foreign policy issue where the small state was deemed to have achieved its goal and one where the small state largely failed to achieve its goal. Each individual case in these two chapters situates the small state's foreign policy within salient asymmetrical relationships. In that sense, each case study addresses the ties between a small state and (at least one) major power. The nested organization allows for variation in issue areas, regions, countries (small and large), and outcomes, providing a broad base of evidence for the theory. The final case chapter, Chapter 7, loosens the more narrowly dyadic organization of evidence to address issues of a more diffuse scope: climate change, human rights, regional organizations, and global public health. These topics bring additional evidence to bear on our treatment of the global environment as emphasized in Chapter 2. They also provide greater scope for assessing how small states' relations with one another—not just with large states—matter. The concluding Chapter 8 draws out comparisons from across our cases, assesses the theory in light of this evidence, and suggests applications for research and policy.

This description of the book's organization should give some sense of the task ahead. It goes without saying, but no single author can be an expert in all small states, regions, or issues, so I have relied on the work and advice of dozens of scholars to construct my case studies and to inform my theory. My hope is that this tradeoff, exchanging country-level depth for cross-regional breadth, furthers the comparative study of small states and their asymmetrical relationships. Likewise, I hope my theoretical approach sheds light on small states' quests for influence in the interstices of asymmetrical relationships, and in doing so brings the study of small states into closer conversation with other debates in IR theory. After all, this is not a story of small states in isolation. It is the story of jousting with giants on the uneven playing field of international politics over matters as fundamental as security, wealth, and the nature of international society.

2

Small States, Big World

From what vantage point should one view small states? For decades, International Relations (IR) scholars' answer to this question helped paint a picture in which small states were largely irrelevant to global affairs. To understand the world's "high politics," many IR scholars agreed, one needed a broad view that encompassed as much of the globe as possible. In this structural perspective, the largest actors dominate the panorama. In doing so, they hide many others in their shadows. But when we change from a systemic to a relational approach, the plurality and diversity of international actors come into focus.

The field of IR has suffered from a great-power bias, which likewise blurred IR's vision of small states. IR's main theories, particularly during the field's Cold War consolidation, were great-power-centric. As a result of Anglo-American dominance, Cold War concerns, and theoretical formalization from the late 1950s through the 1980s, IR's emphasis on the systemic level of analysis became more explicit.[1] The number of great powers and their interactions were the primary concern; small states disappeared from canonical theory. As IR's most influential theorist of the Cold War period argued, "It would be . . . ridiculous to construct a theory of international politics based on Malaysia and Costa Rica. . . . A general theory of international politics is necessarily based on the great powers."[2] The goal of this book is not to develop a "general theory of international politics," but even so, one might ask, what could a supposedly "general" theory so indifferent to the experiences of middle-sized Malaysia or smaller Costa Rica tell us about the conditions of the vast majority of the world's countries?

Small states in International Relations theory

Though structural realism, IR's long-dominant theory, was developed with minimal reference to small states, it nonetheless exercises great influence on how we understand them.[3] A systemic level has much to recommend it; it allows

---

[1] Waltz, *Man, the State, and War.*

[2] Waltz, *Theory of International Politics*, 73, qtd. in Kang, "Getting Asia Wrong."

[3] A classic example is Handel, *Weak States in the International System*. A recent one is Maass, *Small States in World Politics*. For a discussion, see Jesse and Dreyer, *Small States in the International System*, chap. 2.

A Small State's Guide to Influence in World Politics. Tom Long, Oxford University Press. © Oxford University Press 2022. DOI: 10.1093/oso/9780190926205.003.0002

for broad claims that apply, at least in a general sense, no matter where one sits in that system. It is hard to deny that the international system—and the great powers that define it—matter a great deal for small states. As the often-invoked proverb goes: when the elephants fight, it is the grass that suffers most. Systemic studies of small states often ask, in essence, how are small states affected by the relations among the elephants of international politics? This question especially preoccupies studies concerned with the survival of small states, painting the international system as an unforgiving place for its smallest members. This view is founded in core realist assumptions that power—especially military capabilities—matters most in world politics. For systemic realists, the lack of a recognized and effective central authority—international anarchy—is the key ordering principle of international life. Survival is always at stake. In this "self-help" world, a premium is placed on obtaining, possessing, and exercising power—exactly what small states cannot do. Defined by their lack of power, small states' very existence is tenuous. The stylized fact of existential precarity was perhaps the most common feature of the early IR literature on small states.[4]

When detached from micro-level foundations, the systemic view led to important errors of analysis and prediction. As noted, systemic IR theory long held that anarchy was the distinguishing feature of international relations. From the perspective of relations among great powers, this claim is plausible.[5] However, when international politics is examined from the perspective of the majority of the world's states—let alone nonstate actors—that plausibility crumbles. Dynamics of asymmetry and varieties of hierarchical relations come to the fore.[6] By focusing so heavily on great powers, IR suffered from decades of biased case selection, where systemic theories were developed with reference to a handful of largely European states and then presumed to be applicable to all.[7]

It would be wrong to characterize all early studies as presenting small states as helpless. Rothstein starts his classic 1968 study, *Alliances and Small Powers*, with the observation that "Small Powers are something more than or different than Great Powers writ small." That point would gain renewed significance in later decades, but Rothstein's book focuses on the alliance options of small states in proximity to great powers, essentially asking when different types of balancing behaviors may occur.[8] Rothstein wrote before the solidification of structural

---

[4] Vital, *The Inequality of States*; Vital, *The Survival of Small States*; Rothstein, *Alliances and Small Powers*; Handel, *Weak States in the International System*; Fox, *The Power of Small States*; Singer, *Weak States in a World of Power*.

[5] Milner, "The Assumption of Anarchy in International Relations Theory"; Donnelly, "The Discourse of Anarchy in IR."

[6] Mcconaughey, Musgrave, and Nexon, "Beyond Anarchy"; Womack, *Asymmetry and International Relationships*; Musgrave, "Asymmetry, Hierarchy, and the Ecclesiastes Trap."

[7] Sharman, "Sovereignty at the Extremes."

[8] Rothstein, *Alliances and Small Powers*.

realism as IR's leading paradigm, and his study shows the analytical flexibility and historical orientation of Morgenthau's classical realism.[9] In contrast, the influence of Kenneth Waltz's systemic theory is clear from the first page of Michael Handel's influential 1981 book *Weak States in the International System*. Handel grants less attention to differences in *kind* between small and large states, emphasizing instead the distribution of material capabilities. For Handel, the international system is a threatening environment for small states, forcing them to prioritize survival. Domestic factors are relatively unimportant.[10] Cold War–era studies of small states discussed moments of agency and foreign policy success, but systemic constraints loomed large. The realism-inspired emphasis on existential threats to small states overlooked the ways in which tiny polities—sometimes largely unarmed—survived across various eras.[11]

A countercurrent has evolved toward greater appreciation—cynics might say overstatement—of small states' influence. Recent works often invoke the 1959 book *The Power of Small States* by Annette Baker Fox. In her study of small states' efforts to stay out of World War II, Fox emphasized both geographical location and agency, embodied in far-sighted diplomacy.[12] This was small-state agency in a most inauspicious context—the largest war in history is hardly representative—but Fox found diverse outcomes for small states. While there have been some periods in European history where the dire logic of existential threat applied to many small polities—like the Napoleonic wars and the opening years of World War II[13]—generalizing from those extraordinary conditions can misstate the pressures faced by most small states in a world where the shadow of great-power war has receded.

IR theory's paradigmatic turn to liberalism and, later, constructivism suggested greater possibilities for small states. Though his systemic definitional approach emphasized small states' irrelevance, elsewhere the liberal institutionalist Robert Keohane underscored the "big influence of small allies." When small states sought narrower goals vis-à-vis the United States, through leveraging particular assets and exploiting interdependence, they could be quite effective.[14] Keohane could "see" this influence precisely because he loosened his own systemic assumptions and adopted a relational perspective with a consideration of domestic politics. Liberals underscored that power asymmetries in interdependent relationships create greater vulnerabilities for the smaller side. Still, work on complex interdependence opened possibilities for small-state

---

[9] Morgenthau, *Politics among Nations*.
[10] Handel, *Weak States in the International System*.
[11] Sharman, "War, Selection, and Micro-States."
[12] Though showing the category's flexibility, this study included states as large as Spain. Fox, *The Power of Small States*.
[13] Maass, *Small States in World Politics*; Handel, *Weak States in the International System*.
[14] Keohane, "The Big Influence of Small Allies."

influence by facilitating a relational perspective and allowing for the malleability and diversity of states' preferences. It also recognized that issues beyond security were salient to most states, most of the time.[15]

Cold War alliances permitted possibilities for "big influence" through pressuring patrons. But after the fall of the Soviet Union, many foresaw opportunities for small states to make an impact through participation in international organizations (IOs) and by advancing international norms.[16] New approaches to small states emerged from political shifts and theoretical turns. The post–World War II period has been marked by an extraordinary absence of direct war between great powers (though plenty of indirect and other conflict in which small states have been implicated).[17] Though great-power interventions continue, states very rarely "die" anymore;[18] their survival is protected by norms and international law against territorial conquest[19] and a strong bias toward "extantism" (the continuation of existing states).[20] International conditions during the first two decades after the Cold War favored small states' survival and even the creation of units of smaller size, as seen in the emergence of new states like Timor-Leste or (more contentiously) Kosovo, and the potential for new small states from Scotland to Somaliland.[21] The rise of China and other non–North Atlantic powers has underscored the importance of understanding how small states relate to their large and rising neighbors—a fundamental element of many of the case studies later in this book. The increasingly evident diffusion of power away from the United States and Europe has reignited debate over whether the future will resemble the past in terms of frequency and intensity of great-power conflict.[22] One may ask whether the recent decades of relative security for small states represent a real change or merely an aberration in a longer history of conflict—a question to which we will return later.

---

[15] The classic statement is Keohane and Nye, *Power and Interdependence*. There are many applications to small states, including Maris and Sklias, "European Integration and Asymmetric Power"; Garrison and Abdurahmonov, "Explaining the Central Asian Energy Game."

[16] This literature is now immense (though still heavily European). Important contributions include Ingebritsen, "Norm Entrepreneurs"; Panke, *Small States in the European Union*; Archer, Bailes, and Wivel, *Small States and International Security*; Panke and Gurol, "Small States: Challenges and Coping Strategies in the UN General Assembly"; Björkdahl, "Norm Advocacy."

[17] Goertz, Diehl, and Balas, *The Puzzle of Peace*; Freedman, "The Rise and Fall of Great Power Wars"; Goldstein, *Winning the War on War*.

[18] Fazal, *State Death*.

[19] Hathaway and Shapiro, *The Internationalists*; Brooks, "The Globalization of Production and the Changing Benefits of Conquest."

[20] Bartmann, "Meeting the Needs of Microstate Security."

[21] Alesina and Spolaore, *The Size of Nations*; Maass, *Small States in World Politics*; Corbett, "Territory, Islandness, and the Secessionist Imaginary."

[22] Kang, "Hierarchy, Balancing, and Empirical Puzzles in Asian International Relations"; Brooks and Wohlforth, "The Rise and Fall of the Great Powers in the Twenty-First Century"; Layne, "This Time It's Real"; Stuenkel, *Post-Western World*.

With respect to IR theory, the growing influence of constructivism during the 1990s encouraged scholars to consider a greater variety of actors and their nuanced forms of power and influence. As Corbett et al. note: "The key difference between the 1960s and 1970s literature and more recent studies of European small states is the shift from treating these countries as 'objects' in the international system to studying them as 'subjects' capable of exercising agency in creative ways."[23] Initially, the liberal and constructivist focus on small states and international institutions and norms encouraged extensive study of small states in Europe. Until quite recently, there had been much more limited systematic or comparative attention to small states elsewhere.[24] Calls for "Global IR" have illuminated Eurocentric and great-power biases in the field, while bringing actors, theories, and histories from the Global South into focus.[25] As Global IR's proponents might suggest, the study of small states and IR broadly have much to gain through growing global engagement, and the study of small states provides a point of entry to IR debates for scholars beyond North America and Europe.[26]

If an earlier generation of studies largely argued that small states faced a choice between ceding independence and futile resistance to great-power domination, the recent boom in small-states scholarship emphasizes security, agency, and influence. Studies have de-emphasized the international system, instead illustrating how unique domestic conditions matter for small states.[27] With a bit of luck and a great deal of pluck, it seems, small states can "punch above their weight," to use one of the field's favored clichés. Where constraints are recognized, apart from complex geopolitical environments,[28] attention has often been paid to issues like limited diplomatic-bureaucratic capacity. If the systemic approach inspired by structural realism undervalued small states or exaggerated the ubiquity of the threats they faced, the domestic-level foreign policy approach risks understating international constraints.

[23] Corbett et al., "Climate Governance, Policy Entrepreneurs and Small States," 827.

[24] Archer, Bailes, and Wivel, *Small States and International Security*; Baldacchino and Wivel, *Handbook on the Politics of Small States*.

[25] Acharya and Buzan, *The Making of Global International Relations*; Tickner and Smith, *International Relations from the Global South*.

[26] The range of global contributions and coverage of the *Small States & Territories* journal, created in 2018, illustrates this engagement: https://www.um.edu.mt/sst. Relatively early works along these lines include Cooper and Shaw, *The Diplomacies of Small States*; Hey, *Small States in World Politics*.

[27] Corbett and Veenendaal, *Democracy in Small States*; Corbett and Veenendaal, "Why Small States Are Beautiful"; Baldacchino, "Small States: Challenges of Political Economy."

[28] Adhikari, "A Small State between Two Major Powers"; Oskanian, "The Balance Strikes Back."

Setting the scene: Asymmetrical theory and international context

This book's theory and cases emphasize asymmetrical relationships. However, bilateral relationships exist within a broader international context. In our perspective, the international system is not some detached and distant structure; instead, it emerges from the accumulation and accretion of relationships over time, forging a durable network with bonds of varying intensity. What is commonly called the international system or international society emerges from the patterns of relationships among states.[29] Our approach zooms in on specific relationships within that network, without forgetting that they are part of a broader context.[30] Small states need to take this context into account in making decisions and designing foreign policy strategies. In the short term, for the policymakers of small states, the international system appears to be an immutable reality. Can one imagine a small-state leader declaring, as an unnamed U.S. official once did, that "when we act, we create our own reality"?[31] Gradually and collectively, small states shape international society too, but unlike for the largest powers, changing international "reality" is not a plausible short-term goal.

In general terms, the international context has grown more beneficial to small states' survival and success since World War II. If there is an overriding factor that permits the perceived growth in small states' numbers and influence, it is this: few small states today worry about imminent threats to their survival. (The same may not apply to the *rulers* of small states, but that is a somewhat different matter.) Some of those that harbor existential dread are enmeshed in supportive networks: Baltic states may fear Russia, but their efforts are geared toward bolstering North Atlantic Treaty Organization (NATO) commitments rather than preparing for an imminent assault.[32] Today's more permissive international context emerges from patterns of relations among great powers, as well as between great powers and small states, and from the network of relationships among smaller states. An international context that permits the survival of small states is one thing; one that is conducive to their influence and/or wellbeing is another. There is significant evidence that this is also the case.

---

[29] Nexon, "Relationalism and New Systems Theory," 113–14.

[30] When one's focus is on a shorter period of time, it makes sense to pragmatically treat these lasting patterns as structural. See Nexon, "Relationalism and New Systems Theory"; Jackson and Nexon, "Reclaiming the Social."

[31] The quotation originates in Ron Suskind, "Faith, Certainty and the Presidency of George W. Bush," October 17, 2004, *New York Times Magazine.*

[32] Crandall, "Soft Security Threats and Small States"; Hamilton, "The Baltics: Still Punching Above Their Weight"; Bailes, Rickli, and Thorhallsson, "Small States, Survival and Strategy"; Archer, "The Nordic States and Security."

Not all small states are thriving, and many attempts at influence fail. Most small-state policymakers could offer lists of constraints and disappointments. However, variation in success should be expected in an international system composed of a great variety of relationships. By studying some of the world's very small states, Sharman concludes that today's "permissive" international environment allows states as small as Nauru (population 12,704) and the Seychelles (population 96,762) a great degree of latitude to make "strategic choices" in their relations with more powerful states and about how they position themselves internationally. Today's international system protects the security of even very small states, most of the time, while giving them access to the international economic safety net of development assistance and bailout loans.[33] It is imperfect and conditional, but it matters tremendously. However, small states' differing positions mean that some will face greater constraints while others enjoy more security and opportunity. Several aspects of the international system shape small states' agency—which we define as their ability to articulate their identity and interests and to make meaningful (though not unfettered) choices about how to pursue those interests. Because small states possess a degree of choice, some paths will be successful while others will not, even under similar international conditions. Analyzing these systemic features is a first step for policymakers looking to diagnose their state's international position and possibilities.

Great-power politics

Does the international stratosphere of great-power polarity matter today, or is systemic stability at a global level less important than relations with powerful states closer to home? According to most systemic IR theories, the nature of an international system is defined by the number of great powers and the nature of the relations among them. There is no simple answer about what system is preferable for small states. Debates about whether systems with one, two, or many dominant powers are most war-prone remain unresolved; given the limited universe of cases provided by history, they are probably unsolvable.[34] In any case, today's emerging system of multiple major powers in different world regions, but with profound and immediate connection and interdependence, is essentially unprecedented.[35] Instead of assessing the prospects for great-power

---

[33] Sharman, "Sovereignty at the Extremes." Population figures for 2018, World Bank.
[34] Mearsheimer, "Back to the Future"; Waltz, *Theory of International Politics*; Deutsch and Singer, "Multipolar Power Systems and International Stability"; Gaddis, "The Long Peace."
[35] Though Europeans certainly interposed themselves in local balances of power starting with the fifteenth-century expansion, as Sharman notes. On the broader point of global systemic novelty, see Acharya, *The End of American World Order*; Kupchan, *No One's World*.

accommodation or conflict, we identify aspects of the increasingly multipolar international system of greatest relevance for small states.

Seen through the lens of great-power politics, the international system has undergone rapid shifts during the past century. In most instances, system stability is preferable to tumult for small states, regardless of polarity.[36] The multipolar great-power competition of the early twentieth century, first centered on Europe and then spreading across the Atlantic and Pacific, is sufficient reminder of the risks that international turbulence creates for small states. Competition between great powers is often seen as a threat to small states' security; while competition can provide a potential source of leverage, it increases risks. The Concert of Europe created and erased several small states in the name of the greater balance of power. Belgium's existence, as well as its suffering during the world wars, offers a testament to the sword of Damocles created by neighboring great powers. During the Cold War, both the United States and the Soviet Union undermined the sovereignty and security of numerous smaller states; they also showered many with benefits in a competition for their allegiance.[37] The great-power dynamics of the Cold War reshaped incentives and alignments for small states everywhere, often contributing venom and resources to local conflicts. Competitive bipolarity was more permissive of small state emergence than the colonial, multipolar system that preceded it. The global level was intertwined with nationalism in many of the struggles that produced small states from decolonization in Africa, Asia, and the Caribbean.[38] However, to see small states' policies as determined by bipolarity repeats the flawed, Manichean analysis of many U.S. and Soviet policymakers who struggled to differentiate national causes from the political control of their rival. The Cold War shaped and constrained small states' choices more often than it directly determined them, though the intensity of those constraints varied tremendously.

From the vantage of great-power politics, the end of the Cold War produced an uncontested United States. Did small states fare better in this period of U.S. unipolarity? The period saw an expansion in the number of small states, including through the at times bloody re-emergence of states from the former Soviet Union and Yugoslavia. Elsewhere, a U.S.-led and internationally backed military campaign preserved the sovereignty of a small state, Kuwait, against invasion; at nearly the same moment, the United States invaded small Panama to depose its authoritarian leader.[39] Unipolarity facilitated expanding globalization,

---

[36] The exception might be systems that are stable in terms of polarity but with an expanding hegemon that threatens small states' independence. For historical examples of such systems, see Kaufman, Little, and Wohlforth, *The Balance of Power in World History*.

[37] Westad, *The Global Cold War*; Brands, *Latin America's Cold War*.

[38] Suri, "The Cold War, Decolonization, and Global Social Awakenings"; Westad, *The Global Cold War*.

[39] Engel, "A Better World . . . but Don't Get Carried Away."

open markets, and regional integration, which increased both opportunities and volatility for small states. U.S. military aid cuts meant that some small states, especially in Europe, had to take on additional security functions; but the Cold War's end initially granted greater security at a lower price.[40] Unipolarity offered benefits to many small states through international openness and stability—alongside harsh repercussions for those that crossed the lone superpower.[41]

If the 1990s seemed to encapsulate the possible benefits of U.S. unipolarity for small states, the 2000s highlighted the risks created by the United States' global centrality and power.[42] For U.S. policymakers, the attacks of September 11, 2001, suggested that dangers could emanate from corners of the map they had long overlooked.[43] For other parts of the world, the U.S. response to the attacks upset regional security dynamics.[44] Small states were swept into the U.S.-led "global war on terrorism," which created possible benefits but also demanded adherence to U.S. policies.[45] For states deemed "weak" or "failing," sovereignty and regime stability was suddenly threatened.[46] Unipolarity might not be so benign, depending on where one sat. The U.S.-led "war on terror" subjected some small states to intervention and hegemonic discipline, while also providing opportunities for others—including authoritarians initially out of favor in the "unipolar moment"—to attract external support for their own objectives.[47] Traditional indicators of state "size" became less relevant, while state capacity and policy alignment became more important.

The decade ended with a financial crisis that emanated outward from the United States with lasting effects for the global economy. Small and medium states were reminded how decisions at the U.S. Federal Reserve and Treasury Department could suddenly erode their effective policy autonomy. Even high-income small states like Iceland, Ireland, and Greece suffered severe blows, with limited economic policy options to shield themselves.[48] The crisis put an exclamation mark on global shifts in power marked by the rise of China and a general diffusion of relative economic capabilities away from the North Atlantic. If the

---

[40] Archer, "The Nordic States and Security"; Rickli, "European Small States' Military Policies after the Cold War."

[41] Ikenberry, Mastanduno, and Wohlforth, "Unipolarity, State Behavior, and Systemic Consequences"; Jervis, "Unipolarity: A Structural Perspective"; Cooley and Nexon, *Exit from Hegemony*, 72–73.

[42] Chollet and Goldgeier, *America between the Wars.*

[43] An influential statement of this view comes from Robert Kagan. For example, see Kagan, "End of Dreams, Return of History."

[44] Betts, "The Soft Underbelly of American Primacy."

[45] Hinnebusch, "The Iraq War and International Relations"; Emerson, "Radical Neglect?"

[46] Barnett, *The Pentagon's New Map.*

[47] Jourde, "The International Relations of Small Neoauthoritarian States"; Cooley, *Great Games, Local Rules*; Cooley and Nexon, "'The Empire Will Compensate You.'"

[48] Broome, "Negotiating Crisis"; Verdun, "Small States and the Global Economic Crisis."

age of the U.S. unipolarity was not entirely over, it was suddenly easy to imagine its conclusion.[49]

The effects for small states have been significant. The rise of China bound many small states across Asia to its production networks. U.S. retrenchment facilitated Chinese economic expansion in numerous African and South American states.[50] For the moment, the effects are mixed. Some small states in South Asia have managed to maintain substantial policy autonomy and attract astounding levels of investment and aid from India and China, as the two giants conduct a "managed rivalry," but such freedom may be tenuous.[51] Similar dynamics are at work in the Pacific as a result of strategic competition between China and the United States and its ally Australia.

While some commentators have portrayed the power shift of the last fifteen years as "back to the future," either as a U.S.-China cold war or a renewal of pre–World War II multipolar competition, these analogies fall short. As Acharya notes, the geographical distribution of major powers matters; previous iterations of competitive multipolarity were squeezed in and around Europe or extrapolated through overseas imperial competition; today multiple powers are rising across the globe, providing more breathing room.[52] The locus of rising powers is in Asia between China, India, and Russia; the United States enjoys a privileged geographical position. Technological, normative, and institutional changes—as well as the advent of nuclear weapons—suggest a different dynamic than past multilateral eras too. Most small states will retain options to resist great powers' demands, even as large states deploy pressure and incentives to cajole and attract the followership of small states.[53]

Many of the systemic challenges states now face are not defined by traditional great-power competition. Climate change, pandemics, financial crises, expanding migration, and the Arab Spring have dominated headlines and leaders' attention for the past decade, but they are not easily understood through the lens of great-power competition. Such issues will shape the next decade as well. Climate change is the clearest example of a problem where great powers may compete or cooperate, but not to win small states' allegiances. Small states will be deeply affected by great powers' climate actions—especially their

[49] Porter, *The False Promise of Liberal Order*; Mearsheimer, "Bound to Fail"; Acharya, *The End of American World Order*.

[50] Tuman and Shirali, "The Political Economy of Chinese Foreign Direct Investment in Developing Areas"; Urdinez et al., "Chinese Economic Statecraft and US Hegemony in Latin America"; Brautigam, *The Dragon's Gift: The Real Story of China in Africa*.

[51] Paul, "When Balance of Power Meets Globalization"; see also Goh, "Great Powers and Hierarchical Order in Southeast Asia."

[52] Acharya, *The End of American World Order*.

[53] Williams, Lobell, and Jesse, *Beyond Great Powers and Hegemons*.

domestic environmental and energy policies—but thinking of those effects in terms of blocs or alliances would miss the point.

In short, changes in polarity over the past century have had mixed effects on small states' wellbeing and influence. There are no universal laws suggesting what system is "better" for small states. Instead, this will vary depending on states' relationships, locations, levels of development, and goals. Still, there are lessons to be learned, though these lessons must be contextualized to the situations of particular small states. We underscore four general propositions that suggest where to focus when considering the effect of the international system on a given small state.

1. **The nature of competition, not the number of competitors.** While structural realism debated the effects of the number of great-power competitors, we suggest that for small states, the nature of great-power competition is more important.

2. **Private versus club and public goods.** Changing power distributions will reshape elements of global order, including the creation of private, club, and public goods.[54] Private goods are typified by bilateral patron-client relationships, where benefits can be offered or withheld to coerce changes in small-state behavior.[55] Club goods offer benefits to a select group, perhaps by invitation or by virtue of geography. Many "regional public goods" are in fact club goods. In the extreme, club goods can encourage regional blocs; more often they will be regional free trade agreements or customs unions.[56] Though some states are (or can be) excluded, club goods cannot be withdrawn as easily as private goods. True public goods are available to all states. While the United States proclaims itself as a provider of global public goods, oftentimes, these goods were restricted to members of the club. During the 1990s, the club got bigger, and some of the goods became increasingly public.[57] Increasing multipolarity will tend to increase club goods at the expense of public goods. Even in an environment of muted security competition, China and the United States are setting the groundwork for competing clubs.[58] While joining a club appears attractive, often providing direct and higher-profile benefits, a system of public goods

---

[54] Adams and McCormick, "Private Goods, Club Goods, and Public Goods as a Continuum."

[55] This follows the argument of Hirschman, *National Power and the Structure of Foreign Trade*.

[56] Estevadeordal and Goodman, *21st Century Cooperation*; Sandler, "Regional Public Goods and International Organizations."

[57] Ikenberry, *Liberal Leviathan*.

[58] The Belt and Road Initiative has characteristics of such a club, while under the Trump administration, the willingness to provide any international goods has been repeatedly questioned. Jervis et al., *Chaos in the Liberal Order*; Ferdinand, "Westward Ho"; Nordin and Weissmann, "Will Trump Make China Great Again?"

better serves small states. Club goods may foster economic dependence and, long term, reshape a small state's interests in accordance with those of the great power.[59]

3. **Capacity, not size.** In previous multipolar eras, size was seen as the fundamental determinant of a state's importance. That is changing. Small but capable states now demonstrate resilience and international influence, while larger and weak states struggle to cope with multipolar globalization, transnational security issues, and challenges like pandemics and climate change.[60] Small states have some advantages in capacity-building, such as coherence, coordination, and unity; that said, they face risks of "group think"[61] and need greater flexibility to overcome limits on specialization. The growing complexity of international society creates a capacity challenge, as small states struggle to be diplomatically present at the proliferating number of relevant forums, let alone to maintain proficiency in myriad specialized and technical discussions.[62]

4. **Location, location, location.** Location has always been an important factor for small states, as Annette Baker Fox pointed out six decades ago.[63] Place never disappeared, even under peak unipolarity, but its weight on outcomes diminished. The United States carried out airstrikes and major operations from Panama to Iraq, followed by global drone campaigns executed with apparent ease. Multipolarity will make regional powers more salient in the political calculations of small states—whether they embrace their nearest power or cast about for alternatives.[64] But being located next door to hard-power Russia is very different from being next to Brazil, with its more limited military.[65] As Womack notes, "States must bloom where they are planted, and they are planted in pots of different sizes next to larger and smaller neighbors."[66] This observation is particularly germane to a relational approach; location affects the salience of relationships. The characteristics of a small state's salient and proximate larger partners affect which strategies are most likely to work.

---

[59] Abdelal and Kirshner, "Strategy, Economic Relations, and the Definition of National Interests"; cf., Ross, "On the Fungibility of Economic Power."

[60] For related arguments, see Sarapuu and Randma-Liiv, "Small States: Public Management and Policy-Making"; Cooper and Shaw, *The Diplomacies of Small States*.

[61] Janis, *Victims of Groupthink*.

[62] Baldacchino and Wivel, "Small States: Concepts and Theories," 11–12.

[63] Fox, *The Power of Small States*.

[64] Rising powers might not produce coherent regions, notes Garzón, "Multipolarity and the Future of Economic Regionalism."

[65] On Brazilian regional leadership, see Burges, "Revisiting Consensual Hegemony"; Burges, *Brazil in the World*; Gardini and de Almeida, *Foreign Policy Responses to the Rise of Brazil*. On Russia, see Contessi, "Prospects for the Accommodation of a Resurgent Russia"; Libman and Obydenkova, "Regional International Organizations as a Strategy of Autocracy."

[66] Womack, *Asymmetry and International Relationships*, 39.

Traditional indicators of international size are less relevant than a small state's network of relationships—especially its relationships with great powers—for understanding its international influence.[67] Small states' foreign relations are dominated by asymmetry, but not all asymmetrical relationships are equal. They are shaped by identities, history, and interests. Constraints and opportunities are shaped by small states' positions in individual asymmetrical relationships and broader global networks.[68]

Institutionalization

International institutions and organizations have long been perceived as friendly environments for small states. In some, like the UN General Assembly, the vote of the least populous state—Tuvalu (population 11,508)—counts as much as the vote of China (population 1.4 billion). In practice, international democracy is more limited; many major decisions are made in great-power conclaves, in institutions with less egalitarian voting rules, outside of any formal framework, or unilaterally. Even the most egalitarian designs, like the UN General Assembly's one-state one-vote system, provide room for great-power manipulation.[69] Even so, the thicker the web of international laws, norms, and institutions, the costlier the unilateral deployment of coercion. As skeptics note, that might not stop a determined great power, but it shapes their calculations.[70] This web also shapes the options and strategies of small states. Though small states rarely expect to vote their way to victory, IOs provide them a forum to amplify concerns, generate publicity, and coordinate with potential allies. While institutional proliferation increases the demands on small states' foreign ministries, these same institutions allow them to diplomatically network with other states at lower cost. This trend dates back to the world's first multipurpose, multilateral IO—the Pan American Union (PAU). Starting in 1890, the PAU's predecessor facilitated growing contact among a Latin American diplomatic corps that lacked extensive bilateral representation.[71] For many small states, IOs have become important sources of expertise, technical development assistance, intelligence sharing, public health support, climate response, disaster management, and more. For minimal contributions, the specialized agencies, institutes, programs, and coordinating mechanisms of the UN system provide shared access to capabilities that

---

[67] Baxter, Jordan, and Rubin, "How Small States Acquire Status"; Long, "It's Not the Size, It's the Relationship."
[68] This variation is a recurring theme for Womack, *Asymmetry and International Relationships*.
[69] Brazys and Panke, "Why Do States Change Positions in the United Nations General Assembly?"
[70] Martin, "International Institutions."
[71] Carrillo Reveles, "México en la Unión de las Repúblicas Americanas," 22.

individual small states cannot replicate. Other IOs and nongovernmental actors also enhance small states' capacities.[72] While there is great attention to small states' influence or lack thereof in international negotiations, the capabilities-enhancing role of IOs is often mentioned but underexplored.[73] What aspects of the international institutional environment are most relevant for small states' influence?

1. **Density.** A denser web of institutions and norms is more favorable to a small state. Small states value predictability.[74] Institutions manifest predictability through reiterated interactions, which in turn facilitate cooperation.[75] Repeated interactions curtail unilateral impulses and provide a level of security, so even if small states have little influence on the design of specific institutions, a highly institutionalized environment is preferable to a thinly institutionalized one. This is true at both the global and regional level. In the early 1900s, Latin American states helped create new regional institutions to curtail U.S. military interventions from the early 1900s through World War II; a century later, small and middle powers in Southeast Asia created an institutional web with similar intentions.[76]

2. **Institutional design.** Quality of institutions matters as well. Institutional design shapes how much influence small states can gain via institutional channels. If there are formal voting procedures, how are votes distributed and weighted? Within the International Monetary Fund (IMF), small states often rely on an executive director from a middle power to represent their interests, and weighted voting limits their formal influence even en masse. In contrast, within the World Trade Organization (WTO), small states and allies have been able to block actions they oppose under a consensus-based structure, and they have access to dispute settlement mechanisms.[77] Such mechanisms can provide leverage to small states as they negotiate commercial disputes with larger partners.[78] Conversely, small states largely lack the access and information to shape decisions of "soft law" regulatory committees that exercise major, if rarely seen, influence over global economic rules.[79] The more open the process of agenda

---

[72] First-hand accounts are suggestive in this respect. Rosenthal, *Inside the United Nations: Multilateral Diplomacy Up Close.*

[73] Panke, "Small States in Multilateral Negotiations"; Brazys and Panke, "Why Do States Change Positions in the United Nations General Assembly?"

[74] Womack, *Asymmetry and International Relationships.*

[75] Axelrod and Keohane, "Achieving Cooperation under Anarchy: Strategies and Institutions."

[76] Friedman and Long, "Soft Balancing in the Americas"; Goh, "Great Powers and Hierarchical Order in Southeast Asia."

[77] Jackson, "Small States and Compliance Bargaining in the WTO"; Lee and Smith, "The Political Economy of Small African States in the WTO."

[78] Jackson, "Small States and Compliance Bargaining in the WTO."

[79] Grynberg and Silva, "Harmonization without Representation"; Grynberg, *WTO at the Margins.*

setting and the more egalitarian the voting procedures, the more influence small states will exercise.[80]

3. **Issue scope.** Small states must pick and choose how they allocate diplomatic resources, so they will prefer institutional environments that bring important issues together. "Smaller countries can devote disproportionate resources toward certain regimes and issue areas, allowing them to participate, gain experience, and tilt the information playing field in their favor."[81] To do so, however, small states must find institutional niches, specialize, and build coalitions within broad organizations, such as the United Nations.[82] Smaller states will often find even "niche diplomacy" on their own to be an onerous task; institutional environments that both are highly focal and cover a broad array of issues make that engagement feasible.[83]

4. **Priority and preference overlaps.** Even if these factors exist, the precise preference alignments of a small state matter a great deal. If a small state's priorities and preferences are outliers, then institutions are unlikely to provide a favorable field. Protective norms like sovereign equality offer some consolation, but institutions will not offer much influence. States that diverge from accepted norms and great-power preferences can be isolated in IOs and face greater scrutiny of domestic political practices.[84] This scrutiny can have consequences: UN Human Rights Council condemnations reduce aid from multilateral organizations in a way that the existence of violations alone does not.[85] This can make institutions uncomfortable places for states with divergent preferences. But when a small state finds support for its preferences, IOs become very useful—especially when support is broad but not particularly salient for most members. Smaller states can play a role in isolating great powers with opposed preferences, even in issues of security;[86] they can attract attention and raise diplomatic costs, as Panama did in the 1970s by involving the UN Security Council in its canal negotiations with the United States;[87] they can coordinate to reshape international agendas as island states have done regarding climate change.[88]

[80] Corbett, Yi-Chong, and Weller, "Small States and the 'Throughput' Legitimacy of International Organisations."

[81] Carson and Thompson, "The Power in Opacity," 113.

[82] Deitelhoff and Wallbott, "Beyond Soft Balancing."

[83] Cooper, "Niche Diplomacy: A Conceptual Overview."

[84] DeMeritt, "International Organizations and Government Killing."

[85] Lebovic and Voeten, "The Cost of Shame"; Sikkink, *Evidence for Hope*, chap. 6.

[86] Mantilla, "Forum Isolation."

[87] Long, "Putting the Canal on the Map."

[88] Benwell, "The Canaries in the Coalmine"; Betzold, "'Borrowing' Power to Influence International Negotiations"; Corbett et al., "Climate Governance, Policy Entrepreneurs and Small States."

In short, institutions provide forums and tools that small states can use to shape and gain influence in their international relationships. In geographical and thematic areas where there is a high density of institutions and relatively egalitarian designs, and where there is a high degree of overlapping preferences among membership, small states gain influence. Where one or more of these factors is missing, small states will benefit from the predictability that institutions provide, but they will find institutions less useful for pursuing policy goals.

Economic governance

Vulnerabilities stemming from exposure to global economic fluctuations were long seen as daunting for small states.[89] The 2020–21 coronavirus pandemic again made economic liabilities evident: as international travel froze, small states that rely on tourism lost their major economic driver, while simultaneously exposing limits in public health capacity.[90] Small states called for coordinated responses to manage the health crisis and restart the economy.[91] The pandemic's financial cost for small states was severe, although economic pain was hardly limited by state size. As the experience of the pandemic suggested, the vulnerabilities of smallness are real. However, as early as the 1980s, it had become clear that small, developed states showed resilience to global market forces and occupied niches in the global economy.[92] The positions of small developing states seemed more tenuous, given dual vulnerabilities due to their limited internal markets and dependence on fewer commodities, economic sectors, or foreign assistance. For small island developing states, market volatility is exacerbated by difficulties of transportation and exposure to major natural disasters.[93]

However, macroeconomic analyses suggest that smallness on its own is not a crippling economic problem. Small states, on the whole, are better off. They tend to be more open to trade and outperform larger counterparts, despite international economic volatility, Easterly and Kraay found.[94] Despite the caveats, an open international trading system is more beneficial for small states than likely alternatives. The economic logic is simple: given their small markets, small states have inherently limited economies of scale and on their own cannot develop

[89]   Singer, *Weak States in a World of Power*; Sutton, "Lilliput under Threat."
[90]   Sheller, "Reconstructing Tourism in the Caribbean."
[91]   Knight and Reddy, "Caribbean Response to COVID-19."
[92]   Handel, *Weak States in the International System*, chap. 5; Katzenstein, *Small States in World Markets*.
[93]   Briguglio, "Small Island Developing States and Their Economic Vulnerabilities"; Darius et al., "The Fiscal Consequences of Natural Disasters"; Bishop, "The Political Economy of Small States: Enduring Vulnerability?"
[94]   Easterly and Kraay, "Small States, Small Problems?"; Lake and O'Mahony, "The Incredible Shrinking State"; Armstrong and Read, "The Phantom of Liberty?"

substantial functional differentiation. Access to large markets allows small states to achieve both, often occupying niche areas of the economy or plugging into global value chains. Trade globalization has been good for small states, on average. While financial flows add to volatility, numerous small states have found niches in global finance as well, though sometimes drawing the ire of larger states.[95] The expansion of WTO rules has, in some cases, phased out the benefits of older, preferential arrangements (for example, with former colonial metropoles) for small states.[96] While migration has often provided something of a safety net—or even an apparent windfall—for some small states via remittances, this too comes with political and developmental costs.[97] An uptick in mercantilism, protectionism, and nativism in large economies constitutes an economic threat that small states struggle to anticipate or contain. The question, then, is two-sided: what are the economic systemic conditions that allow small states to do well, and what are the conditions that allow them to gain influence?

1. **Open but flexible.** An open system of trade is more advantageous than one of unilateral protectionism or closed blocs. Small states also benefit from flexibility in global economic rules, such as those that provide stability for commodity prices, re-embed aspects of global financial flows, and allow the temporary nurturing of nascent comparative advantages. On the other hand, some special arrangements long prized by small states—such as preferential banana pricing[98] or market access carveouts in exchange for policy cooperation[99]—are more likely to protect entrenched interest groups than to foster better long-term economic performance. In short, small states need a high degree of openness in the global economy to develop productive niches, but also enough flexibility in economic governance to embed their own interests.

2. **Global competition.** Oligopolistic markets are good for the big players, who can fix prices and diminish competitive pressures from new entrants.

[95] Vleck, "The Caribbean Confronts the OECD"; Sharman, "Power and Discourse in Policy Diffusion"; Baldacchino, *Island Enclaves*.

[96] Read, "The Implications of Increasing Globalization and Regionalism for the Economic Growth of Small Island States."

[97] Political costs emerge from vulnerability to changes in host state policies, as Central American states learned with the end of legal protections for temporary protected migrants during the U.S. Trump administration, and as Central Asian states have learned regarding Russian policies. Several studies suggest the development effects of remittances are ambiguous and appear to vary by geography, development level, state size, and exchange-rate regime. Feeny, Iamsiraroj, and McGillivray, "Remittances and Economic Growth"; Ball, Lopez, and Reyes, "Remittances, Inflation and Exchange Rate Regimes in Small Open Economies."

[98] Grynberg, *WTO at the Margins*, chaps. 11–13; c.f., Fridell, "The Case against Cheap Bananas"; Clegg, "Banana Splits and Policy Challenges."

[99] Loveman, *Addicted to Failure*; Jácome and Velasco, "Ecuador: The Evolution of Drug Policies in the Middle of the World."

The U.S.-led liberal order, with its beneficial stability, showed aspects of this oligopolistic collusion—seen, for example, in practices of agenda setting among the "G" groupings. Despite rhetorically championing a "Global South" agenda, the BRICS (Brazil, Russia, India, China, and South Africa) also exhibited oligopolistic decision-making, albeit in partial opposition to the G7.[100] In the global economy, then, having elements of competition instead of collusion among the great powers is likely to provide benefits and opportunities for influence—if economic competition does not spill over into security conflict.

3. **Positionality.** Even in an open and competitive economy, it matters where one is positioned, in terms of geography and economic niche. Positionality can facilitate economic diversification, providing opportunities to enhance resilience.[101] Positionality also refers to how one is placed in relationships with other actors, and that is something small states can influence. The position and actions of the smaller state are just as crucial to defining the nature of a relationship as those of the larger state, even if those choices are made within greater constraints.[102] The policy choices of small states can shape their positions within global economic relationships.

The niche one occupies in global trade or value chains affects how beneficial the arrangement is. Some small states have found economic niches drawing on internet connectivity; a benefit of geographical smallness can be ease in upgrading communications infrastructure.[103] This has helped places like Singapore and Estonia to engage in global services trade at a high level, while allowing other states to develop online services ranging from gambling to customer service. Global markets and economic specialization, reduced transport costs, and international tourism have been a boon to many small island economies. Despite the overall benefits, openness and volatility complicate economic planning and entail significant social disruptions. Balancing the risks of openness with an emphasis on "resilience" has become a major focus for both scholars and policymakers in small states.[104]

---

[100] Hopewell, "The BRICS—Merely a Fable?"; Cooper, "The G20 and Contested Global Governance"; Stuenkel, "The Financial Crisis, Contested Legitimacy, and the Genesis of Intra-BRICS Cooperation."

[101] Thanks to Jack Corbett for pointing out this connection.

[102] Womack, *Asymmetry and International Relationships*; Long, "It's Not the Size, It's the Relationship."

[103] In fact, some small island states have marketed themselves as ideal "work from home" residences to take advantage of greater telecommuting.

[104] Briguglio, Cordina, and Kisanga, *Building the Economic Resilience of Small States*.

Normative environment

The institutional structure of today's international society rests on underpinning normative commitments—to multilateralism, expansive mobility of goods and capital, and loosely rules-based decision-making.[105] These norms were often violated, and the United States granted itself and chosen allies exemptions. Despite its inconsistency, the normative environment shaped patterns of international relationships: it socialized states into understanding their interests in particular ways and expecting certain patterns of behavior.[106] The consequences were momentous even for former leading powers. The possession of formal overseas colonies transformed from being the ideal of great-power status in 1900 to being deviant behavior in the 1970s and taboo in the 2000s.[107] Shifts in the normative environment affect states large and small.[108] What aspects of today's fluctuating international norms will most affect small states' wellbeing and possibilities for influence?

1. **Who can govern?** One of the most important, if taken-for-granted, international norms designates who is considered a legitimate actor, with rights to govern a territory or population and engage in international politics. The norm of international legal recognition shapes who can act and how. During the nineteenth and early twentieth centuries, many non-Western populations were excluded, as were some polities deemed too small—famously, Liechtenstein's application to the League of Nations was rejected.[109] Since World War II, the international franchise has been broadened to recognize more polities as states, but other aspirants are denied recognition and formal participation in the society of states—often due to great-power opposition.[110] Once recognized, small states are adept at utilizing international recognition to assure their survival and seek benefits and influence.[111]

---

[105] Deudney and Ikenberry, "The Nature and Sources of Liberal International Order"; Ikenberry, *Liberal Leviathan*; c.f., Parmar, "The US-Led Liberal Order"; Long, "Latin America and the Liberal International Order."

[106] Ikenberry and Kupchan, "Socialization and Hegemonic Power."

[107] Sharman, *Empires of the Weak*, 144; Philpott, *Revolutions in Sovereignty*.

[108] Hurrell, *On Global Order*.

[109] Schulz, "Civilisation, Barbarism and the Making of Latin America's Place in 19th-Century International Society"; Cha, "The Formation of American Exceptional Identities"; Ingebritsen et al., *Small States in International Relations*. Thanks to Godfrey Baldacchino for suggesting the example.

[110] Pegg, *International Society and the De Facto State*; Coggins, *Power Politics and State Formation in the Twentieth Century*.

[111] Wendt and Barnett, "Dependent State Formation and Third World Militarization"; Jackson, *Quasi-States*; Sharman, "War, Selection, and Micro-States."

2. **Sources of legitimacy.** All international orders rely on some sort of legitimacy that justifies the use of force or seeks to make the use of force unnec-
   essary.[112] The sources of an order's legitimacy shape what arguments are
   persuasive; this affects how small states defend or advance interests. For
   example, international institutions' dependence on the perceived legitimacy of their decision-making processes allows small states to advocate for
   greater voice in the name of procedural legitimacy.[113] The U.S. emphasis
   on political rights and democracy (though unevenly implemented) gave
   small states certain rhetorical tools, while its emphasis on capitalism and
   markets limited the space for appeals based on social welfare rights. Some
   argue that Chinese visions of international order are underpinned less by
   individualism and more by ideals of harmonious society.[114] In that normative context, appeals to political rights would be less effective than those
   predicated on the prevention of discord. Either way, commonly understood sources of international legitimacy shape pathways of influence with
   larger states.

3. **Use of force.** The reduction of the use of force as standard, first-order statecraft has changed the wellbeing and possibilities of small states.[115] This
   includes the de-legitimation of territorial conquest and the normative
   consolidation about rationales for intervention as a tool of regime change.
   These norms were advocated by those at the margins of the international
   system as a means of defense.[116] Normative shifts are buttressed by nuclear deterrence and the tremendous costs of modern state-to-state war
   among great powers. Lacking deterrence, small states must rely on normative compliance. But there are reasons to question how settled these norms
   really are. Evident breaches include Russia's annexation of Crimea, while
   U.S. compliance with nonintervention norms has long been uneven. Both
   the United States and rising powers have cast doubt on central norms by
   renouncing multilateral commitments, including on arms limitations. The
   rise of drone warfare and the possible expansion of unmanned violence
   has changed conflict between states and nonstate actors; it is increasingly
   bleeding into relations between states through proxy conflicts, surveillance, and direct clashes. This violence often occurs in a normative grey
   area. Old norms were not obviously prescriptive for new technologies.
   Looser use of new weapons threatens to erode once-established norms for

---

[112] Hobson and Sharman, "The Enduring Place of Hierarchy in World Politics."

[113] Corbett, Yi-Chong, and Weller, "Small States and the 'Throughput' Legitimacy of International Organisations."

[114] Yan, "Chinese Values vs. Liberalism."

[115] Hathaway and Shapiro, *The Internationalists*; Maass, "Small States: Survival and Proliferation."

[116] Lorca, *Mestizo International Law.*

the conduct of combat. Small states may find themselves vulnerable to this sort of undeclared warfare, which may fail to gain widespread great-power or public attention. Weaker normative constraints on military force erode small states' security and influence.

During the last century, the evolution of the normative environment has been propitious for small states, but the future is less certain. Norms are shaped by the repeated words and practices of the members of the international system. Small states alone cannot determine these norms, but their actions constitute and re-constitute the normative environment. Over time, these actions matter. The emergence of groupings that explicitly adopt a "small state" identity and pres-sure for change is a positive development.[117] While such groupings often pursue concrete goals, they make implicit claims about these normative questions—that small states can govern and participate, that their participation is necessary for an order's legitimacy, and that influence should not be determined by the ability to use force.

Structures, relations, and small states today

The four factors noted previously describe aspects of the environment that small states inhabit. In the broad view of systemic IR theory, the international envi-ronment appears overbearing and determinative for small states. However, when one starts from the nearer-term concerns of specific small states' policymaking, systemic factors are rarely deterministic. The environment imposes constraints on actions but also allows for opportunities.

Here we depart from the traditional dichotomy between IR's emphasis on structure and the Foreign Policy Analysis emphasis on domestic drivers of state action.[118] Instead, we take a "relational turn" to examine small states in the con-text of their most important international relationships.[119] In this view, the con-tent of international relations is found in the various exchanges among actors. The systemic factors described previously are "an analytical shorthand for rel-ative stabilities in patterns of interaction."[120] When the international system is understood as a network of relations among states, small states cannot be irrel-evant to IR theory in the way Waltz suggested. They constitute the majority of

---

[117] Corbett, Xu, and Weller, "Norm Entrepreneurship and Diffusion 'from below' in International Organisations"; Browning, "Small, Smart and Salient?"
[118] On this division, see Kaarbo, "A Foreign Policy Analysis Perspective on the Domestic Politics Turn in IR Theory."
[119] Nexon, "Relationalism and New Systems Theory."
[120] Nexon, "Relationalism and New Systems Theory," 101.

the international network's nodes and participate in its relationships. This relational approach allows us to examine the near-term interactions with states and IOs that occupy much of small-state policymakers' time, without forgetting the broader picture.

Small states' positions in the international network are constituted through asymmetry—small states play a recurring role as the smaller partner in salient relationships. This is what makes them "small states."[121] The emphasis on asymmetry presumes that material divergences exist—in military forces, total gross domestic product, level of development, population, territory, etc.—and impact the dynamics of bilateral relationships and broader patterns of international interaction.

Despite material asymmetries, the post–Cold War international environment generally has been favorable for small states. For two decades or more, a small state's position in the international system was in significant part a function of its relationship with the United States. Now, patterns of international relationships are undergoing rapid changes, highlighted by shifting relations among large states. Relations among great powers, as well as relations between large and small and among small states, are shaped by institutional and normative constraints. Even bilateral ties are affected by the broader network of relationships. That network provides security and voice opportunities for many small states. In economic relations, the broader network, combined with relative openness, provides greater opportunities and policy space for small states than narrow and closed relationships that dominated the past.

None of that means that small states are unconstrained or that their futures are wholly of their own making: they must act "under circumstances already existing," to borrow Marx's phrase. Small states are embedded in networks of international relationships, and "relations endow actors with varying degrees of agency," Nexon writes.[122] Foregrounding asymmetry means exploring those varying degrees of agency and examining the limits and possibilities that small states face in their international relationships. We now turn to that task.

---

[121] Baldacchino and Wivel, "Small States: Concepts and Theories," 7; Long, "It's Not the Size, It's the Relationship."
[122] Nexon, "Relationalism and New Systems Theory," 109.

3

Opportunities and Constraints: Conditions for Success

Despite a favorable global environment, recent shocks suggest the fragility of the open global economy and multilateral diplomacy: the rise of global populism signaled by support for Donald Trump in the United States, Narendra Modi in India, and Brexit in the United Kingdom in 2016; the U.S.-China trade war and lasting tensions over technological exports; and nationalistic responses to COVID-19 in 2020–21; among others. China's assertion of strict controls over Hong Kong and the Armenia-Azerbaijan war over control of the de facto state of Nagorno-Karabakh demonstrate the importance of international legal statehood while worryingly suggesting that the global diffusion of power will be accompanied by more diffuse use of coercive force. With good reason, these events unsettle small states, though they have not (yet) reversed more favorable, historical trends toward greater security. As Wivel and Crandall note, the "permissiveness of the strategic environment" today still provides many small states with greater "action space" than the past.[1]

One should not mistake a permissive international environment for one of equality. Small states enunciate and pursue their goals in the context of power asymmetries. Their ability to achieve those goals is conditioned by those same disparities. When small states' goals do not coincide with the policies and international orientations of larger states, they may need to "overcome asymmetry" in some sense. This chapter asks, what conditions affect the likelihood that small states can achieve their goals and exercise influence?[2] Beyond considering the general conditions of the international system, as we did in the previous chapter, answering that question requires addressing the internal conditions of the small state and the dynamics of its relationships with other states.

Can small states achieve the foreign policy goals they set out? This chapter places small states in the context where power-centric International Relations (IR) theory would generally expect them to be most disadvantaged—in

[1] Wivel and Crandall, "Punching Above Their Weight, but Why?," 396–97.
[2] Achieving one's goals and exercising influence are related but analytically distinct. One can achieve goals without influence if these do not require changing others' behavior—getting an actor to do (or not do) something. If achieving goals implies changes on the part of others, then influence is required.

A Small State's Guide to Influence in World Politics. Tom Long, Oxford University Press. © Oxford University Press 2022. DOI: 10.1093/oso/9780190926205.003.0003

asymmetrical relationships with larger powers.[3] However, the degree of power disparity is just one relevant consideration for assessing small states' "foreign policy power."[4] This chapter expands upon our relational approach and argues that asymmetrical dynamics produce recurring constraints and opportunities for small states. We propose an analytical framework for evaluating the link between relational factors and small states' possibilities for success.

Policymakers can use this framework to diagnose their state's situation. This diagnosis should help policymakers identify strategies that match a state's capabilities with the situation it faces. Those strategies respond to different configurations of conditions (discussed in Chapter 4). After identifying relevant relational conditions individually, we create a typological theory to consider the interactions between these factors. Typological theories offer explanations that are systematic and generalizable, while also allowing for the consideration of multiple, interacting factors. Success and strategies are conditioned by three relational factors: the degree of divergence between small-state preferences and great-power policies, the issue's relational salience, and the cohesiveness of preferences within the great power.[5]

Not all situations are amenable to near-term influence by a small state. When a great power makes an issue a high priority, advocates a policy that diverges widely from the small state's goals, and possesses internal cohesion supporting those policy preferences, the likelihood that a small state will achieve its policy goal is low. The small state may have to adopt a longer-term approach and face near-term frustration—and it may be best served by policies that minimize the costs of this disagreement. However, when these three conditions are not met, the door opens to diverse strategies through which the small state can pursue its priorities.

This chapter has three goals. First, it briefly outlines conditions within small states that affect their possibilities for achieving relational influence. Being explicit about these is important: small states' capacities for international action vary. A small state that possesses unified preferences among decision-making elites and competent administrative institutions has a head start in pursuing its goals. Conversely, a given small state's failure to achieve its goals might have domestic causes—like internal discord—instead of originating in its international relationship. Second, the chapter creates a "scorecard" that identifies relational conditions that favor or disadvantage a small state's foreign policy goals. The dimensions of this rubric reflect the nature of asymmetry—small states face

---

[3] Archer, Bailes, and Wivel, *Small States and International Security*, 8; Womack, *Asymmetry and International Relationships*; Long, "It's Not the Size, It's the Relationship."

[4] Chong and Maass, "The Foreign Policy Power of Small States."

[5] Work on intra-alliance bargaining has sometimes noted similar dimensions. See Resnick, *Allies of Convenience*, chap. 1.

different relational and international pressures than great powers. The greater the asymmetry of the relationship, the more this will apply. However, there is an important corollary to this: all things being equal, the greater the asymmetry of capabilities, the greater the asymmetry of attention. As Womack points out, great powers must divide high-level attention between a whole world of relationships and issues. Most of the time, any given small state will not be a priority for a great power's leaders—but the great power will remain a priority for the small state.[6]

While we are using the terminology of great powers and small states, in reality, asymmetry does not create fixed dichotomies. Size is relationally contingent. A state that is "small" vis-à-vis the United States may be "large" in relation to its own neighbors. Some of the same patterns will occur, though in general, the larger the state, the greater the diversity of relationships and interests that it will seek to manage. Having explored conditions that structure asymmetrical relationships, the chapter's third task is to explore how the interaction of these factors influences whether and how the small state might succeed. This is where typological theory comes into play, illuminating the interactions of these three relational conditions. First, we turn to the small states themselves.

Small-state characteristics and relationships

This book's central argument pertains to asymmetrical relationships, as opposed to small states categorized by population or gross domestic product (GDP).[7] Still, work on small states' foreign policies sheds light on the conditions they face in asymmetrical relationships.[8] These studies suggest there is a need to re-evaluate the perspectives that "equate[s] 'smallness' with a lack of power."[9] Chong and Maass argue that "The challenge lies in identifying the often particular and unconventional sources of small states' foreign policy power."[10] Likewise, Braveboy-Wagner argues for an approach that treats small states as actors in their own rights: "This does not mean that they are not vulnerable in many respects (as are all states to some degree or another) but that they are capable of employing strategies, both foreign and domestic, which allow them to overcome many of these handicaps."[11] Studies along these lines foreground small states' agency as "smart"

---

[6] This point builds on Womack, *Asymmetry and International Relationships*, 47–51.
[7] For a definitional discussion, see Maass, "The Elusive Definition of the Small State."
[8] For recent overviews, see Yee-Kuang Heng, "Small States"; Baldacchino, "Mainstreaming the Study of Small States and Territories."
[9] Browning, "Small, Smart and Salient?"
[10] Chong and Maass, "The Foreign Policy Power of Small States."
[11] Braveboy-Wagner, "Opportunities and Limitations of the Exercise of Foreign Policy Power by a Very Small State."

or "entrepreneurial" international actors.[12] Small states may turn their vulnerabilities into strengths, shaping agendas or petitioning for special resources.[13] Small states play active and significant roles in myriad ways: as effective builders and members of institutions, including the European Union;[14] in international negotiations;[15] through peacekeeping;[16] in climate talks;[17] as promoters of international norms;[18] by recasting Western perceptions of their domestic and regional politics;[19] and through economic assets.[20] Small states have shaped events at the highest tables of world politics, such as nuclear disarmament and the laws of war.[21] Like great powers, small states care about and manage their international status.[22] Under certain circumstances, small states can change how their large neighbors see their own regional roles.[23] Small islands may act as major maritime influences, using their ocean territory and niche knowledge to enhance influence.[24] Even small states in difficult geographies—such as traditional "buffer states"—may profit from crafting a bridge role between great powers.[25] These examples suggest the range of agency and influence that small states may exercise, if one's preconceptions allow it.

Following a "foreign policy power" approach to small states, we define success and failure in terms of the goals small states enunciate and pursue.[26] While this seems simple, it differs from traditional approaches to small states where questions of dependence and independence, constraints and autonomy, and

[12] Browning, "Small, Smart and Salient?"; Pedi and Sarri, "From the 'Small but Smart State' to the 'Small and Entrepreneurial State.'"

[13] Corbett, Xu, and Weller, "Norm Entrepreneurship and Diffusion 'from below' in International Organisations."

[14] Panke and Gurol, "Small States as Agenda-setters?"; Thorhallsson, *The Role of Small States in the European Union*; Steinmetz and Wivel, *Small States in Europe*; Hey, "Luxembourg: Where Small Works (and Wealthy Doesn't Hurt)"; Haugevik and Rieker, "Autonomy or Integration?"; Lupel and Mälksoo, "Necessary Voice."

[15] Panke, "Dwarfs in International Negotiations"; Panke, "Studying Small States in International Security Affairs"; Deitelhoff and Wallbott, "Beyond Soft Balancing."

[16] Pedersen, "Bandwagon for Status"; Jakobsen, "Still Punching Above Their Weight?"; Jenne, "Peacekeeping, Latin America and the UN Charter's Chapter VIII."

[17] Corbett et al., "Climate Governance, Policy Entrepreneurs and Small States"; Benwell, "The Canaries in the Coalmine."

[18] Ingebritsen, "Norm Entrepreneurs"; Fuentes-Julio, "Norm Entrepreneurs in Foreign Policy."

[19] Jourde, "The International Relations of Small Neoauthoritarian States."

[20] Braveboy-Wagner, "Opportunities and Limitations of the Exercise of Foreign Policy Power by a Very Small State"; Kamrava, *Qatar: Small State, Big Politics.*

[21] Jargalsaikhan, "The Role of Small States in Promoting International Security"; O'Driscoll and Walsh, "Ireland and the 1975 NPT Review Conference"; Mantilla, "Forum Isolation."

[22] de Carvalho and Neumann, *Small State Status Seeking*; Wohlforth et al., "Moral Authority and Status in International Relations"; Long and Urdinez, "Status at the Margins."

[23] Guimarães, *A Theory of Master Role Transition.*

[24] Bueger and Wivel, "How Do Small Island States Maximize Influence?"; Chan, "'Large Ocean States.'"

[25] Efremova, "Small States in Great Power Politics."

[26] Chong and Maass, "The Foreign Policy Power of Small States"; Braveboy-Wagner, "Opportunities and Limitations of the Exercise of Foreign Policy Power by a Very Small State."

vulnerability and resilience have been central.[27] We argue that small states' goals should not be treated as exogenously determined. International asymmetry may affect a small state's aims by shaping what its leaders see as necessary and feasible, but a host of domestic conditions also matter. The observable variation in what small states seek, even under similar conditions, helps confirm this.[28] The approach is more applicable to policymaking too, because it sheds light on the pursuit of concrete aims instead of vague, if generalizable, categories like "security." Once foreign policy goals are identified, we ask: can small states shape outcomes in their asymmetrical relationships, and under what conditions? What foreign policy strategies can small states adopt to pursue those goals within and through those relationships? Addressing these questions requires taking small states' preference formation seriously. Before beginning to theorize about international relationships, we first specify our assumptions about small states' preferences and the internal factors that condition the pursuit of international goals (see Table 3.1).

Internal factors

Basing our analysis on small states' goals means we must take both international and domestic sources of preferences and preference formation seriously. Small states (like large states) can identify—through elite consensus, domestic processes, or dictatorial whim—divergent goals to be pursued through their foreign policies. However, small states' preferences are more strongly shaped by the state's position in asymmetrical relationships.[29] Over the long run, asymmetrical relationships may exercise profound effects on preferences: shaping the constitution of national elites through decolonization or determining the availability of resources via asymmetrical economic relationships.[30] In the shorter term, small states' interests will reflect perceptions of what is possible from a position of relative material weakness. For the purposes of this study, empirically demonstrable small states' preferences form the starting point of our research. We adopt a pragmatic approach of inferring preferences from what policymakers said, did, and sought.

Second, we assume that even very small states possess material and ideational resources that can be used to pursue their goals. In our asymmetrical approach,

[27] Fox, *The Power of Small States*; Cooper and Shaw, *The Diplomacies of Small States*; Briguglio et al., *Profiling Vulnerability and Resilience*; Baldacchino, "Small States: Challenges of Political Economy."

[28] Gigleux, "Explaining the Diversity of Small States' Foreign Policies through Role Theory."

[29] Gvalia et al., "Thinking Outside the Bloc."

[30] Abdelal and Kirshner, "Strategy, Economic Relations, and the Definition of National Interests."

Table 3.1 Assumptions

---

1. Small states (like great powers) have and pursue foreign policy goals.

2. Small states possess some material and ideational capabilities.

3. Great powers must prioritize attention and resources between multiple interests relating to other large states and myriad small states.

4. The cohesion of elite preferences (in all, but especially large, states) surrounding any given policy may vary from consensus to fragmentation.

---

the "small state" will always be the relational partner with fewer material capabilities, but we do not deny the diversity among small states. Small states have vastly different attributes of wealth and development, geostrategic positioning, bureaucratic capacity, and more. Many of IR's standard power resources are likely to be relevant—economic development or military capabilities. While some of these capacities are fungible, in the sense that they affect possibilities for influence across many issues, other attributes might be specific and intrinsic to certain issues and relationships. Beyond capabilities, the consistency of support for preferences—often discussed as "resolve" or "commitment"—matters a great deal, particularly when small states face great-power resistance.[31] Some small states may have longstanding relationships through which they can derive power.[32] Overcoming asymmetry will require small states to make exceptional use of the resources—material and otherwise—that they do possess.

Some of these attributes change only over the long term. However, limiting one's analysis to fairly static capabilities risks replicating divides in the existing literature, in which the agency of European small states, and favored outliers like Singapore, receives attention, while for most other states the emphasis is on constraints and vulnerabilities. Finding that higher-income small states are more influential than lower-income small states would have limited implications for small states' policymakers. Such an approach would also assume a generalizable and comparable concept of "influence," instead of relating it to goals and within contexts and relationships. Another reason for departing from a capabilities-counting approach is that a substantial body of evidence suggests that material capabilities do not correlate perfectly—or perhaps even well—with outcomes. This is doubly the case when one recognizes that asymmetry is "priced in" to

---

[31] Habeeb, *Power and Tactics in International Negotiation*, 20–24; Hopmann, "Asymmetrical Bargaining in the Conference on Security and Cooperation in Europe."

[32] Long, "Small States, Great Power?"; Handel, *Weak States in the International System*.

small states' preferences and goals.[33] When examining small states' influence, the question of capabilities is more a qualitative issue of *what types* of capabilities, rather than a quantitative question of *how much* of given capabilities. For that reason, we examine how small states deploy the resources available to them and how certain capabilities matter for achieving specific goals.

External factors

The second two assumptions pertain more closely to small states' larger counterparts in asymmetrical relationships. First, larger powers have diverse interests and must prioritize resources and decision-making attention among them. Although large states typically have larger foreign policy bureaucracies, decision-making remains hierarchical and concentrated. As a result of their more diverse interests and relationships, they must ration decision-making attention. A large state will tend to divide its attention, with attention most consistently focused on other large states. Small states will often gain salience for great powers when they relate to areas of crisis "in an alternating cycle of fixation and inattention."[34] A small state's agenda will be more consistent, with priority given to its large partner. During moments of "fixation," the stakes are raised for the small state; however, these are exceptional occurrences. More common are the fallow periods in which stasis rules in the relationship; drift is the norm. This allows gradual opportunities for small states to prepare and advance their own agendas.[35]

The final assumption relates to preference cohesion in a large states. The degree of support for any given policy will vary within a great power's government, ranging from near consensus to fragmentation of preferences among those who influence decisions.[36] The foreign policy organization and processes of the great power become important to small states. On the one hand, decision makers in a great power could have preferences that are homogenous and tightly held: more colloquially, people agree and care a great deal. On the other hand, preferences could be diffuse and weakly held: people disagree and/or have low levels of investment in a policy. This characteristic is more salient in great

[33] In this sense, one can easily run into problems of endogeneity when trying to assess how the level of capabilities affects the likelihood of successful pursuit of foreign policy goals.

[34] Quote from Pastor, *Exiting the Whirlpool*, 18; on the broader pattern, see Womack, "How Size Matters."

[35] Darnton, "Asymmetry and Agenda-Setting in US-Latin American Relations"; Durant and Diehl, "Agendas, Alternatives, and Public Policy."

[36] In an attempt to make the resulting framework more empirically applicable, I focus on divisions within the government, leaving aside important questions of public opinion and domestic politics. These may be determinant in the longer term (through elections that change leadership, most obviously), but the immediate evaluation is limited to the administration itself.

powers' policy environments. The diversity of relationships and interests that a great power maintains means that most bilateral relationships will not receive regular high-level consideration. Policies may be maintained and implemented even when there is a lack of coherent support.[37] Size generates diverse interests and relationships, and it complicates follow-through across large and complex bureaucracies.

Diverse preferences exist within small states too. Scholars of small states have argued that smallness confers an advantage in this sense—all things being equal, smallness should be related to greater homogeneity of preferences.[38] However, in the world of small states, all things are rarely equal, so preference cohesion and commitment are treated as empirical questions for the small states in our case studies. We emphasize instances where the small state displayed sufficient preference consistency to enunciate cohesive policy demands vis-à-vis its larger partner, building on the discussion of internal characteristics earlier.

These four assumptions emerge from the dynamics of asymmetry, in which differences in material capabilities shape patterns of relationships among states, but without determining the outcomes of specific interactions. Asymmetry shapes how states define and pursue their national interests, but it does not directly determine those interests. A relational and asymmetrical approach is not as deterministic as classic structural accounts that suggest that international structures force small states to be eternally fearful of annihilation. Nor is it as open-ended as purely domestic accounts that see small states' preferences and actions primarily as the product of internal forces. We now turn to a discussion of international asymmetry and its effects at a bilateral level and within networks of asymmetrical and symmetrical relations.

Asymmetrical international relationships

Understanding the interactions of great powers and small states requires an exploration of both sides. While the decisions of great powers typically receive exhaustive study at different levels of analysis, it remains common to assume that the leaders of small states simply "do what they must" or that independent foreign policies are of limited consequence. This ignores how small states shape agendas, reframe problems, advance options, and achieve influence. Regardless of a state's inherent "size," the exercise of power in foreign policy is relationally

---

[37] The classic literature on the bureaucratic politics of U.S. foreign policy illustrated how policies were often maintained despite presidential opposition. Especially, Neustadt, *Presidential Power*.

[38] Katzenstein, *Small States in World Markets*; Alesina and Spolaore, *The Size of Nations*; Dahl and Tufte, *Size and Democracy*; Anckar, "Homogeneity and Smallness."

and contextually dependent. An actor that is relatively weak in one issue area, or in the context of a particular relationship, might be strong elsewhere.

The world's largest states may take disparities in capabilities for granted and instead categorize their relationships with small states according to other factors, such as perceptions of deference, ideological alignment, or connections to another great power. For small states, however, asymmetry is the most salient element in their relationships with great powers. What is meant by asymmetry? No two states are the same, so perfect symmetry does not occur in international relations. Looking at today's two largest powers, the United States and China, we see how one state has an advantage in population and exports while the other possesses greater military capabilities and per capita wealth.[39] However, these differences are not the sort of asymmetry at the heart of this book. Instead, our concept of asymmetry refers to rougher metrics of state "size." State size is a continuum, without clear divisions between small, medium, or large. The degree of asymmetry refers to the distance between two points on that continuum. When referring to *asymmetrical relationships*, we emphasize the interactions of states that are located toward the extremes of dyadic continuums of state size. As with definitions of "small states," trying to fix categories of just how asymmetrical given relationships are may not be helpful or desirable. Cut-offs for asymmetry— for example, that "small" is a tenth of the larger state's GDP—would be as arbitrary as the quantitative definitions of smallness discarded earlier in the book.

As a result, the conditions identified later do not pertain only to a subset of states; nor are the strategies discussed in the next chapter only available to states below an arbitrary point on the state-size continuum. Instead, these conditions and strategies will be increasingly salient in more asymmetrical relationships— dyadic pairings in which states are further apart in terms of capabilities.

One key to understanding asymmetrical relationships is to realize how differences in material capabilities lead to different perceptions of the same relationship, as Brantly Womack notes. From the perspective of each side, the relationship between a large state and a small state is not perceived as one relationship but two: large and small states tend to see one another in tremendously disparate ways.[40] These divergent patterns of perception produce characteristic dynamics of (in)attention, (in)stability, and (in)security. Multiplied across a network of largely asymmetrical relationships, these dynamics of relational asymmetry produce the challenges often attributed to smallness in international politics. Building closely on Womack's theoretical work, we examine these challenges in turn.

[39] Womack, "How Size Matters."
[40] Womack, *Asymmetry and International Relationships*.

- **(In)attention:** The small state is disproportionately exposed to changes or actions of the large state. Facing this risk, the small state's leadership will be highly attentive to the large state. "In effect the top leaders of B [the small state] are all A [large state] experts."[41] This observation rings true particularly for small states in the vicinity of great powers. What Cuban leader has not intimately considered U.S. politics? What Vietnamese leader could ignore Chinese dynamics? Large states can concentrate tremendous attention on a small state—but not on all small states all the time. Even in moments of attentiveness, the top leadership of the large state likely knows little about the small state. Their concerns often regard narrow issues. They may lean on vague and stereotypical representations.[42] This creates possibilities for the small state to advance its preferences through more consistent attention. "The 'asymmetry of attention' greatly enhances the weak actor's issue power position," a scholar of negotiations wrote. "For one it helps increase and sustain commitment, particularly in the face of a hard-line position by the strong actor. Moreover, it enhances the credibility of the weak actor's tactics."[43]

- **(In)stability:** The perception of the relationship's stability also differs in a patterned way. The large state perceives the relationship as stable if the small state is deferential to its core interests (such as excluding rival powers from its "near abroad"). The small state perceives the relationship as stable if the large state is respectful of its independence. In conflictual relationships, both sides' perceptions of the other are often categorized by violent or patronizing stereotypes—David versus Goliath, bully and bullied, adults and children, Gulliver and Lilliputians—that can exacerbate conflict when normalized practices break down.[44] Even in stable relationships, these patterns of perceptions generate frustration with great-power paternalism. Even so, it is often in the interests of both sides to maintain a nonconflictual relationship.[45] Faced with external threats, small states may seek "shelter" from large powers to gain stability even if they must performatively stress their deference to core great-power concerns while protecting their own.[46]

- **(In)security:** The security problems for each side are likewise very different; the small state legitimately worries about a near-existential threat (at least to its regime) from the large state; the large state worries about threats to its interests or credibility. Despite a great power's advantages in material

---

[41] Womack, *Asymmetry and International Relationships*, 51.
[42] Miklian, "International Media's Role on U.S.–Small State Relations"; Jourde, "The International Relations of Small Neoauthoritarian States."
[43] Habeeb, *Power and Tactics in International Negotiation*, 132.
[44] Brenner and Castro, "David and Gulliver."
[45] Womack, *Asymmetry and International Relationships*, 51–58.
[46] Thorhallsson, *Small States and Shelter Theory.*

capabilities, coercing small states in a world characterized by asymmetrical relations is costly. The immediate benefits to be gained from a small state are usually marginal. So are the odds of success. Large states may overestimate their own capabilities of coercion and the likelihood that coercion will achieve desired political changes. The ability to achieve outcomes is lessened by misperceptions. What a great power perceives as transnational threats involving the territory of a small state may be serious internal or domestic security problems for the small state. What a small state perceives as core national interests—like its migrant diaspora or market access—may be considered domestic politics for the relevant great power.[47] Security conflicts with a great power are risky for an asymmetrically exposed small state and generally to be avoided. Therefore, when a small state adopts a conflictual approach, it is often highly committed, complicating the large state's calculations.[48]

In short, asymmetry suggests that relationships between large and small states cannot be boiled down to differences in material capabilities. The indicators of material capabilities that are sometimes synonymous with "power" tell us less about influence over outcomes than is often supposed.[49] In part, this is because power is relational and context dependent, not some absolute attribute possessed by large states. Even more, though, it is because asymmetry produces cross-cutting patterns of attention, security, and stability. When each bilateral relationship is put into the context of the vast network of relationships that states maintain, these dynamics become even more important.

Typological theory and the conditions for relational influence

To move from relational and asymmetrical principles to more specific theoretical statements, we must take another step. To do so, we draw on typological theorizing. Rather than simply trying to link and assess the weight of one cause on one effect, typological theory allows for the contextualized explanation of cases and the inclusion of multiple causal conditions. The analyst highlights salient dimensions and puts these in relation to one another. The combination of these dimensions creates "types." From there, one can construct a theory

[47] Long, "Coloso Fragmentado."

[48] Womack, *Asymmetry and International Relationships*, 76–80; Arreguin-Toft, "How the Weak Win Wars"; Angstrom and Petersson, "Weak Party Escalation"; Long, "It's Not the Size, It's the Relationship," 149–50.

[49] Baldwin, *Power and International Relations*.

about how and why cases develop in certain ways. "Typological theories specify the pathways through which particular types relate to specific outcomes."[50] In terms of research design, typological theorizing usefully combines within-case methods and cross-case comparison. Because the approach facilitates contextualized hypotheses instead of universal (if probabilistic) claims, it is better suited to the needs of policymaking. Policymakers may be interested to know about high levels of correlation between independent and dependent variables; however, in foreign policy decision-making—with its universe of hard-to-define and hard-to-compare cases—it is more helpful to assess how one's situation relates to other cases of a similar nature.

Before moving to the typological theory, we first must be able to diagnose the relevant conditions within a given case. For this reason, we introduce an "analytical scorecard," which facilitates an analysis of how interacting conditions shape small states' possibilities and mechanisms of influence in asymmetrical relationships. These interacting conditions create a typology of cases, from which we theorize about small states' possibilities and strategies for influence. Building on the scorecard, we can assess how the combination of relational conditions creates constraints and opportunities for small states' pursuits of their foreign policy goals.

Our analytical approach is as follows. First, we impute small states' preferences about a given policy issue from the available evidence. Second, we assess the degree and nature of the divergence between the small state's goals and the great power's policy. Third, we gauge the great power's interest in the problem: is the issue on policymakers' agendas? Finally, we examine whether the great power's policymakers have tightly held and coherent preferences on the issue. We explain our choices of these four factors in turn.

One consequence of asymmetry is that the small state is unlikely to seek policy change unless its leadership is fixated on an issue—an effect that should be intensified in more asymmetrical dyads. For an asymmetrically exposed small state, influencing a great power's policy is costly, so small states' leaders are unlikely to pursue change on marginal issues even if policy divergence is great. For that reason, on many issues small states adopt broadly cooperative policies in their dealings with salient great powers—the costs of challenging a great power are often high and the benefits uncertain. However, cooperation does not mean compliance; there is a meaningful middle ground in which small-state leaders pursue their priorities.[51] This path will make sense for many states that lack tools available to larger powers. Small-state interest can be treated as a precondition

---

[50] George and Bennett, *Case Studies and Theory Development in the Social Sciences*, 235.
[51] Womack, *Asymmetry and International Relationships*; Long, *Latin America Confronts the United States*, 12–18; Kat, "Subordinate-State Agency and US Hegemony."

for case selection, allowing a focus on the three remaining conditions: (1) policy divergence, (2) relational salience, and (3) great-power preference cohesion. A visual depiction, stripping away nuance, gives us the "scorecard" shown in Table 3.2.

The scorecard is a descriptive and analytical tool to classify cases according to the theoretically important conditions of an asymmetrical relationship, as perceived by the small state. The assessment of a case reflects one specific conjuncture of conditions—a snapshot. Over a longer span of time, a case may change its location in the typology. That change could occur because a small state is successful in achieving influence or shifts its own preferences (endogenous change) or because unrelated events, like a change of government in the great power, lead to shifting attention or preferences (exogenous change).

The scorecard is not intended to categorize the totality of a small state's relationships or international position. Instead, it refers to divergence and preferences regarding a specific policy goal, vis-à-vis a specific partner. To say that a small state x is "successful" in a given case does not necessarily mean that x is a successful small state. The scorecard and typological theory are not an attempt to build a "theory of everything" for small states; instead, the analytical wager is that for small states, asymmetrical relationships make up a great deal of the "stuff" of international politics, and so a concrete explanation of the most important issues in those relationships offers more value, especially for policymakers, than a theory focused on general correlates of success.

The scorecard helps specify whether a situation is amenable to small-state influence. The dynamics of asymmetry mean that the values of each of these dimensions, high or low, relate closely to the great power. But that does not make the small state a passive object; instead, it means that a small state's leaders will react to these conditions as they perceive them. Over a longer period, small states' leaders may attempt to shape these factors.

Before looking at how combinations on the scorecard shape small-state strategies and case outcomes, I briefly explain each column. Although high salience for small-state leaders is treated as a precondition, small states' interests and goals remain an important object of study. Small states' leaders will most likely pursue changes to great-power policies where the existing policy incurs political

Table 3.2 Analytical scorecard

	Policy divergence (1)	Relational issue salience (2)	Preference cohesion (3)
High (a)			
Low (b)			

costs. Domestic political situations might explain how leaders' interests diverge from the great power's policy, what their goals are, and what domestic political constraints they face in pursuing them. Domestic political factors, along with the resources available, will shape a small state's effectiveness in pursuing its goals. After establishing those goals, the three factors in the scorecard are:

- **Policy divergence:** For the first dimension, the analyst needs to compare great-power policies with the goals of the small state. Is a large change in policy required to satisfy its interests, or would small adjustments do? Of the three, this is the only factor that consistently moves in the same direction as outcome: the greater the divergence, the more difficult it will be for a small state to obtain its preferred policy. In the absence of divergence, the small state would lack a reason to seek change (though it may act to preserve the status quo). If divergence is low but not zero, a small state might seek redress of lesser differences, particularly if expected costs are low. Large asymmetries mean that the rectification of even modest divergences can have significant ramifications for small states—while being almost imperceptible to a large state. In these cases, often broadly cooperative asymmetrical relationships, outcomes, and processes might be of interest. While divergence seems straightforward, it interacts with the two remaining conditions in ways that affect the likelihood of change and the strategies through which small states might achieve it.
- **Relational issue salience:** Does the small state's policy goal matter to the great power? A small state's leaders might direct an inordinate amount of attention to the dealings of a great power, but the inverse is less frequently the case. A frequent effect of asymmetry is that issues of peripheral importance to a great power's policymakers are central to the leaders of smaller states.[52] The corollary is that the central concerns of smaller countries might be marginal to the great power's foreign policy agenda. But if a small state's leader wishes to change a great power's policy, he or she must first have that power's attention.[53] As a result, agenda setting is a perennial challenge for small states in their bilateral relations and in international institutions. On its own, salience is indeterminate—low or high salience could be favorable to a small state's aims. Salience can multiply the effects of policy divergence (positively or negatively). A salient issue with great divergence presents additional risks to the small state. When a great power is inattentive, its

[52] Womack, *Asymmetry and International Relationships*, 47–51; Keohane and Nye, *Power and Interdependence*, 32–33.
[53] In a domestic context, Kingdon noted that getting an issue defined as "a problem" is a political accomplishment and a necessary precursor to policy change. Kingdon, *Agendas, Alternatives, and Public Policies*; Vasquez and Mansbach, "The Issue Cycle."

existing policy could result from policy drift or capture. The interaction between salience, divergence, and cohesion also affects the strategies a small state should consider.

- **Preference cohesion:** The third dimension regards how great-power policymakers view a problem, and whether there is a significant degree of consensus within decision-making circles about how to address that problem.[54] When preferences are undefined, weakly held, or contested, new possibilities for influence emerge. It may seem implausible that this dimension could register as "low" while salience and divergence are high. Though they ideally should overlap, it is important to separate preferences and policy. Policies can be formed or continue even when preferences are unclear, unsettled, or divided. Bureaucracies can be subject to path dependence, putting status quo policies out of step with current demands and preferences. There are three situations in which divisions between preferences and policy are most likely. First, "new" issues appear on the political agenda, but responses are constrained by pre-existing policies. Second, new policymakers may take power, leaving old policies in place because of lack of priority, indecision, or entrenchment. Third, an old "policy paradigm" long applied to a problem may collapse. Moments of crisis can signal a policy's failure, allowing for shifts in both the understanding of a problem and the policies seen as possible solutions to that problem.[55] If a great power's preferences are malleable, this offers an opportunity for small states to influence decisions by shaping the definition of the problem itself.

No single condition sufficiently explains when and how small states will succeed or fail to gain influence in their asymmetrical relationships. The interaction of conditions affects both the likelihood of the outcome and the pathways through which that outcome may occur. To create an explanatory typology, the scorecard simplifies the values into either "high" (designated "a") or "low" ("b") across the three dimensions to fill out the "property space."[56] This results in eight possible types of cases (Table 3.3), which we have given color-coded names as a memory aid (Figure 3.1). Despite obscuring considerable nuance, this rubric allows us to hypothesize about the likelihood of positive or negative outcomes across a group of similar cases, as well as to make systematic observations about "pathways" of small-state strategies and great-power responses.

---

[54] The focus on decision-making circles is not meant to discredit the possibility of other modes of influence, like pressure on legislatures or via transnational advocacy coalitions. These pressures might be reflected in a lack of consensus in the decision-making group and could be an additional "access point." Livingston, "The Politics of International Agenda-Setting," 313–29.

[55] Skidmore, "Explaining State Responses to International Change"; Welch, *Painful Choices.*

[56] Bennett and Elman, "Qualitative Research: Recent Developments in Case Study Methods," 465.

Table 3.3 Typological theory

	Policy divergence (1)	Relational issue salience (2)	Preference cohesion (3)
High (a)			
Low (b)			

Type	Color code	Combination	Description	Degree of opportunity for small state's goal seeking
1	Red	1a, 2a, 3a	Conflict/gridlocked distributional negotiations	Lowest opportunity
2	Orange	1a, 2a, 3b	Crisis or political shift that overturns understanding of a situation or policy paradigm	Medium opportunity
3	Yellow	1a, 2b, 3b	Status quo policy without vested interests	High opportunity
4	Green	1b, 2a, 3a	Problem-solving negotiations within shared problem understanding	Most likely
5	Blue	1b, 2a, 3b	Problem-solving negotiations, but divergent problem understandings	Medium opportunity
6	Violet	1a, 2b, 3a	Status quo policy supported by vested interests	Low opportunity
7	White	1b, 2b, 3a	Status quo policy supported by both countries (but with potential bargaining over benefits)	Status quo likely to be maintained
8	Grey	1b, 2b, 3b	Status quo policy subject to drift	Change unlikely to be sought

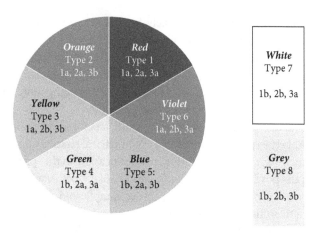

Figure 3.1 Color coding of case types

In assessing changes of great-power policy, we must be cognizant of "equi-finality." Simply put, the great power might change its policy for reasons other than a small state's influence—policy failure, personnel change, changing priorities, or domestic pressure. Past policy might be seen as no longer serving the great power's interests. Here it is important to assess how the great power's interests are defined or redefined, and whether it is the influence of small states or exogenous factors that explain changes in preference or policy. In these cases, one should ask, do the small state's leaders have a hand in shaping interests or providing policy options for their pursuit?

If an issue scores "high" on all three dimensions of the scorecard, near-term change is unlikely. However, other combinations are more propitious. The second and third dimensions interact with the degree of policy divergence to affect the likelihood that the small state can gain influence. In some situation types, small-state strategies focused on agenda setting are better suited to produce a policy change. When divergence between the small state's preference and the great power's status quo policy is high (Column 1) but the great power's leaders do not place a high priority on an issue (Column 2), the small state's leaders must try to get the issue onto the agenda. How they do so will depend largely on the degree of problem clarity (Column 3). In cases of low clarity (3b), they might be able to reshape preferences. If the problem is clearly defined (3a), small-state leaders are more likely to recast their issue to make it fit with an over-arching narrative.[57] On issues where there is low divergence (1b) and high priority (2a), changes in policy are likely because they need only be differences of

---

[57] Jourde, "The International Relations of Small Neoauthoritarian States."

degree. Cooperative negotiations are likely, facilitated by a shared understanding of the problem the new policy is meant to address. Typically, the cases of greatest interest to scholars involve high levels of policy divergence (hard cases for influence) or great uncertainty in problem definition. However, cases of great relevance to small-state policymakers may tend toward managing more cooperative asymmetrical relationships to achieve greater benefits.

On its own, each relational condition is insufficient for understanding when a small state is likely to gain influence in an asymmetrical relationship. The combination of dimensions, and the resulting location of a case in the "property space," shapes both the possibility for influence and the likely pathway to achieving it. While this rubric cannot capture all aspects of complicated cases, it helps to assess similar situations and identify strategies. By employing the scorecard, one can assess the initial status of the case and consider how a small state could successfully influence great-power policy. The typology is intended to be temporal, allowing the analyst to track the evolution of cases over time and to make within-case comparisons. The scorecard and typology could also be employed to choose cases and facilitate cross-case comparison.[58] The combination of these conditions is not deterministic, though it shapes the exercise of agency by the small state.

To make this rather complex scheme a bit easier to recall as we discuss possible strategies and progress through the case studies, we have given each case type a color. The position of each type of case on Figure 3.1 reflects the relative feasibility of attaining policy change. Adapting general "traffic light" conventions, the combination of lowest opportunity (Type 1) is represented as "red"—an indication that stopping may be safer. Across the circle, the most favorable combination (Type 4) is represented as "green"—push ahead with the pursuit of policy change. Like a flashing light, "orange" cases (Type 2) call for attention to changing conditions that create risk and reward. "Yellow" cases (Type 3) sit closer to "green," suggesting a more favorable combination of circumstances and a policy susceptible to change. On the other side, "blue" cases (Type 5) have a medium possibility of change but represent divergent understandings of the problem between small states and great powers. Such cases recall the line from Bob Dylan's masterpiece, "Tangled Up in Blue," where he sings: "We always did feel the same, we just saw it from a different point of view." A step closer to "red," "violet" cases (Type 6) revolve around great-power policies that are often held in place by vested interests.

Types 7 and 8 represent cases of a somewhat different nature, as they normally involve the maintenance of status quo policies instead of attempts to foster

[58] Elman, "Explanatory Typologies in Qualitative Studies of International Politics"; George and Bennett, *Case Studies and Theory Development in the Social Sciences.*

significant policy change. For this reason, they are represented as "white" and "grey," alongside the color wheel's representation of likelihood of change. We will refer back to these types in Chapter 4's discussion of strategies, as well as in the case studies.

Bilateral asymmetrical relationships and international context

The previous scorecard and typology place the agency of the small state in the context of asymmetrical relationships; their most evident use is to study bilateral dynamics. However, even a small state's single most important relationship exists within the context of a broader network of ties (its own and those of the great power). How does one "scale up" a relational, asymmetrical typological theory from the bilateral level to a bigger international picture? One approach is to adopt a more holistic view through statistical network analysis to get a picture of relational networks on one or more dimensions.[59] Where are relationships more intensive in terms of economic, military, or political connections? What states occupy central positions? Several studies with implications for small states have taken this approach, developing what Schulz and Rojas-de-Galarreta call a "relational network approach to peripheral agency."[60] While this is promising for expanding the relational approach to small states and asymmetry, these tools are better suited to assess a state's international position[61] than to examine influence at a more granular level of changing concrete policies.

In pragmatic analytical terms, scaling up to broader networks of relationships is not always necessary. An issue might be adequately contained within a bilateral relationship, making a largely dyadic focus sufficient. For many other issues, that will not be the case. More practically, limiting issues to the bilateral sphere tends to advantage the great power instead of allowing small states to gain leverage through numbers and recourse to multilateral institutions. The answer, in short, is to assess how the international context and network of other relationships affect (1) the small state's preferences, (2) the three analytical dimensions mentioned earlier, and (3) the strategies available to the small state.

1. **Preferences**: While preferences often have internal sources—identity, domestic politics, leadership characteristics, etc.—they are also shaped by international positionality. An asymmetrical relationship with a salient great

[59] For an overview, Hafner-Burton, Kahler, and Montgomery, "Network Analysis for International Relations."
[60] Duque, "Recognizing International Status: A Relational Approach"; Baxter, Jordan, and Jordan, "How Small States Acquire Status"; Schulz and Rojas-De-Galarreta, "Chile as a Transpacific Bridge."
[61] For an example, see Goddard, "Embedded Revisionism."

power matters for positionality, but it is not the only relevant factor. Is the small state part of a community of other small states? Is its positionality affected by other great or middle powers? It will often be hard to understand small states' preferences without taking this context into account.

2. **Analytical dimensions**: International context affects the dimensions of the scorecard:
   - **Divergence**. The degree of divergence between the large and small states' policy preferences might seem intrinsic to the relationship. Out of the dimensions considered, it is the facet most easily assessed in isolation. However, the perception of policy divergence can be relative, with small divergences easily overlooked in the context of a common foe. If the small state believes that it has outside options, it may choose to play up divergence. Even if the degree of divergence remains unchanged, international context can meaningfully affect the perceptions and implications of that divergence.
   - **Salience**. Perhaps most clearly, the broader relational network affects the degree of priority attached to any given issue and relationship. As discussed previously, a great power distributes its attention across many relationships. Instability in a relationship with another large state or a crisis in a different small state will further diminish the "normal" amount of attention that the relationship in question will receive. Without taking international context into account, it is easy to overestimate the salience of an issue/relationship.
   - **Preference cohesion**. The international context can shape preference cohesion in two ways. First, context may shape perceptions of allegiances, blocs, or other groupings among which loyalties lie. Those big-picture schemas might eclipse preferences at the bilateral level in asymmetrical relationships. Second, and related to the discussion on priority, there may be differences regarding how states prioritize a certain relationship—and whether making concessions in one relationship is worthwhile to shore up support and gain allies in the broader picture.

3. **Strategies**: The strategies open to a small state change dramatically depending on international context. While we deal with strategies in greater depth in the next chapter, a word on how strategies connect dyadic asymmetric analyses with the broader picture is warranted. It is helpful to categorize the ways in which small states gain influence: particular-intrinsic, derivative, and collective.[62] Derivative and collective power are

---

[62] For a full treatment, see Long, "Small States, Great Power?"

closely related to international context. Strategies that rely on derivative power use a relationship with a great power to accomplish an objective, either in domestic politics or against a third party. The strategy's efficacy depends on positionality. Can the small state convince the larger state of its importance within a broader international context? International irrelevance is not a winning argument, nor is being positioned as an obsequious client. The "competent performance of vulnerability" might help a state achieve support from larger states or international organizations, creating a base of derivative power, but there must be a reason that vulnerability matters.[63] Collective power too depends on connections outside the bilateral relationship. It requires a small state to act with other small and medium-sized states, at least to gain moral support. More effective still is marshalling the backing of other states through diplomatic coordination and international organizations. This strategy may be deployed to create pressure, even when the issue at hand primarily concerns bilateral negotiations with the great power.

Even when the goal of the analysis is to study small states' most salient, asymmetrical relationships, the bilateral level needs to be situated in a broader international context. Beyond that, there are international issues for which a predominantly bilateral approach is less helpful. For that reason, this book's final empirical chapter examines small states' actions as they relate to more diffuse international features like institutions, norms, and law. In the following chapter, we turn to the strategies that small states adopt in pursuit of their goals.

---

[63] Corbett, Xu, and Weller, "Norm Entrepreneurship and Diffusion 'from below' in International Organisations."

4

Playing Small Ball: Strategies for Success

There are two sides to the coin of small-state agency: the conditions that shape it and the means through which small states act. In previous chapters, we examined how the international environment, internal characteristics, and relational conditions shape small states' possibilities for influence. The typological theory (Chapter 3) will guide our analysis of the interplay between relational conditions and small states' pursuit of influence. Drawing on insights from studies of small states, negotiations, asymmetry, foreign policy, and agenda setting, this chapter focuses more explicitly on the means and strategies available to small states in pursuit of their goals. Theoretically, understanding small states' strategies foregrounds the possibility for (conditioned) agency on behalf of small states. Practically, the question of what strategies may succeed under specific conditions is of significance to policymakers. To achieve its goals, a small state's actions must emerge from its unique material and social capabilities *and* respond to international and relational conditions: namely, the interaction of policy divergence, issue salience, and preference cohesion.

First, this chapter will examine the sources of small states' foreign policy power, which I refer to as particular-intrinsic, derivative, and collective. Small states' foreign policy repertoires and toolkits are inherently more limited than those of large states, and they have less ability to change the international and relational constraints they face in the near term.[1] This encourages an emphasis on strategies that respond to the dynamics of asymmetry. Second, the chapter will locate small-state foreign policy strategies in relation to the typological theory presented in the previous chapter.

Small states' sources of power

Most states are relatively small, and these small states play significant roles in international society through joining international organizations, propagating norms, executing creative diplomacy, and influencing alliances.[2] But do they exercise power? In a world where the anxiety about survival has

---

[1] On statecraft and repertoires, see Goddard, MacDonald, and Nexon, "Repertoires of Statecraft." With application to small states, see Haugevik and Sending, "The Nordic Balance Revisited."
[2] This section draws on Long, "Small States, Great Power?"

A Small State's Guide to Influence in World Politics. Tom Long, Oxford University Press. © Oxford University Press 2022. DOI: 10.1093/oso/9780190926205.003.0004

Table 4.1 Three categories of power

	Particular-intrinsic	Derivative	Collective
Base (source)	Resource inherent to small state	Relationship with great power	Relationships with smaller powers
Means (instrument)	Threat/promise to withhold or grant	Lobbying, framing, patron alliance manipulation	Institutional; ad hoc coalitions
Amount (extent)	Contextually dependent	Potentially great	Depends on coalition
Scope (range)	Directly related to resource, plus linkages	Issue specific	Narrow for ad hoc coalitions; diffuse for institutions

Source: Long, "Small States, Great Power?"

decreased and military coercion only occasionally dominates states' agendas, conceptualizations of both power and the small state are open to reinterpretation. Critical scholars and constructivists have produced insightful visions of power that help us look beyond immediate actions and specific actors to deeper structures that shape international politics in less visible ways.[3]

Our focus is more narrowly relational and somewhat nearer term. For that purpose, returning to Robert Dahl's classic vision of power is useful. Dahl's definition of power is relational, and at first blush coercive, but Dahl implores the analyst to move beyond capabilities—what he calls the base of power—to consider the means, amount, and scope of power. Material capabilities are only a quarter of Dahl's approach.[4] This classic framework helps us assess how small states may achieve power in the sense we mean—affecting the behavior of other actors in ways that increase the small state's ability to achieve goals. These forms of power can be grouped into three categories according to the base of that power: particular-intrinsic, derivative, and collective (Table 4.1). These forms of power are not exclusive to small states—that is, the smaller partner in an asymmetric relationship. However, they are likely to be of greater relative importance to small states, given their deficits in other (perhaps more coercive) forms of power. We examine these in turn, before connecting this discussion of small states' power and strategies to our typological theory.

[3] Lukes, *Power: A Radical View*; Strange, "The Persistent Myth of Lost Hegemony"; Guzzini, "The Concept of Power: A Constructivist Analysis."
[4] Dahl, "The Concept of Power."

Particular-intrinsic

Though small states have a relative deficit in traditional reserves of material power—gross domestic product (GDP), population, or military force—they may possess particular-intrinsic resources. These resources are a potential base of power, but they only become salient in world politics through their exercise (whereas a tremendous military or economic heft has a higher baseline salience). Not commonly understood as power, the resource fades from view until it is given means and applied to a specific goal, or scope. Such resources may include valuable commodities, strategic location, or narrow military capabilities. State administrative capacity is a crucial and flexible particular-intrinsic resource.[5] In perhaps the most visible example, small hydrocarbon producers as different as Qatar and Trinidad and Tobago have used those resources to pursue foreign policy goals.[6] Small but capable or specialized militaries have been used to bolster strategic positions and pursue specific political goals, alone or within alliances.[7] Small states like Singapore and Panama have used their hub positions to bargain with great powers.[8] Several Pacific island states, among the smallest UN members by population, have emphasized that they are "large ocean states," with considerable stakes in international debates on oceans preservation, fisheries, and research. As Chan notes, "Tiny islands dispersed over wide ocean spaces expand the marine territory of a state many times over; the international legal maritime regime thus provides quasi-territorial rights over a considerable proportion of the world's oceans to a handful of small states."[9] Ideationally, small states deploy aspects of their identities to exercise influence, from Scandinavian states that seek influence as international good citizens and exercise "moral authority"[10] to a revolutionary Cuban government that aimed to shape South-South cooperation.[11]

When great powers employ their resources as sticks and carrots, particular-intrinsic resources are often most visible as the base of compulsory power. Although small states are unlikely to turn to compulsion, their particular-intrinsic power can be both broader than and complementary to other forms of

---

[5] Thanks to Anders Wivel for pointing this out.

[6] Kamrava, *Qatar: Small State, Big Politics*; Braveboy-Wagner, "Opportunities and Limitations of the Exercise of Foreign Policy Power by a Very Small State."

[7] Jakobsen, Ringsmose, and Saxi, "Prestige-Seeking Small States"; Wu, *The Defence Capabilities of Small States*; Græger, "From 'Forces for Good' to 'Forces for Status'?"

[8] Acharya, *Singapore's Foreign Policy*; Chong, "Small State Soft Power Strategies"; Long, "Putting the Canal on the Map."

[9] Chan, "'Large Ocean States,'" 541.

[10] Browning, "Small, Smart and Salient?"; Wohlforth et al., "Moral Authority and Status in International Relations."

[11] Kirk, "Cuban Medical Internationalism and Its Role in Cuban Foreign Policy"; Castro Mariño and Pruessen, *Fifty Years of Revolution*.

power.[12] The use of a particular-intrinsic power base can grant a state a central position in an international organization, allowing it to shape rules. An island state may shape maritime institutions: tiny middle-income Seychelles is "recognized as a major facilitator as well as policy entrepreneur and advocate for maritime security and the sustainable development of the oceans."[13] Particular-intrinsic power can combine material resources with identity, such as small states that promote international norms regarding mediation of conflicts or sustainable development by drawing on international perceptions of their "successful" domestic models.[14]

Derivative

Lacking significant material capabilities of their own, small states may derive power by convincing larger states to take actions that boost their interests. This has often been seen as the primary option for small states, described by Keohane as "the big influence of small allies."[15] While Keohane examined examples of intra-alliance bargaining—less generously, patron-client manipulation—derivative power has broader application. Handel, from whom we borrow the term "derivative," considered this the most important facet of small states' strength. "The diplomatic art of the weak states is to obtain, commit, and manipulate, as far as possible, the power of other more powerful states in their own interests."[16]

Derivative power poses a conceptual challenge for orthodox approaches to power. At first glance, it does not seem to have any base at all. However, following Barnett and Duvall, the base of derivative power can be understood as the constitutive relationship between small ally and great power. The means of derivative power will vary according to the small state's goals and its relationship with the great power. Derivative power underpins many of the strategies we discuss later (especially Types 2, 4, and 5), when a small state attempts to frame an issue around potential mutual benefits or seeks access to external resources. Derivative power is likely to have a narrow scope: while it is impractical for a small state to try to change the overall disposition of a great power, it may be possible to change the great power's policy on a specific matter of interest. Denmark and Estonia both behave as "super atlanticists" as a way to gain "security through entrapment"; this has usually entailed close attention to Washington's priorities (not simply acting as North Atlantic Treaty Organization [NATO] institutionalists).[17]

[12] Barnett and Duvall, "Power in International Politics."
[13] Bueger and Wivel, "How Do Small Island States Maximize Influence?"
[14] Ingebritsen, "Norm Entrepreneurs," 11–22.
[15] Keohane, "The Big Influence of Small Allies."
[16] Handel, *Weak States in the International System*, 257.
[17] Wivel and Crandall, "Punching Above Their Weight, but Why?," 413.

The advantage of derivative power is that it offers the possibility of amplifying a small state's influence through the prism of a great power. The drawback is that it entails a concomitant decline in control over outcomes.[18]

Collective

If the fundamental base of derivative power is the relationship between the small state and a great power, collective power is based in a small state's myriad near-symmetrical relationships. Small states' collective power can work in different ways: dedicated institutionalism, single-issue groupings, or ad hoc support for one state's cause. Frequently, the exercise of collective power will be mediated by institutions, in which the combination of rules and negotiating strategies can help small states ameliorate the effects of asymmetry. "Small states try to minimize the costs of conducting foreign policy by initiating more joint action and targeting multi-actor fora."[19] Formal international organizations provide more conducive environments for norm entrepreneurship and small-state diplomacy than bilateral relationships. Global organizations facilitate access to a broad audience, including larger powers, though states need to have capacity and a strategy for achieving influence through international institutions, weighing possible influence against the costs.[20]

For some issues and relationships, however, global bodies might provide less freedom of action for smaller states. Regional organizations serve as forums for policy coordination and as joint mechanisms to press small states' agendas (see Chapter 7). Small states, notably Singapore, have been major players in Association of Southeast Asian Nations (ASEAN).[21] They have been enthusiastic supporters of the European Union, demonstrating their willingness to play by institutional rules to credibly criticize larger states for hypocrisy and double standards.[22] The Caribbean Community brought together very small economies with the goal of increasing resilience to global economic fluctuations.[23] Small states have created their own groupings focused on gaining world attention or changing policies on issues of importance, such as the threat of climate change. They rely on collective power to amass votes and give greater resonance to arguments centered on survival and morality.[24] In another variation of collective

---

[18] For a relevant discussion, see Kat, "Subordinate-State Agency and US Hegemony."
[19] Neumann and Gstöhl, "Lilliputians in Gulliver's World?," 12.
[20] Moraes, "Beyond a Seat at the Table"; Jakobsen, "The United Nations and the Nordic Four."
[21] Kuik, "How Do Weaker States Hedge?"; Goh, "Great Powers and Hierarchical Order in Southeast Asia."
[22] Hey, "Luxembourg: Where Small Works (and Wealthy Doesn't Hurt)."
[23] Braveboy-Wagner, *Small States in Global Affairs*.
[24] Deitelhoff and Wallbott, "Beyond Soft Balancing"; Corbett, Yi-Chong, and Weller, "Climate Change and the Active Participation of Small States in International Organisations."

power, small states gain diplomatic support from other small states to advance their own causes with a great power, making collective power a mirror image of derivative power. Near-unanimous Latin American diplomatic demands and a threatened boycott of the Summit of the Americas added pressure on the United States to alter its policies on Cuba.[25]

In seeking to exercise collective power, small states will deploy agenda setting, the definition of mutual interests, and persuasion. Depending on institutional configurations, small states may be effective at blocking, slowing, or diluting actions they oppose within international organizations. When fundamental interests are at play, a great power may override or ignore a coalition of small states or the rules of an international body. But such coalitions can increase the costs, reputational and otherwise, to a great power for maintaining an undesirable policy. They may nudge other states toward the desired position of the small state, even where they cannot force a reversal. When other states' interests are diffuse or poorly defined, small-state coalitions can affect agendas and influence definitions of interests.

* * *

These forms of power are not exclusive to states under some threshold of material capabilities. They may be more important for all states in today's world. Military force is less acceptable and salient, interdependence is greater, and norms and institutions are more robust. However, the weaker the state in terms of traditionally salient military and economic resources, the more it must specialize in and develop these diverse approaches to power. Rich and poor small states—or, for that matter, territorially small and expansive but low-population states—differ in ways that complicate strict comparison. However, these states' attempts to exert influence share important similarities. To overcome their relative deficits in traditional material capabilities, these states turn to particular-intrinsic, derivative, or collective forms of power. Two of these three forms indicate that small states are less likely to pursue their aims individually. Small states must emphasize relationships to leverage the power of larger allies or enhance their positions through coalitions and institutions. Instead of trying to compare small states as units, these forms of power suggest an analytical strategy that seeks to compare their actions and relationships.

[25] Serbin, "Onstage or Backstage? Latin America and US-Cuban Relations"; de Bhal, "Latin American Regional Integration and the US–Cuba Thaw."

Cases and strategies

We now turn to the challenge of contextualization: When are small states most likely to deploy a certain type of strategy? Through what specific means might they act? This section connects our typological theory with possibilities for small-state influence. The goal is not to predict, ex ante, the strategies a small state will choose but to suggest general strategies most likely to achieve success under specific circumstances.

Small states' pursuit of their goals will be shaped by the degree of divergence between their objectives and the status quo, the salience of the issue at hand, and the preference cohesion of their interlocutors in large states. In situations where there is greater agreement, the governments of small states can provide information and expertise or present themselves as the most effective partner on shared priorities.[26] Small states might fit their priorities into a larger narrative—anti-communism during the Cold War and terrorism after 2001 with respect to the United States, or harmonious development vis-à-vis China today.[27] By redefining a problem in a way that converges with a great power's concerns, the small state may gain status and resources.[28] Cases of divergent priorities and cohesive preferences require bargaining and negotiation. It is usually thought that the party with more material resources gains the lion's share at the negotiating table, in part because greater resources provide states with more acceptable alternatives.[29] However, like in asymmetrical conflicts, weaker forces with cohesive aims can succeed against materially preponderant adversaries and benefit from divisions or relative inattention.[30] The degree of resource mobilization around the issue can be as important as the overall power resources of the actor.[31] Motivated small actors can achieve outcomes that seem surprising if one focuses only on material disparities.

Table 4.2 expands on the typology of the previous chapter. In addition to presenting greater or lesser constraints, each type of case lends itself to a different approach from a small state that seeks change or wants to maintain the status quo. The typological theory helps us understand the relational and situational context in which small states attempt to exercise influence. In the rest of the chapter, we describe each case type and its relationship to small states' foreign policy strategies.

---

[26] Risse-Kappen, *Cooperation among Democracies*.

[27] Jourde, "The International Relations of Small Neoauthoritarian States."

[28] Corbett, Xu, and Weller, "Norm Entrepreneurship and Diffusion 'from below' in International Organisations."

[29] Zartman and Rubin, *Power and Negotiation*; Urlacher, *International Relations as Negotiation*.

[30] Darnton, "Asymmetry and Agenda-Setting in US-Latin American Relations," 64–66; Panke and Gurol, "Small States as Agenda-Setters?"

[31] Evans, Jacobson, and Putnam, *Double-Edged Diplomacy*.

Table 4.2 Case types and small-state strategies

	Policy divergence (1)	Relational issue salience (2)	Preference cohesion (3)
High (a)			
Low (b)			

Type	Color code	Combination	Description	Small-state strategy
1	Red	1a, 2a, 3a	Conflict/gridlocked distributional negotiations	Perseverance, underimplementation, foot-dragging
2	Orange	1a, 2a, 3b	Crisis or political shift that overturns understanding of a situation or policy paradigm	Problem redefinition
3	Yellow	1a, 2b, 3b	Status quo policy without vested interests	Agenda setting for salience
4	Green	1b, 2a, 3a	Problem-solving negotiations within shared problem understanding	Finding mutual benefits
5	Blue	1b, 2a, 3b	Problem-solving negotiations, but divergent problem understandings	"Extraversion"
6	Violet	1a, 2b, 3a	Status quo policy supported by vested interests	Agenda setting and new alternatives
7	White	1b, 2b, 3a	Status quo policy supported by both countries (but with potential bargaining over benefits)	Maintain status quo while seeking additional benefits
8	Grey	1b, 2b, 3b	Status quo policy subject to drift	Buttress support for the status quo

Type 1 (red): Patience and perseverance

A focus on agency should not obscure an important reality: small states cannot get their way in every situation, especially in the short term. They may face steep costs for acting against the preferences of great powers. When a great power is strongly opposed, paying attention, and internally in agreement, possibilities for influence are low. A small state may need to bide its time. International Relations (IR) has something of a conflict bias, so these sorts of cases receive outsize attention. Because their outcomes will often reflect IR's power-based dictums, "red" conditions make for easy confirmatory cases. This type does not lend itself to changes favorable to the small state, so it may seem that no strategy exists: the small state may have to await more favorable winds. However, frustrated national preferences can become a political problem. The management of the domestic consequences of stagnated international negotiations matters. "The weak must not lose hope or become discouraged by even a glaring asymmetry. The strong must not become overconfident or assume that the weak state has no ability to achieve at least some of its objectives."[32] Maintaining the appearance of progress can buy time domestically while laying the groundwork for later international concessions.[33]

In an extreme example, since the collapse of a 2016 diplomatic truce, China has put increasing pressure on Taiwan and peeled away its remaining allies. Taiwan's attempts to find alternate formulas to ensure its security and autonomy have fallen on the deaf ears of a mainland government that radically opposes Taiwanese preferences, considers the issue a "sacred commitment," and brooks no internal discord on the matter.[34] Currently, the issue of Taiwan's status passes through Beijing, so patience and perseverance are fundamental to Taiwanese strategy—but this hardly means passivity. Taiwan's status of partial recognition and incomplete international legal sovereignty make it a unique case; however, many small states face consistent and implacable resistance from salient great powers. Some of these problems are territorial, such as Russian-supported break-away provinces;[35] some reflect economic interests;[36] others reflect institutional patterns, like the great-power dominance of the UN Security Council (UNSC).[37]

The challenges of patience are twofold. First, a small state must maintain preference unity in the face of minimal progress (in the case of negotiations)

[32] Habeeb, *Power and Tactics in International Negotiation*, 140.
[33] Long, "Putting the Canal on the Map"; Habeeb, *Power and Tactics in International Negotiation*, 29.
[34] Didier, "Economic Diplomacy: The 'One–China Policy' Effect on Trade"; Moore, "The Power of 'Sacred Commitments'"; Womack and Yufan, *Rethinking the Triangle*.
[35] Oskanian, "The Balance Strikes Back"; Berg and Vits, "Quest for Survival and Recognition."
[36] O'Sullivan, "Between Internationalism and Empire."
[37] Bourantonis, *The History and Politics of UN Security Council Reform*.

or against a potential threat. The issue at hand may be politicized by opposition leaders who promise they would do a better job. For example, one's credentials to negotiate with the European Union and German creditors became an important part of electoral politics in Greece and other small EU states.[38] The possibilities for patience may be domestically constrained, forcing weaker actors into concessions. Patience and perseverance require political effort. When faced with great-power attempts to compel action, a small state may underperform or foot-drag in its implementation of unwanted changes. In doing so, it takes advantage of asymmetries of attention and the larger state's more diffuse policymaking priorities. Small states must make patience productive by preparing for other possibilities when the winds do change. We turn to those possibilities now.

Type 2 (orange): Problem redefinition

The strategy of problem redefinition is closely connected with "framing," an idea that has been influential across social psychology, behavioral economics, public opinion research, and—most importantly for our purposes—foreign policy analysis.[39] As Mintz and Redd note, framing is an attempt to "insert into the policy debate (or into a group deliberation), organizing themes that will affect how the targets themselves as well as the public and other actors (e.g., media) perceive an issue."[40] To affect framing in an asymmetrical relationship, the issue must be (or become) salient to the great power; this strategy is most relevant when the small state's preferences diverge from the status quo policy but there is not strong cohesion of policy preferences in the great power. For example, if support for the status quo policy has been thrown into doubt due to a crisis or visible policy failure, small states have opportunities to reframe the issue at hand or ideationally reposition themselves.

From the 1990s through the first decade of the 2000s, the issue of how to address climate change divided Global South states. Industrializing heavyweights like Brazil, China, and India opposed binding emissions cuts under the argument that the historic responsibility for climate change belonged to North American and European countries. However, those already suffering most from climate change are also in the Global South. Related droughts, floods, storms, and other disasters are only growing worse. None are more threatened than small island

---

[38] Moschella, "When Some Are More Equal Than Others"; Ardagna and Caselli, "The Political Economy of the Greek Debt Crisis."

[39] For example, see influential work by Tversky and Kahneman, "The Framing of Decisions and the Psychology of Choice"; Garrison, "Framing Foreign Policy Alternatives in the Inner Circle"; Maoz, "Framing the National Interest."

[40] Mintz and Redd, "Framing Effects in International Relations."

developing states, some of whom face a near-term, existential threat from rising sea levels.[41] As the threat of climate change became clear, the issue became both more salient and more divisive for incumbent and rising powers. This created an opening for small island states, who banded together to promote, with some success, a redefinition of the issue from scientific and economic to a moral imperative.[42] Though they reshaped the agenda, maintaining pressure and forcing implementation have proved more difficult. The nature of climate change as a policy problem makes this a particular challenge. It demands a coordinated and lasting shift from many actors, but progress can be undone by domestic political swings in large emitters.

Two types of situations are likely to lead to orange cases: an external crisis that overturns status quo views or a domestic event that provokes internal division in a great power regarding a particular policy course. In the context of domestic politics, John Kingdon long ago observed that there were often many solutions waiting for a problem.[43] This idea has been refined in studies of "political opportunity structures," or the moments that make meaningful action possible and more likely to succeed. Sometimes a small state might recognize that it has the right type of opportunity, but its solution—or the policy change that it needs to meet its goals—does not quite fit. In this case, a small state can adopt strategies of redefinition, in which it reframes its needs to fit with the existing or emerging opportunity structure. But since the small state's preferences differ markedly from the status quo, a major policy change is needed. This differs from "extraversion" discussed later (Type 4/blue), where preferences coincide but salience and resource allocation are the main issues.

Type 3 (yellow): Agenda setting for salience

On low-salience issues, great powers may continue general or status quo policies even without cohesive, high-level support. Such policies can continue for long periods as a matter of special interest capture or bureaucratic routine. As with "violet" cases (Type 5), a small state needs to gain attention and achieve change in a status quo policy. However, in these "yellow" cases (Type 3), the small state is aided by a lack of cohesive preferences in the larger partner, meaning there is greater receptivity to new proposals. As a strategy, agenda setting for salience is more one-dimensional than the previous type. When unrealized common interests exist, the smaller state must gain others' attention to spur action.

---

[41] Pelling and Uitto, "Small Island Developing States"; Campbell and Barnett, *Climate Change and Small Island States.*

[42] Benwell, "The Canaries in the Coalmine"; Deitelhoff and Wallbott, "Beyond Soft Balancing."

[43] Kingdon, *Agendas, Alternatives, and Public Policies.*

Change is more likely when new policies can be persuasively framed as producing mutual benefits. Close and cooperative relationships may allow small states' policymakers to be perceived as sources of ideas and information about shared problems.

Starting in the late 1990s, several Central American governments began advocating for a free trade agreement with the United States. Leaders were concerned that Mexico's access to the U.S. market under the 1994 North American Free Trade Agreement and, later, China's accession to the World Trade Organization would damage their light manufacturing exports. Those events, along with continued threats to their own temporary provisional market access, solidified Central American preferences. The region's leaders began pushing for their own free trade agreement in 1994. For Central America, the economic stakes of access to the U.S. market are enormous; for the United States, the economic gains would be almost imperceptible. Central Americans struggled to gain a place on the U.S. agenda, with a Costa Rican negotiator noting that despite their efforts, the deal was not a priority for the United States.[44] The expansion of free trade in Latin America aligned with broad U.S. preferences, but U.S. policy favored a hemisphere-wide agreement (the Free Trade Area of the Americas [FTAA]). Negotiations opened in 2002, under George W. Bush, when Central Americans made their case as a contrast to the programs of leftist governments led by Venezuelan president Hugo Chávez.

As Mansbach and Vasquez note, "Among the most challenging of foreign-policy tasks for any actor is to determine the issue agendas of other actors and to persuade them of the legitimacy of one's own agenda and the hierarchy of issues it incorporates."[45] In asymmetrical relationships, this task is even more challenging: while unrealized gains may be very large from the small state's perspective, they are likely minor to a great power. Success in agenda setting—even where interests are compatible—is not always likely and rarely easy.

Type 4 (green): Finding mutual benefits

IR has long tended to emphasize contentious, distributive bargaining, as Hopmann notes. Rationalist models have been expanded from negotiations to the explanation of civil and international wars.[46] When preferences are

---

[44] Santa-Cruz, *US Hegemony and the Americas*, 166.

[45] Mansbach and Vasquez, *In Search of Theory*, 94, qtd. in Darnton. "Asymmetry and Agenda-Setting in US-Latin American Relations."

[46] Hopmann, "Two Paradigms of Negotiation"; Fearon, "Bargaining, Enforcement, and International Cooperation"; Powell, "Bargaining Theory and International Conflict"; Schelling, *The Strategy of Conflict*.

proximate and compatible, as in "green" cases, negotiations develop within a basic pattern of agreement. In the classic literature on negotiations, this is conceptualized as "problem-solving" as opposed to distributive bargaining. The impression in IR that hard bargaining is more common than problem-solving seems to originate in biased case selection driven by the visibility of, and fixation on, conflict. Problem-solving cases garner fewer headlines. Many negotiations seek ways to increase total possible gains—the size of the pie—instead of fighting over the slices. States often try to address common challenges or ameliorate risks. Many of these situations fit within Type 4. Such cases represent favorable situations for small states: the powerful partner is paying attention and has cohesive preferences, and its preferences are compatible with the small state's. The trick for a small state is to find and present mutually beneficial solutions.

China's rhetorical emphasis on mutual benefits with its smaller partners, especially in the Belt and Road Initiative and the Asian Infrastructure Investment Bank (AIIB), has been particularly noteworthy.[47] In the creation of the AIIB, potential members were brought together by a belief that important club goods would result. Still, it took substantial creativity to design an organization with heterogeneous members that could satisfy these differing concerns while still meeting Chinese goals.[48] Given the mostly enthusiastic responses these initiatives garnered from partners in Asia, Africa, Latin America, and even Western countries, the perception of potential mutual benefits appears widespread. In bilateral relations, finding mutual benefits is just as important but often not easy. In theory, trade negotiations should offer an ideal venue for mutual benefits; still, finding the right solution has been contentious even for allies as close as the United States and Canada.[49]

A situation with common interests, shared salience, and cohesive preferences might seem like a noncase. What is there to study if everyone agrees? This underestimates the creativity and commitment needed to achieve solutions that improve all actors' positions. Even where there are shared interests and a will to cooperate, levels of cooperation often end up being suboptimal.[50] Zartman and Rubin explain how even cooperative negotiations usually involve several stages: a diagnosis of the challenge, a search for a general formula, and then the creation of a detailed solution.[51] "Arguing" over what is appropriate can occur even in situations where a rationalist might expect agreement on common interests.[52] Within highly institutionalized settings, like the European Union,

[47] Ferdinand, "Westward Ho"; Gong, "The Belt & Road Initiative and China's Influence in Southeast Asia"; Benabdallah, "Contesting the International Order by Integrating It."
[48] Knoerich and Urdinez, "Contesting Contested Multilateralism."
[49] Bow, *The Politics of Linkage*; Hart, *Decision at Midnight*.
[50] Schelling, *The Strategy of Conflict*; Jupille et al., *Institutional Choice and Global Commerce*.
[51] Zartman and Rubin, *Power and Negotiation*.
[52] Müller, "Arguing, Bargaining and All That."

problem-solving approaches such as deliberation and consensus are common and often favorable for small states precisely because these situations start from greater common knowledge.[53] Achieving and maintaining cooperative gains nonetheless requires convincing the large power that changes are worth making—especially since benefits may seem insignificant to a large power.

Type 5 (blue): Extraversion

At the height of the unipolar order and U.S.-led war on terrorism, leaders of weak African states formed alliances with private actors, including companies and transnational organized crime, to ensure their hold on power.[54] Political scientist Cédric Jourde termed this strategy "extraversion." We use the concept of extraversion to refer to strategies in which small states seek international resources by adopting, adapting, and localizing the policy discourses of great powers for their own ends. Extraversion aligns within Handel's idea of derivative power, but with a constructivist focus on how identities, perceptions, policy discourses, and relationships are manipulated for (primarily) domestic gain.

While terms such as "manipulation" perhaps make extraversion appear like the tail is wagging the dog, we can better understand this small-state strategy if we set it in the dynamics of asymmetry. Extraversion is not usually a matter of a wily small state hoodwinking the powerful. Instead, the possibilities for this strategy emerge from an asymmetry of attention that runs inversely to asymmetries of material capabilities. Because a small state will dedicate much of its attention to a large state, it can perceive which discourses will play well there and, oftentimes, who wants to hear them. Extraversion is more than just talking the talk, however. The possibilities for deriving resources through extraversion emerge from a second dynamic: the large state's goals vis-à-vis the small state often emerge from broad imperatives that are ambiguous in their application to specific, local situations. The slippage between the overarching priorities of great powers—and the inconsistent attention dedicated to any given small state—and the translation of those priorities to another state's domestic environment makes extraversion possible. As Jourde points out, consistent with Womack and before him Jervis, though a great power may have bountiful intelligence on a small state, its views and policies are often guided by rudimentary (mis)representations.[55]

---

[53] Elgström and Jönsson, "Negotiation in the European Union"; Panke, "Small States in EU Negotiations"; Warntjen, "Between Bargaining and Deliberation."

[54] Jourde, "The International Relations of Small Neoauthoritarian States"; Carney, "International Patron-Client Relationships."

[55] Jourde, "The International Relations of Small Neoauthoritarian States," 485–86; Jervis, "Hypotheses on Misperception"; Womack, *Asymmetry and International Relationships*; Miklian, "International Media's Role on U.S.–Small State Relations."

During the Cold War, the United States was notoriously overbearing in Latin America, squelching nationalist and communist movements through pressure, covert interventions, and occasional invasion.[56] Despite that, some states developed statist economic programs (sometimes with U.S. support), while others professed anti-communism but disregarded much U.S. advice.[57] When one looks a bit closer, Cold War Latin America provides numerous examples of both authoritarians and democrats strategically deploying the rhetoric of anti-communism.[58] Many of these same leaders portrayed Fidel Castro's Cuba as a Soviet puppet,[59] though Castro and the Kremlin were often at odds. Cuba managed this game with the Soviets too, retaining substantial policy autonomy while benefiting from massive subsidies.[60] Such examples are not limited to Latin America. South Korea's anti-communism and receipt of massive U.S. aid coexisted with radically different domestic programs, a pattern that evolved to new forms after the Cold War.[61] Central Asian authoritarians used the war on terror and U.S.-Russia competition to gain diplomatic deference, military support, and loads of cash that consolidated their domestic positions against a tide of democratization.[62] Ugandan elites position themselves as an aid success story and a U.S. regional ally despite growing corruption and authoritarianism. The strategy has allowed the Ugandan government to maintain substantial autonomy despite seeming dependence. These states were deploying forms of extraversion.

Returning to the typology, this strategy is best suited to situations where policy divergence is low, great-power attention is (perhaps temporarily) high, but preferences are not cohesive. Small states' wishes and status quo policies need not align entirely, but there must be sufficient overlap to allow for rhetorical patches. Because extraversion is about gaining support and resources, at least temporary high salience is required. However, salience combines with uncertainty about how to address the specific situation of the small state. Preference incoherence exacerbates the slippage between a great power's representations and a small state's reality, making small-state rhetorical strategies potentially effective.

---

[56] Rabe, *The Killing Zone.*

[57] In the first category, Costa Rica, Mexico, and at times the Central American Common Market and the Andean Pact. In the second, the notorious Southern Cone dictatorships of the 1970s and 1980s often resisted U.S. pressures while fully embracing anti-communism at home.

[58] Schmitz, *Thank God They're on Our Side;* Clark, *The United States and Somoza, 1933–1956;* Longley, *The Sparrow and the Hawk.*

[59] Harmer, "The 'Cuban Question' and the Cold War in Latin America, 1959–1964."

[60] Gleijeses, "The View from Havana"; Blight and Brenner, *Sad and Luminous Days.*

[61] Shin, Izatt, and Moon, "Asymmetry of Power and Attention in Alliance Politics"; Cha, "Abandonment, Entrapment, and Neoclassical Realism in Asia"; Moon, "Complex Interdependence and Transnational Lobbying."

[62] Cooley, *Great Games, Local Rules.*

Type 6 (violet): Agenda setting and new alternatives

The strategy best suited to "violet" cases has two components. The first relates to putting an issue on the international agenda. A rich body of studies on politics and agenda setting first emerged in the domestic context, where agendas are often more concrete and observable (such as legislative agendas).[63] Agenda setting is often referenced but less developed in IR, outside the more formalized context of the European Union. Even at the summit of international order, the UNSC, there are limited studies of the dynamics of agenda setting.[64] For non-EU regional and issue-specific organizations, we know even less. Though international political agendas are diffuse and harder to pin down than their domestic counterparts, they can be understood as overlapping demands from international actors for the allocation of political stakes.[65] For some issues, they may be evident in the formal agendas of international organizations.[66] In many policy areas, the "agenda" that matters will be even less visible; instead of being captured by an organization's meeting schedule, what matters are the foreign policy priorities of one or several salient states. Still, the point is the same: to change a status quo policy, one needs the attention of relevant policymakers. However, gaining attention does not necessarily produce a positive change from the small state's perspective.

Caught between the export interests of neighboring Russia and the import interests of powerful actors in Western Europe, Slovakia and other small Eastern European states seemed to be fighting a losing battle in opposing—or seeking to delay—the construction of a massive gas pipeline project known as Nordstream II. The pipeline would knit Europe closer to Russian gas and undermine those countries that already host pipelines, Slovakia included. In that position, Slovakia used its EU Council presidency to spur collective opposition to the project. Its ability to shape formal agendas allowed it to put its opposition on large states' radar and keep pipeline approval off the table.[67] Nordic states used European institutions to gain traction for favored "Northern Dimension" policies, which led to greater EU investment.[68] As a non-EU member, Norway lacks access to formal institutional mechanisms for agenda setting; instead, it

---

[63] Scheufele and Tewksbury, "Framing, Agenda Setting, and Priming"; Kingdon, *Agendas, Alternatives, and Public Policies*; Baumgartner and Jones, *Agendas and Instability in American Politics*.
[64] Thorhallsson, "Small States in the UN Security Council"; Joachim and Dalmer, "The United Nations and Agenda Setting."
[65] Vasquez and Mansbach, "The Issue Cycle," 259–60.
[66] Schneider, "Weak States and Institutionalized Bargaining Power in International Organizations."
[67] Bátora, "Reinvigorating the Rotating Presidency."
[68] Magnúsdóttir and Thorhallsson, "The Nordic States and Agenda-Setting in the European Union."

has developed informal relationships with Germany and the United Kingdom to place Norwegian concerns on the EU agenda.[69]

There are two variations of the agenda-setting situation, reflected in "yellow" and "violet" cases (Types 3 and 6). As compared to "yellow" cases, "violet" cases are characterized by greater divergence between status quo policy and the small state's preferences; as a result, the small state must propose new alternatives and gain both attention and support for them—the second element of the strategy. When an issue is a low priority for the great power, small states must influence the agenda in a manner that favors their preferred solution, perhaps by internationalizing a bilateral issue or trying to cast it as a crisis. Small states might be able to reshape a larger power's preferences if these are contested or weakly held.

Types 7 (white) and 8 (grey): Maintaining the status quo

Sometimes, the great power's status quo policy will serve the small state's interests, without requiring substantial change. While such cases might not be salient or easy to observe, the dynamics of continuity deserve attention. Preserving status quo policies may require action by small states. The status quo does not last forever: in domestic and international politics, actors lobby intensely for its prolongation. Small states like Israel and Ireland do not take their friendships with the United States for granted; their leaders have spent decades developing social, legislative, and executive relations to put U.S. support beyond question.[70] North Korean leaders appear to place a similar importance on cultivating their relationship with China through different means.[71]

Maintaining beneficial status quo policies is particularly important when the relevant international context begins to shift. Starting after the 2008 Russia-Georgia war, several small Eastern European members of NATO adopted active strategies to ensure continued support for collective defense. Though U.S. and NATO policies remained unchanged, the external security environment suddenly appeared more threatening. That was true even as U.S. support for NATO remained robust under the Obama administration; the sudden uncertainty caused by the election of Donald Trump led to a redoubling of those efforts (and their expansion to larger, Western European powers). In our typology, U.S. support for European defense in the post–Cold War era had been a Type 7 case—important but not salient, with low divergence, and cohesive preferences.

---

[69] Haugevik, "Diplomacy through the Back Door."
[70] Newhouse, "Diplomacy, Inc."
[71] Kong, "China's Engagement-Oriented Strategy towards North Korea."

Under Trump, U.S. preferences became less cohesive, even though the status quo policy coincided with the preferences of Eastern European and Baltic NATO members.[72]

In politics, the status quo is resistant to change because it represents an equilibrium position and may benefit from path dependence, increasing returns, and the powerful illusion of sunk costs.[73] Dominant ideas are also central to maintaining status quo policies. If a status quo policy becomes discredited, it can be subject to rapid change.[74] To forestall that possibility, a small state may wish to show that "the status quo policy can be demonstrated to be functioning reasonably well" or discredit alternatives as infeasible.[75] Tactics for maintaining support for status quo policies are likely to involve lobbying and broad-based relations with elites—media, think tanks, universities, and the private sector. Depending on the context, these may have a broad focus on maintaining a "special relationship,"[76] or they may be sectoral, with actions targeted to relevant technocrats, regulators, businesses, and nongovernmental organizations (NGOs). Asymmetry gives the small states an important advantage, precisely because persistence and attention can outweigh capabilities.

Applying the theory: Case selection and methods

The typological theory in Chapter 3 and the strategies described earlier marry the constraints faced by small states with the ways in which they can exercise agency in pursuit of their goals. Small states retain options, despite a lack of power in the traditional sense. The conditions highlighted in the different case types make success more or less likely; however, there is room for meaningful action and different routes through which small states can exploit the policy space they possess. That makes small states' particular-intrinsic, derivative, and collective power important. The same holds for the strategies adopted by small states.

Case selection and methods

While the first three chapters have developed their theoretical points with frequent reference to examples, in the next three chapters, we explore the dynamics

---

[72] Sloan, "Donald Trump and NATO."
[73] Pierson, "When Effect Becomes Cause"; Pierson, "Increasing Returns, Path Dependence, and the Study of Politics"; Hall, "Policy Paradigms, Social Learning, and the State."
[74] Baumgartner, "Ideas and Policy Change."
[75] Baumgartner, "Ideas and Policy Change," 4.
[76] Haugevik, Special Relationships in World Politics.

of asymmetry in a more systematic range of empirical settings. We now describe our research design and methodological approach.

One goal of this book is to provide a global and comparative analysis of the international relationships of small states, bridging regions and issue areas. As such, each of the empirical chapters addresses a broad theme in world politics; within each chapter, we examine cases by region before making cross-regional comparisons in the conclusions. In the first two empirical chapters, covering security and political economy, the cases examine small states' relationships with one or two great powers, or in some cases with coherent blocs (whether international organizations like NATO or several actors united in negotiations such as the "Troika" in the European debt crisis or a "consultative group" in foreign aid and debt talks). In most cases, the larger actor is the local regional power, though in some cases they are global powers (the United States), groups of powers, or influential former colonial powers (France).

Within that structure, we have chosen two cases for each region, intentionally selecting one case of prima facie small-state success and one of small-state failure. The basic logic of the research design follows John Stuart Mill's classic "method of difference." Within each region, cases are selected for having a different outcome while possessing similarities across other relevant conditions.[77] This being the real world of international politics, our ability to "control" for those conditions is limited, and there are certainly omitted conditions not captured in the case selection. These imperfections are common in IR; we recognize and address these limitations through the analytical narratives in the cases themselves. This produces sixteen cases across the security and economics chapters, with reference to additional cases to make clarifying points. The final empirical chapter on norms, laws, and international institutions looks at small states' efforts to achieve change on issues of a more systemic nature; this also allows for examination in greater detail of how the network of relationships among small states matters to the pursuit of broad international goals.

In all three chapters, the case studies proceed through an analytic narrative.[78] Using the academic and policy literature, supplemented by news sources and documentation, the cases track the processes through which a small state pursued specific goals. First, we seek to identify the small state's goal, relying on statements corroborated by supporting actions where possible. Second, we assess the case according to the "scorecard" described earlier. This requires determining the status quo policy and the degree of divergence from small-state

[77] Eckstein, "Case Study and Theory in Political Science"; Gerring, "What Is a Case Study and What Is It Good For?"; Bennett and Elman, "Case Study Methods in the International Relations Subfield"; Seawright and Gerring, "Case Selection Techniques in Case Study Research."

[78] George and Bennett, *Case Studies and Theory Development in the Social Sciences*, chap. 5; Büthe, "Taking Temporality Seriously."

preferences, the relational salience of the issue, and the preference cohesion in support of that policy in the great power. From there, we track the development of the issue within the relationship to see how the small state pursued its goals, whether it achieved its aims, and through what process this occurred. Finally, we assess both the cases' results and the processes that connect that small state's efforts to eventual outcomes, successful or unsuccessful.

5

Small-State Security

Introduction

Recent studies of small states' agency often emphasize their influence in niche areas associated with "low politics." Core security concerns, where military capabilities remain prominent and the shadow of coercion looms, present something of a hard case for small-state influence. A recent realist study noted: "The security dilemma can be more acute for small states due to the nature of their smallness." Their limited capabilities mean they cannot escape their insecurity "solely through their own actions."[1] If great powers are preoccupied with security threats, the situation would seem dire for international society's weakest members.

The focus on traditional state security was the primary reason for pessimism in classic small-state studies, whose questions were shaped by realist theory. How could small states survive in a world characterized by threat and power? When would small states balance against, or bandwagon with, the great powers? Small states were understood to be playing for high—often existential—stakes.[2] Even when state survival is not at stake, conventional wisdom ties control of resources to security outcomes. However, such dire predictions have been largely unfounded since World War II. The security situation of the vast majority of small states has improved further since the end of the Cold War. Even essentially defenseless, very small states that faced invasion in the past seem little concerned about traditional interstate security.[3] Small states have not been as endangered or as helpless as was sometimes implied. But have they been able to achieve their security objectives?

To provide an answer to that question, this chapter explores security from the perspectives of small states. These case studies show the possibilities and limits for small states' influence in asymmetrical relationships in matters of security, as well as the ways small states pursue their goals. The chapter examines both successful and unsuccessful security policies, including attempts at security diversification

---

[1] Jesse and Dreyer, *Small States in the International System*, 21.

[2] Fox, *The Power of Small States*; Rothstein, *Alliances and Small Powers*; Handel, *Weak States in the International System*. For a recent study focused on small states and major conflicts, see Jesse and Dreyer, *Small States in the International System*.

[3] Sharman, "War, Selection, and Micro-States"; Maass, *Small States in World Politics*.

A Small State's Guide to Influence in World Politics. Tom Long, Oxford University Press. © Oxford University Press 2022.
DOI: 10.1093/oso/9780190926205.003.0005

in Africa, management of foreign military bases in Central America, alliance management in Eastern Europe, and responses to rising powers in Asia.

Africa: Asymmetry and security diversification

In a context often marked by regional insecurity and weak state consolidation, many African states must balance competing security aims. Colonial legacies and postcolonial relationships deeply shaped the security forces of many emerging states. At times, conceding security treaties and overseas bases was part of the independence bargain. These arrangements curtail independent leaders' autonomy, however, and can be a source of resentment. Proximity to former colonial powers may be a political liability, pointed to by the opposition to question leaders' nationalist credentials. But such arrangements can also provide significant benefits. A ruling regime may gain funds, military equipment and training, and political support to deflect external threats or hold power against potential rivals. Today, many states seek autonomy from former colonial powers but fear the consequences of lost resources and backing for state security and regime stability. Our first cases consider the attempts of Francophone African states, Djibouti and Gabon, to reduce security dependence on France.

Success: Djibouti finds new partners

Tiny Djibouti is an unlikely success story for security diversification. Located at the crux of the Red Sea and Gulf of Aden, it has fewer than one million residents and its territory is dwarfed by larger neighbors. It has high levels of poverty and inequality, despite having doubled its per capita income during the 2010s (to about US$3,000), and a history of sectarian conflict.[4] Despite these limitations, the ruling authoritarian regime has managed its geopolitical niche astutely (if to its own narrow benefit).

When Djibouti gained independence in 1977, it retained strong military and security reliance on France. A large French military base sat near the capital city. Next door, large, landlocked Ethiopia posed a territorial threat, given its reliance on Djibouti's ports for its trade. The new country's two major security objectives—reducing the reliance on France and balancing Ethiopia—were in tension.[5] In addition, Djibouti has had recurring border conflicts with neighboring

---

[4] Data from the World Bank Data Bank, National Accounts, Djibouti.
[5] Styan, "Djibouti: Small State Strategy at a Crossroads," 80–83; Le Gouriellec, "Djibouti's Foreign Policy in International Institutions," 391–94.

Eritrea.[6] Internal divisions within Djibouti, tracing to French rule, complicated matters further. Tensions between the two largest groups, the Issa and the Afar, continued after independence. In the early 1990s, fighting pitted Afar insurgents against the state.[7] Internal dissent and external threats incentivized continued security dependence on France. Djibouti's leaders needed the military backing of an external power. France had long played that role, and it seemed keen on retaining it.

Still, Djiboutian leaders were concerned about wavering French support in the longer term.[8] Djibouti took advantage of coinciding domestic regime stability and French strategic retrenchment to press for security diversification. This has lessened its dependence on France, though other external actors play a large role (by invitation). From the late 1990s and early 2000s, French policy was marked by lower prioritization and fragmented preferences regarding its African presence. France's status quo policy was to maintain security ties as a key element of the neocolonial *Françafrique* framework; however, there was dissent within the French political sphere over these commitments. Superficial policy continuity was marked by growing dissent and turmoil underneath. Dramatic changes upset the traditionally cozy ties between France and many postcolonial African leaders during the 1990s. The Cold War's end and the shock of the 1994 Rwandan genocide led France to re-evaluate its African commitments: "members of France's governing elites and sections of the French press increasingly questioned the benefits to France of the relationship."[9] France devalued the CFA franc, cut its military budget, and restructured key bureaucracies. Growing European integration limited some of France's old policy tools, imposed budget constraints, and consumed leaders' attention.[10] Nonetheless, there was significant divergence between France's status quo, *Françafrique* policy of a near monopoly on security ties, and the preferences of Djibouti for diversification. Many within France fretted over increased U.S. attention to Africa. But generally, the issue's salience fell for French policymakers and preference cohesion was shattered.[11] As such, this "yellow" case was marked by high policy divergence but low salience and preference cohesion for the more powerful French state.

Djibouti's response to this combination of changes in the French policy-making environment was adept. Instead of kicking France out—France retains a base—Djibouti invited others in, while also expanding its own engagement

---

[6] Mesfin, "The Eritrea-Djibouti Border Dispute."

[7] Schraeder, "Ethnic Politics in Djibouti"; Yasin, "Regional Dynamics of Inter-Ethnic Conflicts in the Horn of Africa," 110–21.

[8] Le Gouriellec, "Djibouti's Foreign Policy in International Institutions," 395.

[9] Chafer, "Chirac and 'La Francafrique,'" 13. Also, Chafer, "Franco-African Relations," 810–11.

[10] Yates, "France and Africa"; Gardinier, "France and Gabon since 1993," 239.

[11] This makes the case "yellow," or Type 3 (1a, 2b, 3b), according to the earlier typology.

in regional and international forums.[12] This approach lessened the salience of policy divergence, allowing Djibouti to pursue creative methods of diversification. In effect, Djibouti presented new solutions and shaped the agenda to its benefit, exploiting the possibilities of greater multilateralism in Francophone Africa's security structures. Djibouti's tactical embrace of the U.S.-led war on terror led to the hosting of a permanent U.S. military presence. That force sat alongside French facilities, then overshadowed it as the U.S. role grew.[13] For the United States, Djibouti became a higher priority, and one where preferences overlapped with those of the Djiboutian government under the decades-long rule of Ismail Omar Guelleh. As anti-piracy joined counterterrorism as a salient mission, Djibouti diversified its security ties further by hosting multilateral campaigns and Japanese and Chinese maritime forces.[14] Djibouti has not been satisfied to play base host. It has drawn on this external support to upgrade its own coastal defenses. In turn, it portrays itself as a good citizen through participation in EU-led anti-piracy efforts and by exercising agency in the West African Intergovernmental Authority on Development (IGAD). IGAD has been a weak catalyst for integration efforts,[15] but it creates another bridge for Djibouti to connect with international partners.

Djibouti took advantage of a window of lower priority and preference fragmentation for France; it found alternatives for diversification that ameliorated the policy divergence with France. It helped that Djibouti's goal was not to evict France, but to reduce security dependency. That made expansion of security ties through joint U.S.- and EU-led initiatives a feasible option, with France retaining a role. From there, Djibouti broadened bilateral ties with rising maritime powers under the international rubric of anti-piracy. These ties reduced security dependency on the former colonial power and helped Djibouti upgrade its ports and infrastructure in ways that facilitated economic expansion, including links to China's Belt and Road Initiative.[16] This bolstered the regime and set the stage for greater diversification.

The benefits of "success" in security diversification can be ambiguous for the larger population. Security successes often entrench the governing elites who capture the lion's share of material and political benefits.[17] This cautionary note is particularly relevant in a polity marked by authoritarian government, ethnic tensions, and socioeconomic divisions, but it is an important caveat in interpreting all cases. Success here is from the regime's point of view.

---

[12] Le Gouriellec, "Djibouti's Foreign Policy in International Institutions."
[13] Styan, "Djibouti: Small State Strategy at a Crossroads," 83–84.
[14] Mason, "Djibouti and Beyond."
[15] Bereketeab, "The Intergovernmental Authority on Development."
[16] Styan, "China's Maritime Silk Road and Small States."
[17] Styan, "Djibouti: Changing Influence in the Horn's Strategic Hub."

Diversification helped secure the governing elite and its economic allies. From the opposition's point of view, neither dependence on France nor successful diversification is necessarily advantageous.

While Djibouti has become a particular hub for security cooperation, it is not alone within Francophone Africa in its successful pursuit of security diversification. Senegal, a country of twelve million on the West African coast, also reduced reliance on France. Like Djibouti, Senegal has experienced internal conflict, particularly a recurrent insurgency in its isolated, southern Casamance region. Unlike Djibouti, Senegal's political history has been comparatively democratic since gaining independence in 1960. Senegal lacks the territorial advantages of Djibouti, which serves as a key to the strait between the Red Sea and the Gulf of Aden.

Like much of Francophone Africa, Senegal emerged with deep security ties to France. The country's capital of Dakar has been home to a large French base and deployment since colonial times.[18] But "France's recent attempts to reduce its military presence in Africa have coincided with attempts by [Senegalese president Abdoulaye] Wade to assert greater independence from the former colonial ruler."[19] In that context, Senegal has developed bilateral security relations with the United States while also opening ties with China after 2005. Senegal broadened its circle of allies to Middle Eastern states, while also engaging in regional mediation efforts and multilateral security institutions. All of this has allowed the country to diversify without displacing France.[20] Together, Djibouti and Senegal suggest how small states can enhance security diversification through agenda management that allowed them to advance an effective frame for their preferred options.

Failure: Gabon deepens dependence

Diversification is not easy, however. It goes counter to path-dependent relationships. It can alienate important allies while inviting scrutiny from new partners. A determined major power will possess multiple levers—economic asymmetries, investments, and sympathetic factions—that it may employ to maintain exclusivity. Achieving diversification requires a state apparatus with sufficient distance from the traditional major power to conceive and execute such a strategy. We now examine another case in Francophone Africa, in which Gabonese leaders sought greater diversification but failed to achieve it despite

---

[18] Chafer, "France and Senegal."
[19] Arieff, "Senegal: Background and US Relations," 13–14.
[20] Bodian and Kelly, "Senegalese Foreign Policy"; Chafer, "France and Senegal"; Arieff, "Senegal: Background and US Relations," 13–18.

contextual factors similar to those that facilitated Djibouti's quest. Though it sought incipient ties with China and made moves to diversify, Gabon's governing regime remains highly dependent on French military support. We briefly consider an additional case, in Mali, in which a crisis provoked deepened dependence.

Gabon, an oil-exporting nation of 2.1 million people, gained independence from France in 1960. Still, Gabon "maintained a clientist relationship with its French patron within a neo-colonialist framework," based on cooperation agreements, tight security ties, and French involvement in the oil sector.[21] From independence to 2020, the country has had but three presidents—with Omar Bongo ruling from 1967 until his death in 2009, followed by his son Ali Bongo. Omar Bongo gained power with the direct intervention of Charles de Gaulle, and the Bongo family cultivated close ties with France. These ties have always had a military element.[22] France ensures the state's integrity through formal defense treaties and via a permanent military deployment. The arrangement has helped the Bongo family hold off challengers while boosting France's regional power projection.[23] Though the relationship was not without dissent, Gabon's Omar Bongo largely seemed content to maintain security dependency. Though France scaled back financial and military aid in the 1990s, French president Jacques Chirac made few demands for democratic reforms and tolerated vote-rigging in Gabon. This comity helps explain why Gabon did not immediately seek new partners despite deteriorating levels of material support from France.[24]

By the late 2000s, however, Gabon began to seek diversity in its economic and security ties to gain greater autonomy and leverage. French resource allocations had declined. Then, critical French official and media statements regarding dubious elections and corruption in 2008–2009 and again in 2016 created tensions with the new—and weaker—Ali Bongo government. After the 2009 elections, President Sarkozy offered tepid support for Ali Bongo, partially walking back official criticism. Under pressure from authoritarian leaders in Gabon and Cameroon, Sarkozy ousted a French minister who had been particularly vocal in his criticism of the authoritarian governments.[25] Despite Sarkozy's tepid turnaround, uncertainty had been sowed. A French commitment to democratization would spell trouble for a regime constructed on decades of French support.

Diminished French material and political support added impetus to Gabon's desires for security diversification. Given its oil reserves and strategic coastal

---

[21] Gardinier, "France and Gabon since 1993," 225.

[22] Gardinier, "France and Gabon since 1993," 228–29.

[23] Moncrieff, "French Relations with Sub Saharan Africa under President Sarkozy," 33–34.

[24] Gardinier, "France and Gabon since 1993," 230–32.

[25] Moncrieff, "French Relations with Sub Saharan Africa under President Sarkozy," 33; Cumming, "Nicolas Sarkozy's Africa Policy," 28.

position, the country does not lack for suitors. Engagement with China grew during the 2010s, including visits from Chinese military forces and some arms purchases.[26] Sino-Gabonese security relations built on growing economic ties, including investments in oil and mining, and growing trade.[27] In 2018, Ali Bongo met with the Chinese defense minister in the Gabonese capital of Libreville, and Bongo called publicly for greater defense cooperation.[28]

Divergence between France's status quo policy and emerging Gabonese interests in diversification, especially with China, was high. The issue was rarely salient for French policymakers, however. And after Gabon missed the window of opportunity in the 1990s, France's preferences grew increasingly cohesive. Following France's 2002 elections, the government renewed political ties with leaders in many postcolonial states, ameliorating the strains of the 1990s.[29] A new policy framework was consolidated after 2010.[30] Worried about being displaced by the Pentagon, France re-established a greater preference consensus on preserving its influence in Africa by Europeanizing some of its commitments, while also showing renewed willingness to engage militarily.[31] In this "violet" case, the status quo policy diverged from Gabonese preferences; despite low salience, those policies had cohesive support from French interests.

In 2016, the French prime minister expressed doubts about Gabon's democracy following fraudulent elections to keep Ali Bongo in power. Gabon recalled its ambassador in protest.[32] It seemed a tipping point might have been reached. Instead, France used questions about the 2016 vote to rebuild its ties with Bongo by accepting the results—France viewed the Gabonese opposition as anti-French.[33] Gabonese reliance on France remained. In January 2019, an ailing and absent Ali Bongo faced an attempted coup d'état from junior officers. The shadow of French support of the Bongo government was evident. The French Foreign Ministry condemned the coup attempt and called for stability; French president Emmanuel Macron made statements supportive of Bongo in the following weeks.[34]

---

[26] Nantulya, "Chinese Hard Power Supports Its Growing Strategic Interests in Africa."

[27] Alden, "China in Africa"; Alves, "China and Gabon."

[28] Xinhua, "Interview: Gabon Seeks More Cooperation with China: Gabonese President," September 1, 2018, http://www.xinhuanet.com/english/2018-09/01/c_137436077.htm; China Military Online, "Gabonese President Meets with Chinese Defense Minister," February 26, 2018, http://eng.chinamil.com.cn/view/2018-02/26/content_7952675.htm.

[29] Chafer, "Chirac and 'La Francafrique,'" 17–18.

[30] This makes the case "violet," or Type 6 (1a, 2b, 3a), according to the earlier typology.

[31] Chafer, "Franco-African Relations," 811–13.

[32] The Economist, "A French-African Quarrel with the Former Coloniser," January 26, 2016.

[33] Nicolas Haque, "A Week in Post-Election Gabon," Al Jazeera, October 1, 2016, https://www.aljazeera.com/blogs/africa/2016/10/week-post-election-gabon-161001064825797.html.

[34] Ruth Maclean, "Gabon Detains Soldiers after Failed Coup," The Guardian, January 7, 2019, https://www.theguardian.com/world/2019/jan/07/gabon-military-seize-national-radio-station-in-apparent-coup-attempt; Florent Mbadinga, "France—Gabon, la petite phrase d'Emmanuel Macron

After a decade in power and numerous diplomatic spats with France, Ali Bongo has managed little effective security diversification. Why has Gabon's security diversification been so limited compared to Djibouti or Senegal? According to one analyst, Gabon's "political class, haunted by its own dependency and corruption, is still unable to articulate a vision of national independence" from France.[35] Given Bongo's reliance on the loyalty of security forces to retain power, and those security forces' long and close relations with their French counterparts, the bilateral relationship remains a pillar of regime stability.

If regime *stability* is central to Gabon's limited diversification, regime *instability* has reversed Mali's relatively diverse security ties. After its independence in 1960, Mali's new socialist government took a "hostile" view of relations with its former colonizer. Mali broke with France's regional currency zone and limited security cooperation. In later decades, Malian foreign policy goals were shaped by the need to maintain favorable ties with international donors and gain international backing in recurring separatist conflicts in the country's north, including through official support for the U.S.-led war on terrorism.[36] In exchange for hard currency and development funding, "the Malian government has adopted a strategy of compliance aimed at maximizing aid flows coming into the country."[37]

The Malian army valued international ties but also retained some autonomy from international actors. Mali's military government signed a military cooperation agreement with France in 1985, but it also built close relations with the United States during the same period. However, diversification and autonomy did not produce a more effective military or better civil-military relations. In the 2000s, a Tuareg separatist insurgency grew. In addition, radical armed Islamic groups gained ground in the country's north. Violence provoked a mass exodus. In response, the military launched a coup in 2012. That initiated a shift in security relations.[38] The United States temporarily cut military and most economic aid. Flows from other donors were also interrupted.[39]

France took a different approach. Despite French president Hollande's initial lack of interest, by late 2012, Mali became a highly salient issue. Given French concerns about terrorism and migration, threats to its investments, and pressure

au sujet d'Ali Bongo," La Libreville, March 14, 2019, https://lalibreville.com/video-france-gabon-pet ite-phrase-demmanuel-macron-dali-bongo-on-lui/.

[35] Moncrieff, "French Relations with Sub Saharan Africa under President Sarkozy," 34.
[36] Lecocq and Schrijver, "The War on Terror in a Haze of Dust," 156; Gutelius, "Islam in Northern Mali and the War on Terror," 66–67.
[37] Bergamaschi, "The Fall of a Donor Darling"; quote from Bergamaschi, "Mali: Patterns and Limits of Donor-Driven Ownership," 5.
[38] Bleck and Michelitch, "The 2012 Crisis in Mali"; Wing, "Mali: Politics of a Crisis."
[39] "Country/Territory Report—Mali," 14; Fané, "La Politique Étrangère Du Mali: 1960–2008."

from neighboring African presidents, French preferences converged on military action.[40] Officially, French intervention came at the request of Mali's interim president Dioncounda Traoré.[41] Initially installed by coup leaders, Traoré became dependent on France.[42] In a larger sense, France's intervention demonstrated the failure of Mali's security strategy. It also reversed Mali's diversification of security ties and upended attempts to create domestic forces capable of maintaining security independently.[43] The French intervention reversed militants' gains but then devolved into a prolonged presence with a large UN contingent. The ongoing intervention in this "red" case has produced growing tension, recurring violence, and increasing human rights abuses. Mali's security goals seem increasingly separate from policies carried out by the French-led international forces.[44] The outcome is likely to be a weakening of the armed forces and greater reliance on external security actors[45]—a dreadful turn of events for a country once considered by international donors to be a regional model.[46]

Americas: Bases and bargains

The relationships between the United States and Central American republics are characterized by a history of great-power intervention and small-state security dependence.[47] During the nineteenth and early twentieth centuries, the United States launched military interventions and several occupations; in the Cold War, covert intervention and deep involvement in civil conflicts were common. Multilateral security frameworks, like the hemisphere-wide Rio Treaty and the more recent Central American Regional Security Initiative (CARSI), have been complemented by intensive bilateral security ties.[48] For decades, there were few sustained Central American attempts at security diversification, aside from the revolutionary Sandinistas in the 1970s and 1980s.[49] Instead, bargaining for the

---

[40] Marchal, "Briefing: Military (Mis)Adventures in Mali," 487–90, offers a close read of the French decision and downplays economic motivations. Henke, "Why Did France Intervene in Mali in 2013" sees these concerns in a regional context and emphasizes Defense Ministry advocacy of a unilateral French action.
[41] Wing, "Mali: Politics of a Crisis"; Marchal, "Briefing: Military (Mis)Adventures in Mali."
[42] Henke, "Why Did France Intervene in Mali in 2013," 8, 11.
[43] In the broader sense, then, the case is Type 1 (1a, 2a, 3a) according to the earlier typology. Under the immediate postcoup government, preference divergence was low (1b), but this was short-lived.
[44] Tull, "Rebuilding Mali's Army."
[45] Bleck and Michelitch, "The 2012 Crisis in Mali," 25. On extraversion, see Jourde, "The International Relations of Small Neoauthoritarian States."
[46] Bergamaschi, "The Fall of a Donor Darling."
[47] For an overview, see Long, "Small States in Central America."
[48] Rivera and Aravena, "Central America and the United States"; Rosenberg and Solís, *The United States and Central America.*
[49] Pastor, *Not Condemned to Repetition.*

benefits of cooperation has been more common. In the two cases that follow, we draw out the small states' goals regarding the place of U.S. bases in bilateral security relations and assess relative degrees of success in achieving material benefits, political support, and autonomy.

Success: El Salvador gains benefits and action space

Situated on the Pacific Coast of the Central American isthmus, El Salvador is a densely populated state with some six million residents. Two facets of its long security relationship with the United States bear mention. First, the United States was deeply involved in El Salvador's civil conflict. The U.S.-backed Salvadoran government and paramilitaries fought leftist guerrillas inspired by the Cuban and Nicaraguan revolutions. The war reached a bloody crescendo in the 1980s, killing an estimated 75,000 civilians.[50] In the early 1990s, the demobilized guerrillas (FMLN) were incorporated as a political party. They twice won the presidency in the 2000s. A second fundamental feature of the U.S.-Salvador relationship, linked to that conflict, is the presence of 1.3 million Salvadoran-born migrants in the United States. Many have tenuous legal status. The remittances Salvadorans send home reach 20% of gross domestic product (GDP) in some years.[51]

Since 2000, El Salvador has hosted a U.S. military presence at its Comalapa Air Base, described in a recent study as a "tiny annex to a civilian airport," near the capital city.[52] Though the U.S. Southern Command emphasizes that Comalapa and similar locations "are not bases," such small facilities serve as key nodes in the U.S. projection of military capabilities, especially in support of drug interdiction.[53] In El Salvador's negotiations over the terms and benefits of hosting a U.S.-run "forward operating location," there has been relatively little divergence between U.S. and Salvadoran positions. The matter garners U.S. attention only in the moment when negotiations arise. The United States has cohesive, bureaucratically driven preferences to maintain or moderately expand the facility. The introduction of Salvadoran relations with China and contentious discussions on migration have produced often contradictory U.S. preferences

---

[50] The FMLN is the Faribundo Martí National Liberation Front, in its Spanish initials. On U.S. involvement in the conflict, see LeoGrande, *Our Own Backyard*; Crandall, *The Salvador Option*.

[51] "Personal Remittances, Received (% of GDP)—El Salvador," World Bank; "Facts on Hispanics of Salvadoran Origin in the United States, 2017," Pew Research Center, https://www.pewresearch.org/hispanic/fact-sheet/u-s-hispanics-facts-on-salvadoran-origin-latinos/.

[52] Bitar, *US Military Bases, Quasi-Bases, and Domestic Politics in Latin America*, 25.

[53] U.S. Southern Command, "Cooperative Security Locations," n.d., https://www.southcom.mil/Media/Special-Coverage/Cooperative-Security-Locations/.

in the broader relationship, which El Salvador has sought to exploit.[54] In this "grey" case, El Salvador has used the base, on which there is fundamental agreement and cohesive preferences, to gain benefits and achieve other goals. These include maintaining some "relational autonomy" in other policy ambits whenever U.S. attention declines.[55]

In the late 1990s, the United States sought facilities around the region to offset the loss of major bases in Panama.[56] Although the proposed U.S. presence in El Salvador drew some dissent from the FMLN, now the major opposition party, the Salvadoran government approved a slightly modified agreement. Over a series of renewals since 2000, El Salvador has maintained a small U.S. presence—often only some 15 U.S. service members.[57] A political consensus emerged that this small presence was desirable. The agreement has been renewed with the support of Salvadoran governments of three different stripes—the traditional elite's conservative party, the leftist FMLN, and in 2019 populist president Nayib Bukele. Hosting a U.S. presence helped these different governments maintain a positive relationship with the United States, including support for a Salvadoran military that remains a key powerbroker. These governments have also retained somewhat greater political autonomy than their neighbors.

The first extension of the agreement in 2008–2009 offered an opportunity for renegotiating terms and benefits. Initially, the U.S. proposed expanding its facilities and presence at Comalapa. In El Salvador, both the outgoing conservatives and the incoming FMLN administration favored renewal. But the Salvadorans rejected the proposed expansion due to sovereignty concerns and logistical worries caused by the facility's suburban location. Despite that, the Salvadoran government suggested replicating the Comalapa agreement at other locations. The U.S. ambassador wrote that "the [Salvadoran] Defense Minister wants a permanent U.S. military presence beyond Comalapa—as a way to obtain more resources for the El Salvador Armed Forces."[58] Though no new sites were officially developed, there was an expansion of U.S. counternarcotics aid to the tune of $200 million. In El Salvador, the bipartisan support for the U.S. presence at Comalapa was a "symbol of the continuation of the special relationship between San Salvador and Washington."[59]

---

[54] Throughout the period, the basing issue is generally "grey," or Type 8 (1b, 2b, 3b), according to the earlier typology, though in occasional moments, greater salience gives it the characteristics of a "blue," or Type 4 (1b, 2a, 3b), case.

[55] Russell and Tokatlian, "From Antagonistic Autonomy to Relational Autonomy."

[56] David Gonzalez, "Salvadorans Balk at American Plans to Use Airport," New York Times, July 4, 2000, https://www.nytimes.com/2000/07/04/world/salvadorans-balk-at-american-plan-to-use-airport.html.

[57] Lindsay-Poland, "US Military Bases in Latin America and the Caribbean," 86; Bitar, *US Military Bases, Quasi-Bases, and Domestic Politics in Latin America*, 67–75.

[58] U.S. Embassy in San Salvador, "GOES Agrees to Five-Year Comalapa Extension," April 2, 2009, https://wikileaks.org/plusd/cables/09SANSALVADOR301_a.html.

[59] Bitar, *US Military Bases, Quasi-Bases, and Domestic Politics in Latin America*, 74.

That special relationship implied significant Salvadoran deference to U.S. security priorities in the region, but it was not ubiquitous subordination. Starting in 2018, El Salvador took steps to change its diplomatic recognition from Taiwan to China—a crucial issue for demonstrating Salvadoran foreign policy autonomy. When the decision was announced by left-leaning president Salvador Sánchez Cerén, he was berated by the U.S. ambassador, several Trump administration officials, and key Republicans in Congress. Despite U.S. pressure, the new Bukele administration reiterated support for the changed recognition. Via Twitter, Bukele insisted that autonomy had paid off, trumpeting a massive Chinese aid and investment package.[60] But Bukele also made overtures to maintain favor with U.S. president Donald Trump. The renegotiation of Comalapa was a helpful card. Military ties enjoyed support among the same U.S. constituencies most miffed by the recognition of China. Using the more amicable issue of Comalapa, Bukele could emphasize mutual benefits. With substantial fanfare, Bukele and visiting secretary of state Mike Pompeo signed a five-year extension of the agreement for the U.S. use of facilities at the Comalapa airport. Bukele also used the tacit support—and practical inattention—of the Trump administration to solidify his increasingly authoritarian control over Salvadoran politics.

However, there is little doubt that El Salvador's hand was weaker on the transnational issue of migration than on base negotiations. The Temporary Protected Status (TPS) of hundreds of thousands of Salvadoran migrants in the United States came under threat from the Trump administration. In 2019, both sides avoided publicly linking the legal status of Salvadoran immigrants with the extension of Comalapa. However, a partial extension of TPS followed on the heels of the Comalapa renewal and related agreements on gangs and migration enforcement.[61] Announcements of security cooperation agreements between Bukele and the Trump administration highlighted "dangerous irregular migration," organized crime, and border security in the same sentence.[62] More definitive evidence regarding the 2019 talks remains classified; however, in previous

[60] Nelson Renteria, "China Signs on for 'Gigantic' Investment in El Salvador Infrastructure," Reuters, December 4, 2019, https://www.reuters.com/article/el-salvador-china/update-1-china-signs-on-for-gigantic-investment-in-el-salvador-infrastructure-idUSL1N28E00J.

[61] Karen DeYoung and Mary Beth Sheridan, "During Pompeo's Visit, El Salvador's New President Says Migrant Problem 'Starts with Us,'" Washington Post, July 22, 2019, https://www.washingtonpost.com/national-security/during-pompeos-visit-el-salvadors-new-president-says-migrant-problem-starts-with-us/2019/07/22/3cda343e-ac25-11e9-bc5c-e73b603e7f38_story.html; "EE.UU. renovará con el país acuerdo para la base antidrogas," Diario El Mundo, July 20, 2019, https://elmundo.sv/ee-uu-renovara-con-el-pais-acuerdo-para-la-base-antidrogas/; Nicole Nerea, "Salvadorans on TPS Will Now Be Able to Stay in the US for Another Year," Vox, https://www.vox.com/policy-and-politics/2019/10/28/20936782/el-salvador-tps-us-agreement-asylum-dhs-uscis.

[62] U.S. Department of Homeland Security, "Joint Statement between the U.S. Government and the Government of El Salvador," September 20, 2019, https://www.dhs.gov/news/2019/09/20/joint-statement-between-us-government-and-government-el-salvador. Also see Galbraith, "Trump Administration Takes Domestic and International Measures to Restrict Asylum."

extension talks, leaked cables show that basing and migratory status were discussed together.[63] More generally, Bukele employed Comalapa and some visible concessions on regional migration to preserve autonomy on China policy and deflect scrutiny of his domestic politics. Even in the difficult context of Trump's anti-immigration pressure on Central America, El Salvador extracted benefits from a U.S. presence that is perceived as desirable across the Salvadoran political spectrum and military, while retaining some foreign policy autonomy.

Failure: Honduras's declining benefits at a higher cost

Even within similar patterns of asymmetrical alignment, small states' ability to derive benefits and maintain some autonomy varies widely. This is evident in the U.S.-Honduran security relationship, of which the U.S. military presence at the Soto Cano base is just one element. Honduras is situated in the heart of Central America, sharing land borders with three states, including El Salvador. With a territory five times larger than El Salvador, Honduras is home to some nine million people. The United States has been deeply involved in Honduras for over a century. During the 1980s, Honduras was a key platform for U.S. involvement in regional conflicts. U.S. forces began operating from the Soto Cano airfield, where they have remained ever since. The base remains the major U.S. staging ground in Central America. It now hosts between 500 and 1,500 U.S. personnel at any given moment, granting it a strategic importance greater than Comalapa. In 2019, the U.S. task force commander at Soto Cano noted, "If we weren't here it's hard to see how SOUTHCOM can have relations with partner nations outside of the embassies."[64] The United States has smaller "forward operating locations" in several places, especially on Honduras's Caribbean coast.[65] This presence creates U.S. bureaucratic support for status quo policies with considerable preference

---

[63] On a 2008 visit to El Salvador, U.S. Deputy Secretary John Negroponte moved immediately from mentioning open talks on Comalapa and counternarcotics to "recogniz[ing] El Salvador's desire to extend Temporary Protected Status (TPS) for Salvadorans in the U.S." U.S. Embassy in San Salvador, "Deputy Secretary Negroponte Meeting with Salvadoran Foreign Minister Marisol Argueta," June 28, 2008, https://wikileaks.org/plusd/cables/08SANSALVADOR723_a.html.

[64] Army Col. Steven Barry, qtd. in Todd South, "Deep in the Mountains of Honduras, Few Know What This US Military Task Force Does," Army Times, https://www.armytimes.com/news/your-army/2019/08/12/deep-in-the-mountains-of-honduras-few-know-what-this-us-military-task-force-does/.

[65] The locations include Mocoron, Caratasca, and Guanaja. Bitar, US Military Bases, Quasi-Bases, and Domestic Politics in Latin America, 160–62. See reports from Thom Shanker, "US Turns Its Focus to Drug Smuggling in Honduras," New York Times, May 6, 2012; Zeina Awad, "The Soldiers in America's War on Drugs," Al Jazeera, https://www.aljazeera.com/blogs/americas/2012/08/31596. html; "Abrirán nueva base naval en Isla de Guanaja," La Prensa, November 11, 2011, https://www. laprensa.hn/csp/mediapool/sites/LaPrensa/Honduras/Apertura/story.csp?cid=328725&sid= 267&fid=98.

cohesion. However, Honduras rarely gains high-level attention in the United States (with a partial exception for migration).

Soto Cano's regional, strategic importance has not given Honduras greater leverage; it has derived fewer benefits and preserved less autonomy than El Salvador in the last two decades. What has Honduras sought? The general pattern displays similarities to El Salvador.[66] Hosting U.S. military facilities signals alignment and acts as a beacon for aid. U.S. security aid and facilities upgrades are welcomed by a military that long invested little in equipment.[67] Honduran security cooperation generates support in the U.S. Congress, even in the face of problems including the conviction in U.S. courts of the president's brother for drug trafficking, the murders of high-profiled activists, and the discovery of police engaged in contract killing—though there are analogs for many of these unenviable demerits in El Salvador as well. Welcoming counternarcotics missions provided some cover from U.S. pressure over the country's role as a major transit point for northbound cocaine and regarding involvement of high-ranking officials and their families in organized crime.[68]

In exchange, the United States has been granted free reign. Though formally U.S. personnel are restricted in their actions, those restrictions have had little weight in practice. Honduran governments have offered access to U.S. armed forces and close alignment with U.S. policies in exchange for political backing. At a minimal level, the Honduran government retained U.S. support, but even this wavered according to shifting winds in Washington. In 2009, a military coup toppled Honduran president Manuel Zelaya. Though Zelaya was somewhat critical of U.S. policy—and denounced by opponents as an acolyte of Venezuela's Hugo Chávez—the United States withheld much assistance from the pro-U.S. postcoup government. Nonrecognition created a significant threat to Honduran interests. In response, subsequent Honduran governments have sought to safeguard relations with the United States. U.S.-Honduran relations again became close, with a restoration and then expansion of aid. In late 2017, the United States recognized the re-election of President Juan Orlando Hernández, pushing aside international denunciations of fraud and violence. But other forms of support have dwindled. U.S. aid has fallen sharply from a 2016 peak.[69] On several occasions, Trump threatened to withhold all remaining aid to coerce compliance with his anti-migration policies, while also cancelling TPS for 57,000 Hondurans the United States.[70]

---

[66] The case can be understood as Type 7 (1b, 2b, 3a) according to the earlier typology.

[67] Meyer, "Honduras: Background and U.S. Relations."

[68] Dudley, "Honduras Elites and Organized Crime."

[69] Meyer, "Honduras: Background and U.S. Relations," 10–12.

[70] Pew Research Center estimates that there are about 425,000 undocumented Hondurans in the United States; these 57,000 were granted a temporary—but long-extended—right to stay in the United States. The cancellation was held up in U.S. courts as of early 2020.

Honduras sacrificed more autonomy for this declining support. The post-coup years saw an expansion of U.S. facilities and operations on Honduran soil, despite bloody episodes of U.S. counternarcotics overreach. Hernández's weak second-term government followed the Trump administration in recognizing Jerusalem as the Israeli capital and starting a process to move its embassy there.[71] Hernández signed a widely maligned and politically costly migration agreement, seen as more domestically punitive than the agreement signed by El Salvador, and without the accompanying considerations on TPS.[72] Encouraged by the United States, Hernández has been profusely pro-Taiwan. Even so, U.S. defenses of the Honduran government's record on drug trafficking have grown increasingly feeble, with a rejection of the Honduran defense of the president's brother. Pressure grows amidst attention to the president's complicity.[73] Remaining U.S. aid under Trump was more narrowly focused on U.S. objectives—especially bolstering borders and policing drug flows.[74] The Biden administration has announced anti-corruption measures and aid that would bypass the Honduran government. This is widely seen as a shot at governing elites. Honduras has few options for building supportive coalitions or developing alternative international partnerships just as its primary benefactor is increasing scrutiny and turning off the aid spigot. Honduras's security bargaining has tenuously maintained U.S. tolerance of the incumbent government—with few benefits for the population—at a high cost to autonomy.

Asia: Managing change in the Himalayas

Being landlocked, tucked among some of the world's highest peaks, and sandwiched between the world's two most populous powers is not an easy geopolitical position for a small state. Yet, it is precisely the situation of both Nepal and Bhutan. These states border only India and China, divided from one another by the Indian state of Sikkim. Until 1975, Sikkim was a nominally independent kingdom. After a royal deposition and a plebiscite, Sikkim was absorbed

---

[71] Tovah Lazaroff, "Netanyahu: Honduras on Path to Opening J'lem Embassy with Trade Office," Jerusalem Post, September 1, 2019, https://www.jpost.com/Israel-News/Netanyahu-Honduras-on-path-to-opening-Jlem-embassy-with-trade-office-600268.

[72] Guatemala also signed such an agreement on asylum claims, similar in effect to a "safe third country" agreement. The three Central America agreements are very similar, but El Salvador's location means it is not a major conduit for transmigration. The agreements have been challenged in U.S. courts and derided by international human rights bodies. Galbraith, "Trump Administration Takes Domestic and International Measures to Restrict Asylum."

[73] Emily Palmer and Elisabeth Malkin, "Honduran President's Brother Is Found Guilty of Drug Trafficking," New York Times, October 18, 2019, https://www.nytimes.com/2019/10/18/world/americas/honduras-president-brother-drug-trafficking.html.

[74] Hiemstra, "Pushing the US-Mexico Border South," 49.

by India—a reminder to the neighboring monarchies about the fragility of dynasties and small states. India protects its own security vis-à-vis China through the management of asymmetrical relations with these small neighbors on its northern, Himalayan border. Caught between India, competing regional powers, and interested extra-regional powers, Bhutan and Nepal balance desires for autonomy and material benefits with the risks of upsetting their large—and often interventionist—Indian neighbor.[75]

The two Himalayan states have used different strategies of distance and approximation to manage their relations with the giants next door. They have not always been successful. Nepal suffered notable failures in its most strident attempts to achieve greater autonomy vis-à-vis India. We examine this important episode (though some see Nepal's policy as more successful today[76]). Smaller Bhutan has been cautious in exercising its independence, setting limited and specific goals for reshaping its relationship with India. In doing so, its conservative monarchy has avoided crises, ensured its position, and gained benefits—though at the price of only gradually loosening security dependency.

Success: Bhutan benefits from alignment

The Himalayan Kingdom of Bhutan, population 800,000, has age-old roots as a Buddhist theocracy with deep connections to neighboring Tibet. As the British expanded their empire in India and South Asia, Bhutan formally accepted British management of its foreign affairs in exchange for maintaining independence at home. Elements of that relationship continued when India gained independence in 1947, most evidently in the India-Bhutan Treaty of Friendship in 1949. That pact served as the legal framework for bilateral relations during the next sixty years and shaped Bhutan's international engagement.[77] The treaty's second article stipulated that India would not interfere "in the internal administration of Bhutan," while Bhutan "agree[d] to be guided by the advice of the government of India in regard to its external relations." The treaty limited Bhutan's right to import arms, effectively granting India a monopoly and veto.[78] In exchange, Bhutanese nationals received equal treatment in India. India assured that landlocked Bhutan's trade and transit through India would be unimpeded, and India returned to Bhutan a small territory long occupied by the British.[79]

---

[75] Mazumdar, "India's South Asia Policy in the Twenty-First Century"; Paul, "When Balance of Power Meets Globalization."

[76] Paul, "When Balance of Power Meets Globalization," 3–4.

[77] Kumar, "Sino-Bhutanese Relations"; Penjore, "Security of Bhutan," 110–17.

[78] Treaty of Friendship between India and Bhutan, August 8, 1949, https://www.refworld.org/docid/3ae6b4d620.html.

[79] Choudhury, "The India–Bhutan Relationship."

Since independence, India has seen Bhutan as integral to its own security. And Bhutan was eager to step under the large country's security umbrella. Mao's revolution in China and the subsequent incorporation and repression of neighboring Tibet in the 1950s preoccupied Bhutan's royals. Following a 1958 visit to Bhutan, India's founding prime minister Jawaharlal Nehru declared that "the protection of the borders and territorial integrity of Bhutan was the responsibility of India and that India would consider any aggression on Bhutan as an aggression on India."[80] A military training mission gave India an armed presence in Bhutan. However, India's decisive defeat in the 1962 war with China was a wake-up call for security-dependent Bhutan. Its king took tentative steps to increase the country's limited international independence and engagement through diplomatic means; however, economic dependence on India grew.[81]

In recent years, Bhutan has sought greater equality in relations with India, resolution of outstanding border controversies with China, and economic gains.[82] On treaty relations, Bhutan achieved greater de jure equality with India in 2007. On borders, though Bhutan has ameliorated conflict with China, it has struggled to bring these disputes to a successful resolution, in part because of concerns about India's reaction. Growing tension over borders between the two giants creates significant risks to Bhutan, including frequent incursions into Bhutanese territory. Though we set aside economic issues here, Bhutan has achieved remarkable economic growth since the mid-1990s, but in a context of deep dependence. Some 90 percent of Bhutan's trade is with India. Bhutan's growth has been driven by hydroelectric projects, built and funded by India, to produce power for the Indian market. Economic asymmetries are deep and salient for Bhutan; these economic asymmetries condition Bhutan's latitude in security matters as well.[83] Though Bhutan rarely rejects Indian leadership in explicit terms, policy and preference divergence has been clear in both treaty relations and the border dispute. Bhutan sought revision of the treaty and seeks settlement of the border dispute, which it views as a major risk. India's preferences regarding treaty relations have often been divided, with salient voices in favor of updating arrangements, while other interests hold on to the status quo; though salience varied, it was generally as a "yellow" case amenable to shifting the agenda. In contrast, the border generally was an inauspicious "red" case, in which Indian

---

[80] Kharat and Bhutia, "Changing Dynamics of India–Bhutan Relations," 39.

[81] Kharat and Bhutia, "Changing Dynamics of India–Bhutan Relations"; Malik and Sheikh, "Changing Dynamics of Indo-Bhutan Relations"; Choudhury, "The India–Bhutan Relationship."

[82] On Bhutanese goals, including outside the triangular relationship with its neighbors, see Kaul, "Beyond India and China: Bhutan as a Small State in International Relations."

[83] On economic issues, especially hydropower, see Bisht, "Bhutan–India Power Cooperation"; Bisht, "The Rupee Crunch"; Bisht, "India–Bhutan Relations"; Kharat and Bhutia, "Changing Dynamics of India–Bhutan Relations"; Taneja et al., "India-Bhutan Economic Relations."

preferences and policies consistently opposed any resolution that grants territories to China.[84] The issue's salience for India has varied dramatically over time, often in accord with India's broader South Asian foreign policies.[85]

By the 1970s, Bhutan began seeking revisions—and asserting a reinterpretation—of sections of the 1949 treaty.[86] This coincided with Bhutan's initial engagement on the broader international stage. Bhutan joined the United Nations in 1971, began promoting the idea of "Gross National Happiness" in 1972, and invited 154 countries' diplomatic representatives to the coronation of its king in 1974.[87] In 1975, India's incorporation of neighboring Sikkim raised alarms in Bhutan. In 1979, the new Bhutanese king publicly called for bringing the 1949 treaty "up to date." The king downplayed Article II's restrictions on Bhutan's foreign policy and criticized the treaty as being open to "loose interpretations."[88] Bhutan took several initiatives without consulting India.[89] However, on matters close to Indian security, deference was the rule. In 2003, Bhutan demonstrated its continued attentiveness to India's security concerns by cracking down on crossborder insurgents who had set up camps in Bhutan.[90] Bhutan has avoided major changes in arms acquisitions policies.

Initially, the treaty was not enough of a problem for Bhutan's monarchy to seriously pursue changes. The monarchy remained on good terms with India. However, from the 1980s, Bhutan entered a process of managed political opening. In 2001, it took steps toward becoming a constitutional monarchy, with elections held in 2007.[91] These changes permitted greater political debate and criticism of India's dominant role, as well as discussion of potential gains from establishing ties with a rising China. Bhutan's preferences for revisions of the 1949 treaty gained momentum. Bhutan felt restricted by the treaty, especially in a context where India's role was drawing domestic criticism. The old treaty

[84] On the typology, the question of "priority" varied substantially over the long term; however, as an approximation, the treaty is a "yellow," or Type 3, case (1a, 2b, 3b); the border question is a Type 1 case (1a, 2a, 3a).

[85] Mazumdar, "India's South Asia Policy in the Twenty-First Century"; Mazumdar, *Indian Foreign Policy in Transition*; Paul, "When Balance of Power Meets Globalization"; Ranjan, *India in South Asia: Challenges and Management*.

[86] Choudhury, "The India–Bhutan Relationship"; Kharat and Bhutia, "Changing Dynamics of India–Bhutan Relations," 40–44; Bisht, "Bhutan's Foreign Policy Determinants."

[87] Kharat and Bhutia, "Changing Dynamics of India–Bhutan Relations," 40.

[88] Qtd. in Saeed Naqvi, "Wide Angle: Bhutan & China: Clues to Crisis from 1979," August 4, 2017, Deccan Chronicle, https://www.deccanchronicle.com/opinion/op-ed/040817/wide-angle-bhutan-china-clues-to-crisis-from-1979.html.

[89] Bisht, "Bhutan's Foreign Policy Determinants," 61–62; Stobdan, *India and Bhutan*, 8.

[90] Mazumdar, "Bhutan's Military Action against Indian Insurgents."

[91] In practice, this was a highly guarded transition, with parties loyal to the monarchy; there has also been large-scale repression of minorities and migrants. Turner, Chuki, and Tshering, "Democratization by Decree: The Case of Bhutan"; more critically, Rizal, "Bhutan–India Relations." Freedom House classed Bhutan as "partially free" in 2019, criticizing discrimination against ethnic Nepalis. See https://freedomhouse.org/country/bhutan/freedom-world/2019.

imposed political costs on the monarchy's attempts to guide a transition that protected its prerogatives.[92]

During the 2000s, Indian preferences on the treaty fragmented. The terms of the treaty invited Chinese criticism of India's seemingly outdated, paternalistic policies toward smaller states. Negotiations came to fruition with a new treaty, signed in 2007, which removed the requirement for Indian "guidance" of Bhutan's foreign policy and approval for Bhutanese arms purchases.[93]

> Bhutan has been quietly raising the issue of revising the treaty with India for several years, and although India did realize that this was necessary, little was done about it. What has prompted New Delhi to act now is the fact that Bhutan is democratizing—it has a new constitution and the Bhutanese will elect representatives to Parliament in an election likely to be held next year—and that India needs to acknowledge Bhutan's full sovereignty formally. This appears to have provided momentum to the process of revising the treaty.[94]

Though the treaty negotiations fulfilled Bhutan's ambitions, caution remained evident in Bhutan's dealings with China. As of 2021, the mountain kingdom still does not have diplomatic relations with its neighbor to the north; instead, it suffers from a considerable irritant in the form of an unsettled, disputed border. India has its own border disputes with China. The powers clashed over the tri-border Doklam Plateau as recently as 2017, involving Bhutan directly. Dozens of soldiers were killed elsewhere in clashes between the two giants in June 2020.

Until the early 1980s, Bhutan's disputes had been discussed alongside India and China's border conflict. The Sino-Bhutanese dispute sits near the narrow Siliguri Corridor that connects most of India with its strategically isolated northeastern provinces.[95] After pressure from Bhutan, India acquiesced to bilateral border talks between Bhutan and China—though with close Indian consultation and without diplomatic relations between Bhutan and China.[96] Talks started formally in 1984, with a round held annually (with some interruptions). In 1998, the countries signed the Agreement to Maintain Peace and Tranquility on the Bhutan-China border, their first bilateral agreement. China explicitly recognized Bhutan's sovereignty.[97] In later rounds, China offered a "package deal," including

[92] Nga et al., "India–Bhutan Treaties of 1949 and 2007"; Ramachandran, "India, Bhutan: No More Unequal Treaties."
[93] For a comparison of the 1949 and 2007 treaties, see Nga et al., "India–Bhutan Treaties of 1949 and 2007."
[94] Ramachandran, "India, Bhutan: No More Unequal Treaties."
[95] Stobdan, *India and Bhutan*, 17–24; Pant, "Delhi Needs to Up Its Game with Smaller Neighbours"; Bisht, "Sino-Bhutan Boundary Negotiations."
[96] Kumar, "Sino-Bhutanese Relations"; Kumar Sahu, "Future of India–Nepal Relations."
[97] Bisht, "Sino-Bhutan Boundary Negotiations"; Kharat and Bhutia, "Changing Dynamics of India–Bhutan Relations," 48.

a territorial swap and, perhaps, diplomatic and economic relations. The offer was attractive to elements of the Bhutanese government eager to remove the insecurity caused by the dispute. However, India casts a long shadow. After Bhutan's prime minister met with the Chinese premier in 2012, some Indian officials criticized Bhutan for "playing the China card to both balance India and extract more concessions from it." India cut fuel subsidies during an electoral campaign. The perceived interference drew strong condemnation within Bhutan.[98] But a Bhutanese critic concluded that "the contemptuous manoeuver worked," helping elect a pro-India government.[99] As border negotiations stagnated, there were small incursions into disputed areas—apparently Chinese pressure to conclude the talks. In 2017, Bhutan detected Chinese military efforts to construct a road in disputed territory near the Bhutan-China-India tri-border area. Bhutan sided with India, calling for its assistance.[100] The border dispute remains unresolved, and Bhutan's ultimate reliance on India is clear.

While Bhutan achieved longstanding goals in its 2007 treaty negotiations, its ongoing border negotiations have been less successful. Bhutan faces constraints imposed by asymmetry and the risk of being pulled into virulent Sino-Indian contestation. Bhutan achieved some stability and recognition in direct talks, but a definitive settlement remains elusive. Continued economic and security dependence limits Bhutan's ability to resolve disputes without China without first getting India on board.

Failure: Nepal—Arms, embargos, and asymmetry

Nepal shares important commonalities with Bhutan: a monarchical history, an avoidance of formal colonization under British tutelage, and a situation as a Himalayan "buffer" between India and China. It remains party to a now-criticized "unequal" treaty with India. Like Bhutan, Nepal depends on Indian markets, aid, and tolerance of its migrants. It possesses an Indian-dominated hydroelectric sector, though this is a smaller part of its economy.[101] However, the states have important differences. Nepal, with a population of twenty-eight million, is many times larger than Bhutan. Bhutan is three times wealthier on a per capita basis.[102] While Bhutan's trajectory has been marked by gradual, steady progression based on an implicit recognition of Indian leadership, Nepal's

---

[98] Stobdan, *India and Bhutan*, 14.

[99] Rizal, "Bhutan–India Relations," 159.

[100] Ganguly and Scobell, "The Himalayan Impasse"; Joshi, "Doklam: To Start at the Very Beginning."

[101] Mazumdar, *Indian Foreign Policy in Transition*, 143–48.

[102] In 2018, Nepal had a per capita GDP of US$1,033; Bhutan, US$3,243. World Bank National Accounts Data.

domestic politics, economic development, and international relations have seen dramatic swings.[103]

In foreign affairs, Nepal and Bhutan have adopted markedly different strategies. Bhutan has sought benefits through close alignment with India; Nepal has sought balanced neutrality between China and India, even as it remains closely bound to India. India and Nepal signed a Treaty of Friendship in 1950, accompanied by secret letters that included restrictions on Nepal's foreign relations and arms imports.[104] This was accompanied by agreements on commerce. But Nepal began to contest these restrictions much earlier than Bhutan, opening internationally by joining the United Nations in 1955. Nepal established relations with China, signed a border settlement treaty, and sought to remain at the margins of the India-China war.[105] In 1975, Nepal sought to institutionalize its neutrality by declaring a Zone of Peace, later incorporated into its constitution. India viewed neutrality as "supported by actors inimical to the Indian interests."[106] China has sought to offset India's dominance in Nepal while also exhibiting great concern about the activities of Tibetan refugees there.[107] "Nepalese nationalists [were] keen to chart an independent path. . . . In response, India has attempted to pressure Nepal to limit its contacts with outside powers."[108] Nepal's attempts at balance were limited by its integration with India.[109] This section examines one illustrative failure of those balancing efforts.

In 1965, Nepal signed a secret agreement under which India was to arm Nepalese forces. But India rejected Nepal's requests in 1972 and 1976 to purchase anti-aircraft guns. When subsequent requests for arms apparently went unanswered, Nepal turned to China.[110] Getting wind of this, India reiterated its opposition. Still, Nepal and China inked a deal in March 1988 and deliveries began in June.[111] India insisted on a halt to the arms transfers and assurances that Nepal would respect the Indian interpretation of the 1950 treaty and the 1965 agreement. Nepal's King "Birendra refused to give any such assurances, insisting that it was Nepal's sovereign right to purchase weapons it considered necessary for its defense."[112] The two sides insisted on different interpretations of the 1950

---

[103] For a helpful overview, see Mazumdar, *Indian Foreign Policy in Transition*, chap. 7.
[104] Subedi, "India-Nepal Security Relations and the 1950 Treaty," 275; Chand and Danner, "Implications of the Dragon's Rise for South Asia," 35; Thapliyal, "India and Nepal Treaty of 1950." The treaty, letter, and 1965 secret agreement are helpfully included in Mazumdar, *Indian Foreign Policy in Transition*, appendix E.
[105] Thapliyal, "India and Nepal Relations," 78–80.
[106] Thapliyal, "India and Nepal Treaty of 1950," 123.
[107] Chand and Danner, "Implications of the Dragon's Rise for South Asia," 30–32.
[108] Mazumdar, *Indian Foreign Policy in Transition*, 137.
[109] Dabhade and Pant, "Coping with Challenges to Sovereignty"; Kumar Sahu, "Future of India–Nepal Relations"; Chand and Danner, "Implications of the Dragon's Rise for South Asia."
[110] Garver, "China-India Rivalry in Nepal," 960.
[111] Garver, "China-India Rivalry in Nepal," 960–61.
[112] Garver, "China-India Rivalry in Nepal," 963.

treaty.[113] Clearly, Nepal's goals diverged from India's status quo policy. Indian intelligence reports about the arms deal increased the issue's salience and consolidated the preferences of the country's leaders.[114] Newfound salience shifted the case from a backburner "violet" case to an increasingly oppositional "red."

Driven by "fears of Nepal becoming another Pakistan," India took harsh measures.[115] Nepal's commercial agreements with India were set to expire, as the arms dispute raged. Despite Nepal's protestations that economic and security issues should be negotiated separately, Indian prime minister Rajiv Gandhi had no plan to forfeit that leverage.[116] "If Nepal wanted a special economic relationship with India, and the generous economic treatment that implied, it also would have to accept a special security relationship."[117] In March 1989, India let commercial agreements lapse and shut almost all ports of entry with Nepal. Given its near-total dependence on India for trade—infrastructure connections with China were limited—Nepal felt the squeeze.[118] China, ensconced in a post-Tiananmen crisis, could not offset the blow.[119]

Soon, the economic pressure gained a political dimension. Nepal's monarchy was opposed by pro-democracy groups and a strong Maoist party. Unlike in Bhutan, India had little sympathy for Nepal's monarchy. Many Nepalese pro-democracy parties and activists had close ties to India's long-dominant Congress Party.[120] As the economic crisis escalated, India backed Nepal's democratic opposition. The monarchy killed over fifty demonstrators as they marched on the palace in April 1990.[121] The violence solidified domestic and international opposition, forcing King Birendra to end a three-decade prohibition on political parties and accept a constitutional monarchy. Birendra had overplayed his hand, both in the Sino-Indian-Nepalese triangle and in domestic politics.

Nepal's post-1990 government acknowledged Indian concerns. The new constitution omitted the previous call for a Zone of Peace. During the new Nepalese prime minister's first visit, India offered a return to the pre-1987 status quo economic arrangements. It used the visit "to remind [Nepal] of its obligations under the treaty of peace and friendship" of 1950.[122] The next year, the countries

---

[113] Subedi, "India-Nepal Security Relations and the 1950 Treaty," 275.

[114] Following the earlier typology, the case moved from Type 6 (1a, 2b, 3a) to Type 1 (1a, 2a, 3a) as Indian policymakers began to fear a potential Nepalese realignment.

[115] Mazumdar, *Indian Foreign Policy in Transition*, 140.

[116] Garver, "China-India Rivalry in Nepal," 964.

[117] Garver, "China-India Rivalry in Nepal," 958.

[118] Mazumdar, "Bhutan's Military Action against Indian Insurgents," 140.

[119] Verma, "Rise of China and India," 167–68.

[120] Ganguly and Shoup, "Nepal: Between Dictatorship and Anarchy," 131; Thapliyal, "India and Nepal Relations."

[121] Garver, "China-India Rivalry in Nepal," 970; "Nepal King Bows to Protests," The Guardian, April 9, 2015, https://www.theguardian.com/world/2015/apr/09/nepal-king-birendra-democr acy-1990.

[122] Subedi, "India-Nepal Security Relations and the 1950 Treaty," 277–78; Mazumdar, *Indian Foreign Policy in Transition*, 140.

renegotiated their commercial and transit agreements, "offering substantive economic concessions."[123] In the 1990s, Nepal's governments focused on positive relations with India. At home they were overwhelmed by a growing Maoist insurgency.[124] "Throughout the 1990s, one frail government after another fumbled while the country's economic and political problems grew worse."[125] In 2006, a royalist power-grab backfired. A more unified opposition incorporated the Maoists into politics through a peace agreement, dismissed the monarchy, and formed a republic. Though the country struggled to agree on a new constitutional compact, the late 2000s saw relative stability.

India's role in Nepal remains controversial. Objections to the 1950 treaty are prominent across Nepal's political spectrum. Fearing a repeat of the 1989–1991 crisis, however, Nepal has never exercised its prerogative to abrogate the treaty: "once in power, political parties have invariably toned down the anti-India rhetoric."[126] While the treaty is a major issue for parties in Nepal, it is rarely mentioned in India—a pattern typical of asymmetrical relationships.[127] The experience of 1989–1991 is a cautionary lesson. Nepal received a reminder in 2015 when an "informal blockade" by pro-India groups seemed to reflect India's opposition to Nepal's new constitution.[128] For Nepal, the goal of diversifying its ties remains.[129] With India watching warily, however, the seventy-year-old Friendship Treaty retains its relevance.

Europe: Autonomy at geopolitical crossroads

Europe's dense institutions have transformed the region's security environment. This has not erased small states' fears, but it has reshaped their interests and strategies. Instead of pursuing autonomy or neutrality in the post–Cold War era, many small states in Europe have been institution joiners and builders—unable to or unwilling to act as security "free riders," as they are sometimes characterized.[130] This section examines Estonia and Moldova. The two countries emerged from Soviet control at the same juncture and faced similar challenges, yet they have had differing levels of success.

[123] Dabhade and Pant, "Coping with Challenges to Sovereignty," 165.
[124] Thapliyal, "India and Nepal Relations," 80–81.
[125] Ganguly and Shoup, "Nepal: Between Dictatorship and Anarchy," 129.
[126] Mazumdar, *Indian Foreign Policy in Transition*, 142.
[127] Thapliyal, "India and Nepal Treaty of 1950"; Subedi, "India-Nepal Security Relations and the 1950 Treaty."
[128] Thapliyal, "India and Nepal Relations," 77, 81–83. PTI, "Nepal Blockade Ends," Indian Express, December 25, 2015, https://indianexpress.com/article/world/world-news/nepal-blockade-ends-tru cks-carrying-essential-supplies-from-india-enter-country/.
[129] Murton and Lord, "Trans-Himalayan Power Corridors."
[130] Rickli, "European Small States' Military Policies after the Cold War," 315.

Success: Estonia between Russia and the North Atlantic
Treaty Organization

Historically, Estonia faced great-power threats and invasions of the very nature that animated pessimistic views of small states' international possibilities. Estonia suffered a Soviet occupation that started in 1940 under the infamous Molotov-Ribbentrop Pact and lasted until the disintegration of the USSR.[131] After Estonia re-emerged as an independent state in August 1991, threats to its territorial integrity and sovereignty remained, with Soviet troops stationed in the country. Deadly repression of an independence movement in neighboring Lithuania in January 1991 demonstrated that escape from a Soviet/Russian sphere was not assured. Estonia feared occupation or annexation from a great power, even as it struggled to establish its independence, institutions, and identity.[132]

Though today Estonia is an economic success story, in the early 1990s it experienced a severe, post-Soviet economic shock. Estonia's population, 1.5 million at independence, declined for a decade due to emigration—particularly of a Russian minority—before stabilizing at 1.3 million in 2014.[133] It was economically dependent on Russia, particularly for energy. Regardless, Estonia's foreign policy toward Russia has been the "most conflictual" and "adversarial" in the Baltic region.[134] Estonian elites prioritized approximation and membership in the North Atlantic Treaty Organization (NATO) and European political and economic institutions. This section examines Estonia's immediate postindependence security strategies for managing asymmetrical relationships with Russia and the West before turning to Estonia's "super atlanticist" approach since the early 2000s.[135]

At independence, Estonia's security goals were clear and pro-Western.[136] First, Estonia sought the withdrawal of Soviet/Russian troops. Voluntary withdrawal was hardly guaranteed, as the lasting Russian military presence in post-Soviet states including Moldova and Georgia shows. Second, it sought NATO membership. This was stated publicly by high-ranking Estonian officials as early as October 1991—two months after independence.[137] Estonia's aspirations were a

---

[131] The annexation of Estonia and its Baltic neighbors was never recognized by the West, unlike with many Soviet bloc states.

[132] Riim, "Estonia and NATO"; Praks, "Estonia's First Steps in the Direction of NATO and National Defence"; Lauristin and Vihalemm, "The Political Agenda during Different Periods of Estonian Transformation."

[133] Kuus, "European Integration in Identity Narratives in Estonia," 102.

[134] Grigas, "Explaining the Policies of the Baltic States towards Russia, 1994–2010," 13, 19. Grigas, however, sees greater Estonian pragmatism around economic issues.

[135] Wivel and Crandall, "Punching Above Their Weight, but Why?"

[136] Lanko, "The Regional Approach in the Policy of the Russian Federation towards the Republic of Estonia," 40–42.

[137] Riim, "Estonia and NATO," 34–35; Praks, "Estonia's First Steps in the Direction of NATO and National Defence," 113–14.

"thorny issue" for Russian policymakers, who accorded the Baltic states an importance "disproportionate" to their sizes. Russia had political, commercial, and
military interests in the Baltic. The region was central to Russia's overseas trade
and crucial for access to the noncontiguous enclave of Kaliningrad. Russian opposition to Estonian NATO membership was strong and cohesive; it was a classic
"red" case.[138]

With potential Western allies, the case was different, with rapidly shifting
conditions creating an "orange" case for Estonia. Baltic security was a priority
for NATO, but preferences were divided. Estonian preferences diverged from
NATO's early 1990s status quo policy.[139] Russian opposition weighed heavily on
NATO decision makers and member states.[140] Similar divisions existed within
the United States. Some State Department officials questioned the benefits of
NATO expansion; the Department of Defense "unanimously" opposed rapid enlargement in late 1993.[141] When the United States signaled support for NATO
enlargement, Baltic states were omitted from the first round. NATO was "not
in a hurry" to expand to the Baltic states, and the possibility of Baltic membership was "treated with considerable skepticism" by NATO leaders as late as early
1995.[142] Defending Estonia, with its proximity to Russian population centers,
was understood to be a challenge. The small country—which was still creating
its own Ministry of Defense—was in no position to burden-share, despite its
Atlanticist enthusiasm.[143] NATO expansion was understood to risk Russian ire.
It could threaten the tenuous pro-liberalization coalition within Russia itself at a
moment when the United States was supporting President Boris Yeltsin with economic and security aid.[144]

Nonetheless, Estonia steadfastly pursued membership in NATO and
European institutions. Given the unlikelihood of achieving Russian accommodation of Estonia's core goals, this was a smart approach—even though NATO's
acceptance was far from guaranteed. Estonia sought out contacts with NATO
even as Russian troops remained. With no guarantee of membership, Estonia

[138] Lanko, "The Regional Approach in the Policy of the Russian Federation towards the Republic
of Estonia," 41; Mezhevich, "Russia and the Baltic States," 6. Regarding Estonia-Russian relations, the
case is Type 1 (1a, 2a, 3a) according to the earlier typology, suggesting that the possibility of changing
Russian policy was quite low.
[139] Estonia-NATO relations were of Type 2 (1a, 2a, 3b) according to the earlier typology.
[140] Kuzio, "NATO Enlargement: The View from the East"; Schimmelfennig, "NATO
Enlargement: A Constructivist Explanation," esp. 206–9. For influential contemporary arguments
against expansion, see Gaddis, "History, Grand Strategy and NATO Enlargement."
[141] Goldgeier, "NATO Expansion: The Anatomy of a Decision"; c.f., Shifrinson, "NATO
Enlargement and US Foreign Policy."
[142] Riim, "Estonia and NATO," 40; Männik, "Small States: Invited to NATO—Able to
Contribute?," 25.
[143] Männik, "Small States: Invited to NATO—Able to Contribute?"; Praks, "Estonia's First Steps in
the Direction of NATO and National Defence."
[144] Goldgeier, "NATO Expansion: The Anatomy of a Decision."

purchased NATO-compatible weapons from Israel in 1993. This helped break defense dependence on Russia. Estonia's "Prime Minister [Mart] Laar compared [the arms purchase] to the introduction of the country's own currency in term of strategic importance."[145] When initial bids for quick membership were rebuffed, Estonia embraced NATO's "Partnership for Peace" program. Despite a miniscule defense budget and scarcity of personnel, Estonia prioritized engagement with NATO. Estonia sent officers and officials to NATO seminars, events, and postings. It supported NATO operations in the former Yugoslavia.[146] Estonia rejected Russian offers for security guarantees out of hand in 1997—the same year it started talks on NATO membership. Estonian elites adopted aspects of NATO's evolving identity into its own.[147] Estonia built pro-NATO relationships with small members like Denmark and cooperated with Scandinavian and Baltic countries to develop regional defense capabilities.[148] A leading Estonian security analyst emphasized that the creation of a Baltic peacekeeping force "was the clearest expression of the understanding of the Baltic states that they would have to contribute to international security." The joint force served as a conduit for Western weapons, expertise, and military values.[149] These actions kept Estonia on the NATO agenda and cast it in a favorable light for Western policymakers.

Although Estonia's actions alone did not cause NATO's expansion, its policies—in cooperation with Latvia and Lithuania—made the Baltic states attractive members in a way that their risky geography, weak capabilities, and then-shaky institutions did not suggest. On August 31, 1994, the last Russian troops left Estonia as a result of steadfast domestic opposition and considerable international encouragement. The Russian withdrawal eased Estonia's enthusiastic pursuit of NATO membership. Baltic elites' profession of liberal values led to the U.S.-Baltic Charter in 1998, which included statements on the potential for later Baltic NATO membership.[150] NATO and NATO members, especially the United States, contributed to the construction of Estonia's own security institutions, rebuilt essentially from scratch. A more detailed route to membership emerged in 1999, culminating in membership for Estonia, Latvia, and Lithuania in 2004. With that, Estonia had achieved its two major postindependence goals and gained the considerable deterrence benefit of NATO's Article 5.

---

[145] Praks, "Estonia's First Steps in the Direction of NATO and National Defence," 123.

[146] Praks, "Estonia's First Steps in the Direction of NATO and National Defence," 125–34; Goldgeier, "NATO Expansion: The Anatomy of a Decision," 87–88.

[147] Riim, "Estonia and NATO." Estonia's first defense minister signaled these values (as well as enthusiasm for pre-membership activities) in an article written in late 1995. Öövel, "Estonian Defence Policy, NATO and the European Union."

[148] Wivel and Crandall, "Punching Above Their Weight, but Why?"; Jurkynas, "Security Concerns of the Baltic States in the Twenty-First Century."

[149] Praks, "Estonia's First Steps in the Direction of NATO and National Defence," 135.

[150] "US-Baltic Charter."

Estonia's security conundrum did not end with NATO membership. The country's threat perception and preferred policies toward Russia often diverged moderately from those of the United States and other NATO members. Divergent views were evident after Russian-inspired riots and cyberattacks against Estonia in 2007 and the Russo-Georgian War of 2008.[151] For Estonian policymakers, these conflicts showed that Russia was a threat willing to deploy unconventional means against adversaries.[152] Estonia sought to shift U.S. and NATO perceptions of Russia, including through "lobbying in Brussels and Washington."[153] Estonia continually signaled its NATO commitment including participation in U.S.-led wars in Afghanistan and Iraq, acting as a "model ally" and seeking "security through entrapment."[154] In Estonia's view, its contributions and sacrifices merited greater commitment from NATO. It had some initial success, leading to NATO support through the creation of a cybersecurity center in Estonia.[155] Estonia laid the groundwork for NATO's stronger response to the Ukraine crisis in 2014, including a NATO "enhanced forward presence" in Estonia after 2016.[156] Estonia paid a substantial cost for this support in terms of defense spending, NATO commitments, and lives lost in far-flung conflicts. In return, it has achieved greater security through external support and international contributions to its security capabilities.

Failure: Moldova between Russia and Europe

Emerging from Soviet rule, Estonia and Moldova shared relevant goals and characteristics, including undesired foreign military presences in their territories. Despite economic dependence on Russia, national leaders in both countries favored a turn to the West. Both had large Russian-speaking populations, perceived as possible threats to national consolidation. Moldova seemed to possess one advantage: it does not border Russia. But Moldova's independence was more troubled, and its primary security goal—a withdrawal of Russian troops—has not been achieved to this day. The case permits an exploration of how changes in external environment and small-state strategy shape possibilities for success. An initial phase, 1990–2003, produced an abject failure. The second phase, 2003–2018, saw limited progress toward Moldovan goals.

---

[151] Jurkynas, "Security Concerns of the Baltic States in the Twenty-First Century"; Wivel and Crandall, "Punching Above Their Weight, but Why?," 410–11.

[152] For an Estonian view from this moment, see Mälksoo, "NATO's New Strategic Concept."

[153] Grigas, "Explaining the Policies of the Baltic States towards Russia, 1994–2010," 34.

[154] Wivel and Crandall, "Punching Above Their Weight, but Why?," 408–13.

[155] Crandall, "Soft Security Threats and Small States."

[156] Luik and Praks, "Boosting the Deterrent Effect of Allied Enhanced Forward Presence."

Situated in southeastern Europe, landlocked Moldova is bordered on the west by Romania and enveloped on the northeast and south by Ukraine. A strip of Ukrainian territory separates Moldova from the Black Sea. Moldova depends on its neighbors, especially the Ukrainian port of Odessa, to trade. Moldova has the unwelcome distinction of being the poorest country in Europe, with a per capita GDP of US$3,227 in 2018.[157] Moldova's population of 3.5 million has declined since independence due to emigration.

Moldova's independence movement gained steam under Soviet policies of *perestroika* in the late 1980s. Empowered local elites promoted the national language and symbols.[158] As the Soviet Union disintegrated, Moldova gain independence on August 27, 1991. Even before independence, however, the new Moldovan state faced resistance from enclaves with populations that identified as ethnically Russian, Ukrainian, and Turkic.[159] In September 1990, separatist leaders in the eastern city of Tirasol declared an independent republic, known as Transnistria.[160] Moldova attempted to reintegrate this breakaway territory in 1992. But the Transnistria-based Fourteenth Soviet Army intervened on behalf of the separatists by providing weapons, fighters for local militias, and then direct support—though this likely was not officially sanctioned. Moldova's weak security forces backed down.[161] With Russian support and Ukrainian tolerance, but without diplomatic recognition from any state in the world, Transnistria has survived three decades as a de facto state.[162]

Despite its chaotic independence, Moldova's security goals vis-à-vis Russia were clear. Its 1991 declaration of independence called on the USSR to "terminate the illegal state of occupation" and remove its troops. This was formalized in Article 11 of its 1994 Constitution: Moldova declared itself a neutral state that would host no "foreign military troops on its territory."[163] Moldova has reiterated

---

[157] Data from the World Bank Data Bank.

[158] The national language is Moldovan, which closely resembles Romanian. Soviet policies had promoted Russification and subordinated Moldovan politicians to Russian policy, favoring a small Russian-speaking elite.

[159] A largely Turkic region, Gagauzia, has also troubled Moldovan authorities, though to a lesser degree than Transnistria.

[160] Transnistria, also spelled Transdniestra, was officially declared as Pridnestrovskaya Moldavskaya Respublika. For background, see Tkach, "Moldova and Transdniestria," 130–50; Vahl and Emerson, "Moldova and the Transnistrian Conflict," 2–9; Demirdirek, "In the Minority in Moldova." For a perspective closer to Transnistria, see Istomin and Bolgova, "Transnistrian Strategy in the Context of Russian–Ukrainian Relations." On elites in Transnistria, see Balmaceda, "Privatization and Elite Defection in De Facto States."

[161] Mörike, "The Military as a Political Actor in Russia"; Istomin and Bolgova, "Transnistrian Strategy in the Context of Russian–Ukrainian Relations," 170–76.

[162] De Waal, *Uncertain Ground*, chap. 2.

[163] The declaration and constitution are available online: https://www.md.undp.org/content/dam/moldova/docs/Publications/Constitutia%20RM%20format%20mic%20Engl%20Tipar%2014-07-2016.pdf.

its requests for the withdrawal of Russian forces from Moldova.[164] Russia's goals have also been clear: the Transnistrian foothold is Russia's "key to the Balkans."[165] Russia wants to prevent Moldova's movement toward the European Union and NATO, maintain influence over Moldovan politics, and retain a military presence. The supposed intractability of the Transnistrian conflict creates a rationale to avoid complete withdrawal, although Russia's presence contravenes Moldovan demands, Western pressure, and international law.[166] Moldova and Russia have diverged sharply on key policies (with a partial exception from 2001 to 2003, discussed later). Moldova was highly salient for Russian policymakers, and Russia held cohesive preferences against Moldovan integration with Western blocs. This "red" case was not an auspicious set of circumstances for Moldova.[167]

After its 1992 defeat by separatists, the central Moldovan government accepted Russian mediation and peacekeeping, which limited violence but favored Transnistria. Transnistria became dependent on Russian gas, subsidies, passports, and remittances. Moldova tried to internationalize the situation but could not offset Russia's advantages. The Organization for Security and Cooperation in Europe (OSCE) joined the Moldova-Transnistria dialogue, but Russia dominated the conversations. In October 1994, Russia committed to withdrawing its troops from Moldova, but it tied this withdrawal to a (favorable) political settlement of the separatist conflict. From 1994 to 1998, Moldovan concessions of regional autonomy failed to satisfy Transnistria or its Russian patrons.[168]

Briefly, in 1999, it appeared that Moldova's strategy of neutrality and internationalization might pay off. Russia committed at an OSCE summit to withdraw its troops within three years. Suddenly, Russia retracted this commitment.[169] In 2001, the Moldovan Party of Communists was elected in a landslide, bringing President Vladimir Voronin to office. The party had longstanding ties and a deep affinity for Moscow. Voronin started his term by rejecting Western ties. "Moldova must resist Europe as Cuba resists on the American continent," Voronin declared.[170] After years of tension, it appeared that Moldovan preferences might

[164] Popescu, "The EU in Moldova-Settling Conflicts in the Neighbourhood," 19; Crandall, "Hierarchy in Moldova-Russia Relations," 4–6.

[165] The phrase was used by a Russian general in Transnistria in 1995. Tkach, "Moldova and Transdniestria," 151.

[166] Lupu Dinesen and Wivel, "Georgia and Moldova," 150–51; Tkach, "Moldova and Transdniestria," 147–53; De Waal, Uncertain Ground, 36.

[167] As Type 1 (1a, 2a, 3a) suggests, this is the most difficult alignment for a small state to achieve change.

[168] Istomin and Bolgova, "Transnistrian Strategy in the Context of Russian–Ukrainian Relations," 171; Vahl and Emerson, "Moldova and the Transnistrian Conflict," 10–12.

[169] Vahl and Emerson, "Moldova and the Transnistrian Conflict," 12; Crandall, "Hierarchy in Moldova-Russia Relations," 6.

[170] Cantir and Kennedy, "Balancing on the Shoulders of Giants," 402–3.

fall into line with Russian policy. Moldovan and Transnistrian leaders negotiated a settlement plan under the guidance of a close aide of Russian president Putin. The resulting "Kozak Memorandum" proposed reintegrating Transnistria into Moldova, though with disproportionate representation, a veto over international treaties, a right to secede under certain conditions, and regularization of the Russian military presence.[171]

The Kozak Memorandum was a turning point—but not in the direction Moscow had intended. When the plan leaked, Moldovan civil society groups protested vociferously, and Western international organizations and governments made their disagreement known.[172] When Voronin backed away from the plan, Moscow retaliated with sanctions and restrictions on gas exports. Moldova doubled down on its move away from Russia, requesting a NATO Individual Partnership Action Plan in June 2004; Voronin made a visit to NATO headquarters the following year.[173] Conflict escalated as Russia levied sanctions against Moldovan wine and agricultural products. Moldova initiated a joint border mission with the European Union in response. With cooperation from a new pro-Western government in Ukraine, Moldova and the European Union tightened controls on Transnistria's trade and grey-market economy.[174] Voronin changed his line, declaring that Moldova would "never be a part of a post-Soviet security space."[175] Divergent preferences with Russia returned the case to "red."

While Moldovan-Russian relations remained similar during both periods, Moldova's relations with the West shifted after 2003–2004. Moldovan and European policies remained relatively aligned, but preferences grew more cohesive in support of those policies. In Moldova, the Communists' Western turn narrowed the pro-Russian space in Moldovan politics. The bigger change, though, was Moldova's salience for European policymakers. During the 1990s, it was clear that the small state was more salient for Russia than for Western Europe.[176] Though the European Union remained cautious, the issue took on aspects of a favorable "green" case with aligning preferences and growing salience and (imperfect) preference coherence. A combination of Moldovan actions and external factors made Moldova a higher priority for EU and NATO policymakers during the next decade. EU and NATO expansion to Romania in the mid-2000s

[171] Cantir and Kennedy, "Balancing on the Shoulders of Giants," 410–12; Kennedy, "The Limits of Soft Balancing," 516; De Waal, *Uncertain Ground*, 40.

[172] Popescu, "The EU in Moldova-Settling Conflicts in the Neighbourhood," 31.

[173] Crandall, "Hierarchy in Moldova-Russia Relations," 7–8.

[174] Sanchez, "The 'Frozen' Southeast," 170–72; Cantir and Kennedy, "Balancing on the Shoulders of Giants," 403–8; Levy, "Managing Moldova"; Dias, "The EU's Post-Liberal Approach to Peace."

[175] Voronin, qtd. in Cantir and Kennedy, "Balancing on the Shoulders of Giants," 403.

[176] Kennedy, "The Limits of Soft Balancing," 513–14. Also, Lupu Dinesen and Wivel, "Georgia and Moldova," 152–55.

put Moldova on the immediate border of European institutions.[177] After the Kozak debacle, Moldova initiated a concerted European strategy, leading to agreements and exchanges with NATO and a 2014 Association Agreement with the European Union. Moldova grew connected to the European market through trade and labor mobility, which increased pressure on Transnistrian businesses to comply with Moldovan and European rules to access the single market.[178] The aftermath of Russia's 2014 annexation of Crimea furthered weakened Transnistria, as Russia reduced subsidies due to its own recession. An anti-Russian Ukrainian government took a tougher stance on the separatists and became more cooperative with Moldova and the European Union.[179]

In the first period, Moldova's strategy of neutrality and Russian actions kept Transnistria and Moldova in a "limbo situation" that "froze" the conflict and limited Moldovan ties to allies. Since 2004, Moldova has watered down its neutrality by building closer ties to Europe. Moldova's active engagement—and diminished neutrality—has borne some fruit. Its concerns have risen on the European agenda, and it has achieved economic, political, and security gains through European partnership. However, given fears of "unfreezing" the Transnistrian conflict, the embrace remains tepid.[180] Engagement has not yet achieved foundational, postindependence security goals. Russian troops remain in Moldova and support the de facto independence of Transnistria. The failures of the 1990s weigh heavily on Moldova's attempt to overcome this fait accompli.

Conclusions

Although existential threats have greatly diminished, small states continue to face serious constraints in their asymmetrical security relations. However, there is substantial variation in how small states respond to these challenges. Some, like Bhutan, have sought benefits through alignment, while seeking niches of autonomy, in ways that support their regimes. The long-term effects of asymmetry can be seen in how national interests are defined, and even in the historical constitution of the state itself. This asymmetry leads to more limited, if successful, foreign policy goals and strategies. Other states, like Djibouti and Estonia, have

[177] In 2002, NATO agreed to Romanian membership, effective in 2004. Around 2004, Romania's path to 2007 accession to the European Union became clear. Sanchez, "The 'mFrozen' Southeast"; Istomin and Bolgova, "Transnistrian Strategy in the Context of Russian–Ukrainian Relations," 183–84.

[178] Schmidtke and Chira-Pascanut, "The Promise of Europe"; Perju and Crudu, "The Evolution of Economic Relations between the Republic of Moldova and the European Union in the Period of 2007–2018."

[179] De Waal, *Uncertain Ground*, 42–44; Kennedy, "The Limits of Soft Balancing," 518.

[180] Lupu Dinesen and Wivel, "Georgia and Moldova," 160; Sanchez, "The 'Frozen' Southeast"; Kennedy, "The Limits of Soft Balancing."

diminished their dependence on a historically dominant power through greater diversification. In both cases, leaders adapted their strategies to moments of opportunity in the relevant asymmetrical relationship—finding conjunctures when policy divergence, issue salience, and preference cohesion created openings to pursue their goals. Other states have been limited by regime weakness (Mali, Moldova) or corruption and complicity (Honduras). A lack of capacity and foreign policy vision meant opportunities were not seen or could not be seized (Gabon). In other cases, the opportunity structure was misread (Nepal), leading to poorly timed actions and reprisals.

6

Small States in a Global Economy

There are two disparate views on how small states relate to the global economy. In a liberal view, state size is not a hindrance to economic success. If small states lower their own trade barriers and engage with an open global economy, they can reap benefits. Trade allows small states to overcome the limitations of small market size. International financial mobility permits access to capital, skills, and technology that small states may lack on their own. A global economy thrives on functional differentiation and there are niches available for small states. They only need to find and exploit their comparative advantages. Along these lines, prominent economists have argued that small states are greater beneficiaries of globalization's increased trade and financial flows than most large states.[1]

On the other hand, a great deal of scholarship focused on small states in the Global South draws on a more critical heritage, such as dependency theory, to argue that small states are doubly marginalized. "Size" in International Relations is not just a matter of population or territory, but a reflection of power—and the global economy is profoundly shaped by the configuration of power. International economic rules and relations are not neutral. Nor did they start yesterday. Across the Global South, many small states' international economies were effectively created by colonialism. Those legacies still shape small countries' productive structures and institutions.[2] While small states in Europe may benefit from closely knit societies and more communal governance institutions, as Katzenstein argued decades ago, that is not the case in much of the world.[3] Instead of emphasizing comparative advantages, this scholarship highlights small states' economic vulnerabilities. As a recent survey noted: "The absence of economies of scale, the existence of tight, clannish and stubbornly networked communities, the obligation to export or perish, and a ubiquitous (often meddlesome) government, in their various combinations and with their various implications, prove challenging to the economic prospects of small states."[4] Openness to trade and investment may also mean dependence on money and markets beyond one's control, leaving small states vulnerable to pressures.

---

[1] Alesina and Spolaore, *The Size of Nations*; Easterly and Kraay, "Small States, Small Problems?"
[2] Braveboy-Wagner, *The Foreign Policies of the Global South*; Moon, "The Foreign Policy of the Dependent State"; Persaud, *Counter-Hegemony and Foreign Policy*.
[3] Katzenstein, *Small States in World Markets*.
[4] Baldacchino, "Small States: Challenges of Political Economy," 73.

A Small State's Guide to Influence in World Politics. Tom Long, Oxford University Press. © Oxford University Press 2022.
DOI: 10.1093/oso/9780190926205.003.0006

This chapter will not try to settle that debate, exactly. Instead of weighing states' comparative prosperity, it examines how small states pursue their economic priorities in the context of asymmetrical relationships. As in the previous chapter, the cases reflect successes and failures, coming from four world regions. They cover a variety of economic issues: bargaining over foreign assistance, negotiations over infrastructure investments, and the management of debt crises. In all of these, small states pursue their goals through cooperation and contestation with the larger, wealthier states that dominate regional and global economies. By comparing cases within regions, the chapter suggests that success is not determined just by location, history, or wealth. These factors shape the constraints and opportunities that small states face, but the nature of asymmetrical relations and small states' own actions have more proximate effects.

Africa

For many Sub-Saharan African states, development assistance has been a crucial part of international economic relations since their independence. Development aid implies a form of asymmetry. When wealthy states provide assistance to poorer states, there are normally strings attached. Those conditions may limit how the money can be spent or is delivered; they may demand profound changes in recipient country policies or shifts in its diplomatic alignment. When aid originates from great powers or is provided by international financial institutions like the World Bank and International Monetary Fund (IMF), asymmetries may be even starker. With the former, security and diplomatic interests are salient. With the latter, disparities in legitimacy and expertise can mean that an IMF decision effectively determines access even to private international credit markets.

However, these asymmetries do not mean that aid recipients are passive. In her pathbreaking study of how donors and recipients bargain over aid, Haley Swedlund notes: "donor agencies have tried to use foreign aid to leverage reforms, while recipient governments have pushed backed against such pressures. . . . [Recipients] use whatever strategies are available to them to resist donor demands and intrusions, trying to carve out as much space for their own preferences as possible." In general terms, recipients prefer to increase the amount of aid received while retaining discretion over spending and minimizing donor influence on policy.[5] The following section examines two cases of aid management, in Rwanda and Zambia. In both cases, new regimes depended heavily on foreign assistance during the 1990s and early 2000s. While Rwanda largely maximized aid flows and policy space, in Zambia, large—but highly

---

[5] Swedlund, *The Development Dance*, 11.

volatile—flows of aid eroded policy independence and control over economic policy.

Success: Rwandan aid and autonomy

In 1994, political turmoil and civil war exploded into a genocide in Rwanda, taking as many as a million lives. From the violence, a new government emerged, led by the Rwandan Patriotic Force (RPF), a rebel army–turned–governing party that halted the genocide and took control of the capital.[6] Almost immediately, recriminations emerged about the complicity of foreign donors with the previous government and the failure of the United Nations and powerful states to prevent the bloodshed. Rwanda saw an avalanche of foreign aid, especially urgent humanitarian assistance, in the aftermath of the genocide. In this postconflict context, one might have expected a weak Rwandan state to become heavily dependent on aid and subject to the donor whims that often characterize highly asymmetric aid relationships.

Rwanda did—and does—rely on aid to fund its government and spur its economy. Despite that, the country's leaders have at times told officials in donor states, literally, "to go to hell."[7] Rwanda's RPF government—which as of 2021 still retains power—has not shied away from confrontations with donors regarding its aggressive regional security policies, domestic authoritarianism, or unpopular aspects of its economic policies. It even broke diplomatic relations with France in 2006. Yet, decades after the genocide, Rwanda received higher per capita levels of aid than its neighbors. One scholar calls this a "paradox of aid dependence coupled with policy independence."[8] While the legacy of the genocide exercises a lasting effect, that history guarantees neither aid nor agency. What matters is how the RPF used that—and other—narratives and strategies to shape its foreign relationships in ways that made the country a "donor darling" while retaining considerable policy autonomy.[9]

Rwanda is a landlocked and densely populated country of twelve million in the Great Lakes region of central Africa.[10] It remains beset by, and implicated in, regional instability, especially involving its expansive and fractious neighbor,

---

[6] Uvin, "Difficult Choices in the New Post-Conflict Agenda"; Hayman, "Rwanda: Milking the Cow," 159–64.

[7] Rwanda's president directed the words to a Spanish judge investigating RPF rights violations. Qtd. in Reyntjens, "Governance in Post-Genocide Rwanda," 24.

[8] Zorbas, "Aid Dependence and Policy Independence."

[9] Swedlund, "Narratives and Negotiations in Foreign Aid"; Desrosiers and Swedlund, "Rwanda's Post-Genocide Foreign Aid Relations."

[10] For a concise history, see Reyntjens, "Understanding Rwandan Politics through the Longue Durée."

the Democratic Republic of Congo. Rwanda remains poor, with a per capita gross domestic product (GDP) of roughly $800, despite drawing on aid and relative stability to spur high rates of economic growth since the early 2000s.[11] Since the early 1990s, Rwanda has been ruled by an effective one-party state under the strong hand of President Paul Kagame. Political repression is widespread. Nevertheless, the government maintained the strong support of dozens of Western donors, with mostly muted criticism.[12] Myriad countries and international organizations provide aid to Rwanda, with funding often reaching a quarter of national income and half of government expenditure. We focus here on Rwanda's asymmetrical relationships with the United States and United Kingdom, which emerged as the largest bilateral donors in the postgenocide period, despite their minimal engagement before 1990. However, one cannot consider the two countries in isolation; at times, the plethora of donors has provided Rwanda with strategic choices.[13]

In the genocide's wake, Rwanda became a high priority for the United States and United Kingdom. Although Rwanda eventually fell from the top of the U.S. and UK policy agendas—policy attention spans are short, even for atrocities—one key to Rwanda's success is how it adapted its approach to remain salient for these countries' development priorities. In the mid-1990s, there was both high salience and widespread preference incoherence among donors over policy approaches. In this context, the Rwandan government moved key donors toward its own priorities.[14] Although there was often substantial preference divergence between Rwanda and its donors, very often Rwanda was able to "mask" areas of disagreement with others where convergence was possible.[15]

Superficially, the case appeared to be "blue," focused on extraversion with many donors. However, the appearance of low policy divergence reflects Rwandan success. Across the donor community, preference cohesion has eroded since the 1990s. In the United States and United Kingdom, however, preferences remained cohesive much longer. From roughly 2001 to 2012, the case is "green" between Rwanda and the United States and United Kingdom—but this reflects the small country's successes. Swedlund notes, "International donors have often seemed hesitant to play hardball with Rwanda, continuing to offer vast amounts of support to the country and often engaging with the government on its own

---

[11] Data from World Bank national accounts, GDP in current U.S. dollars.

[12] There is remarkable agreement among scholars on this point. Beswick, "Aiding State Building and Sacrificing Peace Building?"; Reyntjens, "Governance in Post-Genocide Rwanda"; Hayman, "Rwanda: Milking the Cow."

[13] Marriage, "Aid to Rwanda"; Grimm, "Aid Dependency as a Limitation to National Development Policy?"; Beswick, "From Weak State to Savvy International Player?"

[14] Uvin, "Difficult Choices in the New Post-Conflict Agenda," 178–79.

[15] Hayman, "Rwanda: Milking the Cow," 157. This makes the case Type 5 (1b, 2a, 3b) with many donors and Type 4 (1b, 2a, 3a) with the United States and United Kingdom.

terms."[16] The most critical voices argue that "the international community fell prey to the RPF's spin, by allowing itself to be manipulated" by an increasingly repressive Rwandan government.[17] Others emphasize the country's material progress and note that donor motives are more complex than guilt over the genocide.[18] But from 1994 to 2012, Rwanda shaped its interactions with donors in increasingly assertive ways. How?

In the United Nations and Western capitals, there was handwringing over international inaction in the face of genocide. Guilt, along with the undeniable scale of suffering, provoked an aid influx. Initially much of that funding went to refugee camps and humanitarian relief, channeled through nongovernmental organizations (NGOs) or aid contractors. Less went to government coffers, where the RPF could exercise direct influence. However, the RPF moved quickly to consolidate its power. Within a year, an internationally backed unity government crumbled, and the RPF became the uncontested power broker. The RPF's origins as a hierarchical, disciplined military organization served it well, and it made the most of donors' willingness to provide funds despite the high degree of uncertainty.[19] The party dominated national and international narratives about the genocide, minimizing references to its own violence. The government pushed back against pressure to democratize, playing to donors' concerns about the return of instability and violence. At the same time, it launched military campaigns against its neighbors.

Starting in the late 1990s, the Rwandan government managed to shift the terms of aid provision in ways that allowed it to gain more from aid flows.[20] Aid increasingly passed through government-guided projects or funds that were allocated to budget support, funneling money to the central treasury or ministry budgets. Although budget support implies negotiations, conditions, and deep donor involvement, Rwanda managed these astutely.[21] It limits donors to operating in three sectors each, shaping aid commitments in line with its priorities. The RPF positioned itself as a trustworthy aid recipient, effective in meeting donor metrics. "Kagame's language—efficiency, partnership, alignment, national development objectives—mirrors closely that of the 2005 Paris Principles on Aid Effectiveness."[22] Despite tightening authoritarianism, the Rwandan government emphasized its "good governance," perceived low levels of corruption, and broad

---

[16] Swedlund, "Narratives and Negotiations in Foreign Aid."
[17] Reyntjens, "Governance in Post-Genocide Rwanda," 3.
[18] Desrosiers and Swedlund, "Rwanda's Post-Genocide Foreign Aid Relations"; Zorbas, "Aid Dependence and Policy Independence."
[19] Curtis, "Development Assistance and the Lasting Legacies of Rebellion in Burundi and Rwanda," 1366, 1370–74.
[20] Hayman, "Rwanda: Milking the Cow," 165.
[21] On the politics of budget support, see Swedlund, The Development Dance, chap. 6.
[22] Zorbas, "Aid Dependence and Policy Independence," 108.

alignment with liberal economic principles. Rwandan success with the United States and United Kingdom is notable. High-profile leaders in both countries grew invested in Rwanda during the mid-1990s, despite limited pregenocide aid ties. Though those leaders are gone, Rwanda cemented its place in U.S. and UK aid landscapes. The RPF also cultivated military and intelligence ties with the United States and United Kingdom, broadening the base of support in those governments.[23] Even as some international organizations and donor countries became more critical of Rwanda's government, the United States and United Kingdom largely downplayed disagreements.[24] A U.S. diplomat once claimed the superpower was "almost held hostage" by the Rwandans.[25] A remarkable ten-year aid agreement with the United Kingdom granted the Rwandan government exceptional flexibility.[26]

Beyond invocations of Western culpability for the genocide, the Rwandan government deployed several strategies. First, it took advantage of the RPF's own hierarchical, centralized governance structures to demand donor coordination on its terms. Though the Rwandan government crafts its aid policies with donor input, it also corrals donors to the areas and projects that match government priorities. Second, Rwandan leaders mix an astute use of development discourse with assertions of government independence. Finally, Rwanda shapes its self-presentation to fit with donor priorities, while developing parallel processes that advance RPF goals.[27] Rwanda recognizes the donor community's need for success stories, and the RPF has made some donors feel it is indispensable to that success. Its postgenocide stability and economic growth allow the RPF to sell that story, despite an authoritarian political climate and rising inequality.[28]

Rwanda's exceptional status as a postgenocide state may suggest that the case holds limited lessons for others. But in other ways, Rwanda fits with a broader group of favored aid recipients.[29] Nor is it alone as a state emerging from severe conflict that attracts the attention of the international community. Rwanda's government has turned seeming weaknesses to its advantage, allowing it to access substantial international resources and getting donor states to help fund the RPF's own, partisan vision of the national interest. As Kagame's rule enters a third decade, however, Rwanda may find its record harder to defend. It is already turning to other strategies, including ties with nontraditional donors.

[23] Curtis, "Development Assistance and the Lasting Legacies of Rebellion in Burundi and Rwanda," 1373.
[24] Uvin, "Difficult Choices in the New Post-Conflict Agenda," 179.
[25] Qtd. in Reyntjens, "Governance in Post-Genocide Rwanda," 27.
[26] Zorbas, "Aid Dependence and Policy Independence," 109.
[27] Hayman, "Rwanda: Milking the Cow," 159–61.
[28] Zorbas, "Aid Dependence and Policy Independence."
[29] Desrosiers and Swedlund, "Rwanda's Post-Genocide Foreign Aid Relations."

Failure: Aid and policy dependency in Zambia

In 1991, Zambia seemed poised to become the sort of African success story that the international aid community craved. A new government—the Movement for Multi-party Democracy (MMD)—replaced a decades-old dictatorship in democratic elections. The MMD promised economic and political liberalization with the cooperation of the international community. It aimed to manage crushing foreign debt, restructure its state-centric economy, and spur development. This followed a contentious relationship between the IMF and World Bank and former leader Kenneth Kaunda. The MMD's "dual transition" in economics and politics offered a new start.[30]

Within a decade, the Zambia-donor relationships had grown tense. For Zambia, failures at three levels outstripped any successes. First, economically, the period was a major disappointment despite huge infusions of international aid. Poverty rose, per capita income fell, and debt dependence remained.[31] Second, due to donor pressure, the Zambian government enacted several economic policies that it had previously opposed. The government often paid a price in withheld aid when it resisted external pressures.[32] Third, at a more technical level, Zambia struggled to channel the aid it received. As development expert Alastair Fraser argued, "Since the mid-1980s, Zambia has been identified as an emblematic case of a country dominated by its donors. Massive debt and aid dependency have weakened the government's ability to negotiate with external actors, to set its own policies, and to act on the wishes of its citizens."[33] Donors were running the show.

Zambia is a landlocked country in southern central Africa. Geographically expansive, it was home to about eight million people in 1991—though its fast-growing population approaches eighteen million today. As the population grew, per capita income plummeted during the 1990s from about US$500 to just US$335.[34] From colonial times, the Zambian economy has depended heavily on copper exports; from the mid-1970s to the mid-2000s, it also depended on foreign aid and loans, which it struggled to repay. While Zambia's donors were not a single bloc, they coordinated policy decisions, meeting with the MMD through a joint Consultative Group.[35]

---

[30]   Fraser, "Zambia: Back to the Future," 302–3.

[31]   Rakner, van de Walle, and Mulaisho, "Zambia."

[32]   Rakner, *Political and Economic Liberalisation in Zambia 1991–2001*; Fraser, "Zambia: Back to the Future"; Chisala, "Foreign Aid Dependency: The Case of Zambia."

[33]   Fraser, "Zambia: Back to the Future," 299. Comparative studies also score Zambia as among the most aid-dependent countries, with the lowest policy autonomy. See Whitfield, *The Politics of Aid*, 345.

[34]   Figures from World Bank national accounts data.

[35]   Rakner, *Political and Economic Liberalisation in Zambia 1991–2001*, 135.

When the MMD took power in 1991, its goals seemed to coincide with donor preferences. President Frederick Chiluba and his party made bold commitments to political liberalization and negotiated closely with donors, even before being elected, on liberal economic reforms to marketize the country's centralized, state-dominated economy. The MMD was united by its advocacy of electoral democracy, but divisions became apparent and affected Zambia's ability to enunciate and pursue goals vis-à-vis donors. By the mid-1990s, divergence between the Zambian government and international donors—particularly Western bilateral donors—had increased. Divergence was greater on political matters than on economic policy, but differences had grown in both areas. For large donors, Zambia remained relatively salient. Left unassisted, Zambia would likely have defaulted on its debts to the IMF, World Bank, and Paris Club lenders. Donors hoped to revive Zambia's standing as an aid showcase. However, donor preferences grew less cohesive as divisions emerged between multilateral lenders and bilateral donors over what to emphasize in assessing Zambia—democratic governance or economic liberalization.[36] Donor divisions created some room for maneuver, but Zambian policy gains were minimal. Instead, donors' preference incoherence made aid more volatile, as the case shifted from "green" to "orange."[37]

After the transition, donors extended hundreds of millions of dollars in new support, "'buying' the MMD an extended political honeymoon."[38] Despite the apparent convergence of interests, aid to Zambia came with strict conditionality that the Zambian government struggled to shape. Chiluba promised adherence to conditions in a December 1991 meeting with donors in the capital of Lusaka.[39] "The need to restore international confidence and to increase the level of donor funding was therefore of paramount importance for the government."[40] The MMD committed to liberalizing fiscal and exchange rate policies. Zambia implemented a strictly controlled cash budget months after donors suggested it in a December 1992 Consultative Group meeting. Rakner describes an "uncritical acceptance" of donor preferences during the early 1990s.[41] Zambia reorganized its economic bureaucracy to appease donors, dismantling planning capacities that might have articulated economic positions.[42] This set the stage for a loss of administrative control over aid. Not only did donors negotiate projects without concern for central government coordination, but also they often

---

[36] Rakner, *Political and Economic Liberalisation in Zambia 1991–2001*, 148.

[37] In 1991, the case can be understood as Type 4 (1b, 2a, 3a). By the mid-1990s, the case shifted to Type 2 (1a, 2a, 3b) as preferences conflicts worsened and donor preferences fragmented.

[38] Fraser, "Zambia: Back to the Future," 306.

[39] Rakner, *Political and Economic Liberalisation in Zambia 1991–2001*, 137.

[40] Rakner, *Political and Economic Liberalisation in Zambia 1991–2001*, 135.

[41] Chisala, "Foreign Aid Dependency: The Case of Zambia," 214; Rakner, *Political and Economic Liberalisation in Zambia 1991–2001*, 154–55.

[42] Chisala, "Foreign Aid Dependency: The Case of Zambia," 154.

maintained private bank accounts for these projects and operated them with their own partners. The Ministry of Finance could not even track the number of projects or amount of aid; its own projections and budgeting of aid bore little resemblance to reality.[43]

The most important clashes in the economic realm concerned privatization of Zambia's largest parastatal companies, particularly the national airline, mining company, holding entity, and large utilities. Despite some resistance and delays, Zambia complied with donor preferences in all these areas—even where it had made public statements against them. After several years of resistance, the government sold the assets of the national mining company under unfavorable market conditions. Donors used conditionality on aid commitments and debt relief to encourage the government to act.

More serious disputes, leading to larger aid cuts, arose from political issues. In late 1992, donors pressured the MMD to dismiss ministers who were allegedly linked to drug trafficking.[44] By late 1995, politics often dominated the aid agenda. Several large donors were angered by what they perceived as the MMD's drift from its democratic commitments. The dispute boiled over when the MMD amended the constitution to block former president Kaunda from running, excluding its most potent adversary. Chiluba won re-election in 1996, but donors criticized the elections. Bilateral aid for balance-of-payments support "declined by as much as 70 percent" amid these criticisms.[45] In October 1997, the Chiluba administration foiled an attempted coup. It then responded with a crackdown, arresting Kaunda and implementing a state of emergency.[46] International condemnations intensified.

At this same juncture, international initiatives to provide debt relief and forgiveness to highly indebted economies offered an opportunity for Zambia to escape its longstanding dependence. In 1996, Zambia initiated participation in the IMF- and World Bank–led Heavily Indebted Poor Countries (HIPC) initiative. While the HIPC promised significant assistance for Zambia, it also created new sources of leverage for donors. To access debt relief, Zambia had to hit a list of donor-set targets. "From 1996 to 2006, this [HIPC] was the main instrument through which traditional partners controlled the behaviour of the Zambian government."[47] Under pressure on governance, in need of greater aid, and desperate to start the HIPC, the Zambian government agreed to the privatization

[43] Chisala, "Foreign Aid Dependency: The Case of Zambia," chap. 5.
[44] Rakner, *Political and Economic Liberalisation in Zambia 1991–2001*, 148; Chisala, "Foreign Aid Dependency: The Case of Zambia," 216.
[45] Wohlgemuth and Saasa, "Changing Aid Relations in Zambia," 3.
[46] Chisala, "Foreign Aid Dependency: The Case of Zambia," 218; Rakner, *Political and Economic Liberalisation in Zambia 1991–2001*, 152.
[47] Kragelund, "'Donors Go Home': Non-Traditional State Actors and the Creation of Development Space in Zambia," 154.

of the mining sector.[48] Reflecting on this, a former finance minister said, "Our priorities are determined by Washington. . . . A country under pressure with no resources has no room for self-generated priorities."[49] The privatization process experienced fits and starts over the next three years, but at each stage, donor pressure played a significant role in pushing the government.

In 2001, a new president, Levy Mwanawasa, took office after Zambian civil society successfully blocked Chiluba from extending his mandate. Though this might have provided an opportunity for a reset, little changed in terms of Zambia-donor relations. When Mwanawasa announced that several large utilities would remain state owned, "the IMF responded by stating the government risked forfeiting US$1 billion of debt relief if it did not proceed with the privatization." The utilities were sold.[50]

During the first fifteen years after its transition, Zambia received substantial foreign assistance. It eventually gained a measure of debt relief. However, in other ways, the results were dismal. Much of the aid during the 1990s effectively went to repaying the IMF and World Bank—staving off a painful default but doing little to alleviate poverty or restore growth. Aid likely helped the MMD stay in power, but its popularity slipped, and the party fragmented for reasons in part connected to donor-backed policies. MMD leadership accepted donor priorities and compromised their stated positions even when political stakes were high. The government struggled to determine, shape, or even monitor donor activities in the country. As Fraser noted, "The Zambian government has found it almost uniquely difficult to assert its own preferences."[51]

Americas

During the Cold War, Brazil's importance as a regional power drew infrequent attention outside South America. The Amazonian giant disappeared behind the long shadow of the United States. The Brazil-Argentina rivalry awoke some concern,[52] but few paid attention to Brazil's relations with South American small states.[53] Only after the turn of the century did Brazil's inclusion in the BRICS (Brazil, Russia, India, China, and South Africa) grouping of global rising powers

[48] Fraser, "Zambia: Back to the Future," 307.
[49] Qtd. in Chisala, "Foreign Aid Dependency: The Case of Zambia," 203–4.
[50] Chisala, "Foreign Aid Dependency: The Case of Zambia," 253.
[51] Fraser, "Zambia: Back to the Future," 301.
[52] Schenoni, "The Argentina-Brazil Regional Power Transition"; Darnton, *Rivalry and Alliance Politics in Cold War Latin America*, chap. 3.
[53] For a recent overview, see Wehner, "The Foreign Policy of South American Small Powers in Regional and International Politics."

draw attention to its role as a regional power.[54] Brazilians often suggested their approach to regional management was friendlier, less coercive, less hegemonic, and more consensual than those of other regional powers—a narrative that gained considerable acceptance.[55] But Brazil was not always perceived as such by its neighbors, especially Bolivia and Paraguay.[56] We turn to two cases of Brazil's economic relations with smaller neighbors. In a 2006 clash over nationalization of the oil and gas sector, Bolivia achieved substantial gains, at Brazil's expense. Conversely, in a 1973 treaty to build the world's largest hydroelectric dam, Paraguay ceded the lion's share of the project's benefits to Brazil over the next five decades.

Success: Bolivia, Brazil, and gas

On May 1, 2006, flag-waving Bolivian soldiers seized two refineries, hanging a banner that read "NATIONALIZED: PROPERTY OF THE BOLIVIANS." That day, Bolivia's recently elected president Evo Morales had decreed that the Bolivian state would reassert control over the country's hydrocarbon production. The two refineries—like much of the Bolivian oil and gas industry—were owned by Brazil's state-controlled oil firm, Petrobras.[57] The lines of the dispute were clear. Bolivia sought greater control of oil and gas production and a much greater share of the profits. Those gains would come at the expense of the dominant foreign oil companies, especially Petrobras. In the mid-2000s, Petrobras was Bolivia's largest company, generating about 22 percent of Bolivian GDP.[58] But Petrobras was not just any foreign oil company. Though it has private shareholders, majority ownership and ultimate control rests with the Brazilian state. Its fortunes were intertwined with Brazilian diplomacy. The nationalization damaged Brazilian economic interests, and the strident rhetoric and military deployment raised the political stakes months before a presidential election in Brazil.

Dramatic asymmetries shape the relationship between Brazil and neighboring Bolivia, a landlocked state in the heart of South America. In 2006, Brazil's GDP outstripped Bolivia's by a multiple of a hundred. Bolivia has long been among the poorest countries in South America; at the time of the nationalization,

---

[54] Gardini and Tavares de Almeida, *Foreign Policy Responses to the Rise of Brazil*; Santos, "Brasil y La Región."

[55] Burges, "Revisiting Consensual Hegemony"; Saraiva, "Brazil's Rise and Its Soft Power Strategy in South America."

[56] Lambert, "The Myth of the Good Neighbour."

[57] Text from photographs accompanying Robert Plummer, "Bolivia Takeover Alarms Powerful Allies," BBC News, http://news.bbc.co.uk/1/hi/business/4964432.stm; Fuser, "O Mito Da 'Generosidade'"; Fuser, "Conflitos e Contratos"; Gordon and Luoma, "Oil and Gas."

[58] Cardoso, "A Energia dos Vizinhos," 114–15.

about 60 percent of the Bolivian population of 9.3 million lived below the national poverty line.[59] The disparity between that poverty and increasingly prominent gas wealth shot through Bolivian politics in the early 2000s. Even before Evo Morales's inauguration, Bolivian preferences diverged substantially from the Brazilian policy of protecting a status quo that had benefited Petrobras. Demands for gas nationalization became central to Bolivia's December 2005 presidential election. That election made Evo Morales president with the largest electoral edge in modern Bolivian history. In Brazil, the gas dispute was already a major priority, but the dramatic May 1 nationalization put it on the front page. Brazilian preferences were initially cohesive, but in 2006 the policy consensus fragmented between the competing priorities of promoting Brazilian companies abroad and building Brazil-led regional institutions.[60] That fragmentation in Brazil changed the gridlocked "red" case to an "orange" case characterized by Brazilian questioning of status quo policies.

In the 1990s, the Bolivian and Brazilian economies underwent deep and rapid liberalization. In Brazil, the partial privatization of Petrobras turned the firm into an international player. When Bolivia opened its lucrative gas fields to foreign investment, Petrobras jumped at the opportunity.[61] A 1996 treaty allowed for construction of a natural gas pipeline from Bolivia to Brazil; soon the pipeline was "at the heart of tensions and cooperation" between the two countries.[62] Brazil offered cash-starved Bolivia capital and a guaranteed market. For Brazil, the pipeline would diversify the country's energy matrix and draw Bolivia into Brazil's economic orbit.[63] Plus, Bolivian gas was tremendously profitable for Petrobras, thanks in part to advantageous arrangements that shrank its tax burden.[64]

The partnership grew unstable as gas became one of Bolivia's hottest political issues. Though gas production expanded and generated new revenues, liberalization reduced the state's share of profits. Bolivian civil society—particularly the surging indigenous movement—mounted mass protests in the early 2000s. The protests were violently repressed but continued to grow, forcing Bolivia's president to resign amid the October 2003 "Gas War."[65] The hyper-liberal regime of the 1990s—so beneficial to Petrobras—was under threat. Brazil perceived these

---

[59] Population and GDP figures from World Bank national accounts data.

[60] On the typology, the case evolves from an inauspicious Type 1 (1a, 2a, 3a) to Type 2 (1a, 2a, 3b). Preference fragmentation created the opportunity for Bolivia to overcome initial divergence in policy preferences. Guimarães and Maitino, "Socializing Brazil into Regional Leadership," highlight preference fragmentation in a similar light.

[61] Webber, "From Naked Barbarism to Barbarism with Benefits," 105–7.

[62] Delgado and Cunha Filho, "Bolivia-Brazil," 131.

[63] For an overview, see Cardoso, "A Energia dos Vizinhos," 105–7.

[64] Fuser, "O Mito Da 'Generosidade,'" 238.

[65] For accounts of the gas war, see Gordon and Luoma, "Oil and Gas"; Perreault, "From the *Guerra del Agua* to the *Guerra del Gas*."

social mobilizations as an attack on its interests. From 2003, "Brasilia's diplomatic efforts . . . turned to the maintenance of the status quo, which favored the interests of Petrobras and Brazilian industry." The Brazilian state "used the asymmetry of economic resources" to defend Petrobras's position at the expense of political stability and democratic processes in Bolivia.[66]

After the forced resignation of his predecessor, Bolivian president Carlos Mesa bowed to demands for a national referendum on hydrocarbons. The Bolivian population voted in July 2004 for the repeal the liberal laws of the 1990s and for increased state control over the oil and gas sector. The referendum's terms were ambiguous enough to leave space for negotiations,[67] and Brazilian diplomats made clear their opposition to higher taxes on production in the large gas fields where Petrobras operated.[68] Caught between international pressure and raging domestic protests, "Mesa governed in the middle of a crossfire."[69] When the Bolivian congress passed a new hydrocarbons law that would raise taxes on foreign oil companies, effectively to 50 percent, Petrobras pushed back in private and public, declaring the law "confiscatory."[70] Mesa refused to sign or veto the law, arguing it would damage Bolivia's international financial position, leaving the validation to the senate. Mesa's waffling satisfied no one.[71] Growing polarization set the stage for Morales's landslide win.[72]

Following Morales's watershed election, Brazilian consensus on policy preferences began to fragment. The narrower (but entrenched) interests of Brazilian corporations clashed with proponents of Brazilian regional projects. Morales was Bolivia's first indigenous president; he emerged from the left and from the labor movement like Brazil's president Luiz Inácio Lula da Silva. Morales strengthened the hand of Brazil's competitor for regional leadership, Venezuela's Hugo Chávez. Morales's stature and anti-imperialist rhetoric—sometimes aimed at Brazil—seemed to detract from Brazil's regional leadership.

In that context, Morales issued his May 1, 2006, nationalization decree. Although the decree did not call for the full absorption of foreign companies into the Bolivia state enterprise, YPBF, the process was contentious. Bolivia and Brazil were at loggerheads over Petrobras's two refineries and control of exports.[73] The Brazilian oil giant froze its investments in Bolivia. However, Brazilian government officials began to separate state-to-state relations from the business interests of Petrobras. Gradually, Brazil agreed to concessions that

---

66 Fuser, "O Mito Da 'Generosidade,'" 239.
67 Arrarás and Deheza, "Referéndum Del Gas En Bolivia 2004."
68 Fuser, "O Mito Da 'Generosidade,'" 241–42.
69 Fuser, "O Mito Da 'Generosidade,'" 241.
70 Fuser, "O Mito Da 'Generosidade,'" 243.
71 Gordon and Luoma, "Oil and Gas"; Fuser, "Conflitos e Contratos," chap. 7.
72 Webber, "Carlos Mesa, Evo Morales, and a Divided Bolivia (2003–2005)."
73 Delgado and Cunha Filho, "Bolivia-Brazil," 138.

it had resolutely opposed from 2003 to 2005. Brazilian foreign minister Celso Amorim's reaction to the May 1 decree was moderate, accepting that Bolivia had legally exercised sovereign rights, while stating Brazilian opposition to the form the actions took.[74] President Lula adopted a similar tone. Petrobras continued to push hard; however, by separating corporate interests from diplomacy (nominally), the Brazilian government reframed the dispute as a division of profits, not a question of Brazilian regional leadership.[75]

Bolivia backed away from its most extreme positions—including an initial refusal to compensate Petrobras for its refineries—but it increased pressure on Petrobras with a provisional 82 percent tax on production from its largest fields.[76] The calibrated pressure paid off. Morales scored "a major political coup" on October 29, 2006, when Bolivia announced thirty-year contracts with a dozen oil companies. The economic benefits to Bolivia and the political benefits to Morales were immense. Bolivian state income from the sector jumped from $338 million in 2004 to $2.7 billion in 2008.[77] On the back of the decree, Morales's party dominated legislative elections in late 2006; his access to resources helped him cut poverty rates in Bolivia while solidifying his political control for a decade. The outcome fell far short of a total nationalization of the sector,[78] but that had not been the goal.

These contracts did not settle all issues, particularly regarding refineries, but they contained the political fallout. Later, Petrobras accepted a loss from the nationalization of the refineries and a price increase on Bolivian gas. It restarted investments in 2012. Brazil's concessions preserved Petrobras's role in Bolivia—heavily taxed but profitable—while advancing Brazilian state aims to maintain gas flows and protect regional integration. "The government saw that it was necessary to concede, and that in the political and economic calculus, Petrobras would shoulder the losses."[79] Despite tremendous asymmetries, Morales leveraged domestic support, an astute reading of the regional context, and the prize of continued access to Bolivian gas to shift the balance with Brazil.

[74] "Bolívia é país estratégico para o Brasil, diz Celso Amorim," OUL Noticias, May 9, 2006, https://noticias.uol.com.br/politica/ultnot/2006/05/09/ult3453u212.jhtm; Bruno Garcez, "Bolívia erra 'na forma, não no conteúdo', diz Amorim," BBC Brasil, September 19, 2006, https://www.bbc.com/portuguese/reporterbbc/story/2006/09/060919_amorimboliviabc.shtml.

[75] Cardoso, "A Energia dos Vizinhos," 108–9; Guimarães and Maitino, "Socializing Brazil into Regional Leadership."

[76] Aresti, "Oil and Gas Revenue Sharing in Bolivia," 15.

[77] Aresti, "Oil and Gas Revenue Sharing in Bolivia."

[78] Webber, "From Naked Barbarism to Barbarism with Benefits."

[79] Cardoso, "A Energia dos Vizinhos," 118. Translation by author.

Failure: Paraguay, Brazil, and Itaipú

In March 2018, Paraguayan political economist Miguel Carter made a bold claim: Paraguay had missed out on US$75 billion—nearly twice its annual GDP—in revenue from the massive hydroelectric dam, Itaipú, that it shares with Brazil. Over three decades, Paraguay earned only 14 percent of the market value of its electricity, Carter estimated. Under the terms of the 1973 Itaipú Treaty, Paraguay had subsidized Brazil's growth at the expense of its own. For Paraguay, poorer and smaller than its neighbor, Carter's argument connected with longstanding grievances and attracted widespread attention.[80] The critique is not mere hindsight; similarly pessimistic projections were made even before the dam opened.[81]

Today, Paraguay is a country of about 7 million people; at the time of the Itaipú negotiations in the early 1970s, it had about 2.5 million residents.[82] Paraguay has been overshadowed by neighboring Argentina and Brazil since its cataclysmic loss in the War of the Triple Alliance (1864–1870). Burdened by defeat and reparations, Paraguay spent a century as a poor buffer state with a succession of short-lived heads of state.[83] In 1954, Paraguay's chronic governmental turnover came to an end. Alfredo Stroessner, a virulently anti-communist general, led a coup and consolidated the backing of the military, landholding elites, and the conservative Colorado Party. He would hold power until 1989. Stroessner's goals and the nature of his sultanistic reign set the context for the Itaipú negotiations.[84]

The Itaipú Dam sits on the Paraná River, which forms the border between Brazil and Paraguay. After the War of the Triple Alliance, Brazil and Paraguay argued for divergent interpretations of their demarcation treaty, leading to a dispute over ownership of massive waterfalls known in Brazil as *Sete Quedas* and in Paraguay as *Saltos de Guairá*. For decades, the issue was secondary—the area was far from population centers in both countries. Then during the 1950s, interest in massive hydroelectric projects grew. To strengthen its claims, Brazil launched feasibility and technical studies in 1956. In the early 1960s, it sent military and police patrols into the disputed territory. In 1962, Brazil "formally declared that it claimed absolute sovereignty" over the falls.[85] Paraguay responded that any unilateral developments of hydroelectric resources in the zone would be protested. In this "red" situation, the small state had a limited capacity for response.

---

[80] Carter, "Itaipú: La Riqueza Energética Perdida Del Paraguay."
[81] Nickson, "The Itaipu Hydro-Electric Project"; Silva, "Brasil-Paraguai"; Soares de Lima, "Political Economy of Brazilian Foreign Policy," 374–79; Canese, *La recuperación de la soberanía hidroeléctrica del Paraguay*.
[82] "Population," World Bank national accounts.
[83] Brezzo, "La Guerra de La Triple Alianza"; Abente, "The War of the Triple Alliance."
[84] On the characteristics of the regime, see Riquelme, "Toward a Weberian Characterization of the Stroessner Regime in Paraguay (1954–1989)."
[85] Nickson, "The Itaipu Hydro-Electric Project," 4; Silva, "Brasil-Paraguai," 73.

For Brazil, Itaipú was a stone useful for killing several birds. High energy costs and dependence on oil imports contributed to Brazilian trade deficits and inflation during the early post–World War II period. The claims played to sovereignty concerns and challenged rival Argentina's regional position. Brazilian policy preferences favoring the construction of a major hydropower dam at Itaipú were cohesive and salient, shared by democratic governments and the military regime that ended democracy in a 1964 coup. Before 1966, Brazilian and Paraguayan preferences on Itaipú clearly diverged due to a dispute over an ill-defined border. As discussed later, Brazil managed to shift the bargaining framework away from the zero-sum issue of territorial division to the seemingly win-win issue of energy production. Eager to embrace this solution, Stroessner's Paraguay underplayed the importance of relative gains in the project.[86]

After the border incursions, a series of high-level meetings calmed tensions between Brazil and Paraguay. In June 1966, Brazil and Paraguay signed the Act of Iguazú, which created a framework for joint hydroelectric projects in the border area based on a principle of shared benefits and "condominium," but without a settlement on the border question. Instead, the deal submerged—first figuratively and then literally—the border dispute under the rubric of cooperation on hydroelectric development. Technical studies and political discussions followed—often over protests from Argentina about downstream effects. Plans coalesced around a single dam, the world's largest, and the flooding of some 1,400 square kilometers, including the *Sete Quedas* waterfalls.[87] In the words of a critic, the 1966 accord "set the seal on the Brazilian diplomatic triumph."[88] The accord made deep distributional divisions appear to be technical matters, backed by strong interests—a "white" case of entrenched policies.

Conflict with Brazil over the falls clashed with Stroessner's strategic goal: to lessen dependence on Argentina by deepening links with Brazil. Paraguayans idealized a "pendular policy" of swinging between the two larger neighbors but in practice had been more closely tied to Argentina. Stroessner hoped overland access to Brazil's Atlantic coast would lessen Argentina's leverage over Paraguay's riverine trade. The dictator prioritized connections to Brazil—bridges, roads, rail, and port access—at the expense of other areas. During the 1960s, Paraguay "put itself unequivocally on the Brazilian side," giving up the bargaining leverage that a truly pendular policy might have achieved.[89] Between 1966 and 1973, ties between Brazil and Paraguay expanded. New bridges were built, and a new

---

[86] Following the typology, before 1966, the case was Type 1 (1a, 2a, 3a), with the countries at odds. Brazil's effective redefinition and side payments, however, reduced policy divergence and effectively routinized the previously conflictual issue, creating an entrenched Type 7 (1b, 2b, 3a) case.

[87] Silva, "Brasil-Paraguai," 74–85.

[88] Nickson, "The Itaipu Hydro-Electric Project," 5.

[89] Silva, "Brasil-Paraguai," 80.

Paraguayan city with the megalomaniacal name of "Puerto Stroessner" was inaugurated in the border region. Physical links were complemented by close support between two authoritarian governments.

On April 26, 1973, Brazil and Paraguay signed the Itaipú Treaty. "The negotiation of the Itaipu Treaty was shrouded in secrecy," Nickson notes. "There was no public debate within Paraguay and only four Paraguayan officials, including the Foreign Minister and the head of ANDE [the Paraguayan state electrical firm] were involved in the negotiation."[90] The treaty included several controversial elements, but none had a greater impact than rules governing the sale of the electricity. In principle, the dam's electricity was to be shared equally between Brazil and Paraguay. In practice, Paraguay's share was many times its own total demand for electricity. Paraguay was required to sell the surplus to Brazil instead of testing the open market (in this case, meaning sales to Argentina). The price was set in relation to operating and capital costs, not market rates for alternative energy sources. Brazil's state company Electrobras bought the Paraguayan share at a bargain-basement cost and then resold the electricity to consumers in Brazil. This generated a windfall.

The deal was not a direct economic loss for Paraguay. Itaipú produced benefits that Paraguay would not otherwise have obtained. Paraguay could not have built the dam alone; it lacked territorial control, capital, and technology for such a megaproject. Brazil advanced and guaranteed loans to construct the dam; these were more costly as Argentina's opposition made it difficult to get lower-cost development loans.[91] While Brazilian companies dominated the construction, Paraguay enjoyed an economic boom. Brazil's support for other infrastructure at the border and concessions of port access might not have been made absent the need for Paraguayan cooperation at Itaipú. But the opportunity cost, regardless of the specific calculation, was tremendous. The treaty precluded the sale of electricity at a higher rate. It had significant environmental and social implications. Given the rate structure, Paraguay was saddled with some questionable debts. And the project limited Paraguay's ability to develop other hydroelectric projects with Argentina.[92]

Stroessner achieved some near-term objectives. The deal pulled Paraguay from Argentina's sphere of influence, and he used the ensuing boom to enrich supporters. However, this international strategy limited Paraguay's ability to negotiate a better deal. Even for Stroessner, many implications were unfavorable. The treaty created a rallying point for opposition to a regime that brooked little dissent. Diplomatically, instead of gaining "pendular" autonomy, Paraguay grew

[90] Nickson, "The Itaipu Hydro-Electric Project," 6.
[91] Soares de Lima, "Political Economy of Brazilian Foreign Policy," 372–74.
[92] Folch, *Hydropolitics*.

dependent on Brazil. Economically, the resources generated were a shadow of what they might have been under a more equitable treaty. Later Paraguayan governments have largely failed to gain redistribution of benefits. But sections of the treaty will expire in 2023,[93] offering Paraguay something that international relations often denies small states—a second chance.

Asia

China's unprecedented economic expansion has made it the international political story of the young twenty-first century. For the small and middle powers in Southeast Asia, China's rise has created a new economic and geopolitical reality, marked by salient asymmetries. China has made its Belt and Road Initiative (BRI) a central component of its rise in its region and beyond. The BRI includes "the land-based Silk Road Economic Belt and the sea-based 21st Century Maritime Silk Road," both announced by China's Xi Jinping in 2013. Though global in scope, the BRI remains concentrated in China's neighborhood, "aiming to forge an integrated and extensive network of regional infrastructure with China at its hub."[94] In Southeast Asia, the BRI builds on earlier Chinese and regional initiatives. Though most scholarship has focused on China's motivations for the BRI and its effects on U.S.-China competition, several scholars examine smaller states' engagement with this central element of China's economic statecraft. Small states in the region must weigh the economic benefits against both strategic and economic risks.[95]

For small states, the BRI may seem a fount of inexhaustible resources. Many small-state leaders have knocked on China's door: "the BRI is not necessarily about a big-power pushing; very often it is also about small-state pull."[96] Through the BRI, China promises infrastructure investment without the intrusive conditionality of Western lenders and institutions like the World Bank and IMF—so prominent in the case of Zambia earlier.[97] But risks remain, leading to diverse reactions across Southeast Asia,[98] including concerns about "debt traps" and deepening Chinese political influence.[99] This section looks at two Southeast Asian states as they seek to manage the economic risks and opportunities of China's rise.

[93] Rojas and Arce, "La Renegociación de Itaipú"; Folch, *Hydropolitics*, chap. 5.
[94] Yu, "China's Belt and Road Initiative and Its Implications for Southeast Asia," 117.
[95] Gong, "The Belt & Road Initiative and China's Influence in Southeast Asia."
[96] Kuik, "Connectivity and Gaps," 80.
[97] Nordin and Weissmann, "Will Trump Make China Great Again?"; Oh, "Power Asymmetry and Threat Points."
[98] Chen, "Regional Responses to China's Maritime Silk Road Initiative in Southeast Asia."
[99] Balding, "Why Democracies Are Turning against Belt and Road."

Success: Malaysia and the Belt and Road Initiative

In 2018, after landmark elections unseated Malaysia's long-ruling party, the country pushed back against the terms of its inclusion in China's BRI. The new coalition government—headed by ninety-two-year-old returning prime minister Matahir Mohamad—suspended billions of dollars of Chinese investment in railways, pipelines, and real estate ventures. It denounced corruption and exaggerated costs, while also criticizing China's overreach in the South China Sea. Malaysia sought the renegotiation of BRI projects, while emphasizing its autonomy in the broader relationship. Instead of accepting a tradeoff between autonomy and material benefits, Malaysia sought to enhance economic benefits while retaining freedom of action.[100] A recent study concludes: "Thus far, Malaysian actors have seemingly captured economic benefits from China while preserving some level of independence in the face of gigantic BRI projects."[101] Doing so is a tall order—but it follows Malaysia's relatively successful interactions with Chinese economic statecraft.

Malaysia is far from the smallest state in Southeast Asia, but its relationship with China is highly asymmetric. "Power asymmetry—a clear disparity in capabilities among state actors—has been the defining feature of Malaysia's relations with China."[102] Since the 2000s, China has been the country's most important partner.[103] Malaysia, a middle-income country of some thirty million, has a bifurcated geography. Half the country, including the major city of Kuala Lumpur, shares the Malay Peninsula with Thailand at the southwest corner of the South China Sea. The rest of the country sits across a stretch of water, sharing the island of Borneo with Indonesia and Brunei. Since recovering from the 1997 Asian financial crisis, Malaysia's per capita income has more than tripled.[104]

Like many of its low- and middle-income Southeast Asian neighbors, Malaysia lacks capital and infrastructure. Given those deficits, Malaysia's turn to the BRI was enthusiastic, but never unconditional, and Malaysia maintained diversified trade and investment partners even as China's importance grew. The country sought to guide Chinese investment to promote economic diversification, especially the growth of nonprimary industries. Perceptions of subservience to China—connected to corruption scandals—have generated political backlash in the democratizing country. The pro-China pursuit of economic payoffs is set in

---

[100] Here, we coincide with Tang, *Small States and Hegemonic Competition in Southeast Asia.*
[101] Liu and Lim, "The Political Economy of a Rising China in Southeast Asia," 230–31.
[102] Kuik, "Making Sense of Malaysia's China Policy," 438.
[103] The country is sometimes considered a middle power. See Buszynski, "Small States, China and the South China Sea."
[104] Data from World Bank national accounts data.

a more hesitant geopolitical approach in which Malaysia hedges its friendliness with China through diversification of economic and security relationships.[105]

Malaysia has sought—albeit somewhat inconsistently—greater national control over the nature of China's BRI investments, producing moderate divergences with Chinese policy. Chinese policymakers have accorded particular importance to Malaysia, which is seen as a key to managing relations with the Association of Southeast Asian Nations (ASEAN) and implementing southern components of the BRI.[106] Malaysia plays a key role in Chinese efforts to enhance energy security, including plans for rail and pipeline infrastructure to lessen China's dependence on traversing the Straits of Malacca.[107] In this generally "green" case, the salience of BRI connections to Malaysia is matched by cohesive Chinese preferences, given that Xi Jinping has made Southeast Asian components of BRI a core element of his international vision.[108]

Because BRI represented more of a deepening than a shift of previous economic ties, Malaysia was engaged with the initiative from the official announcement in 2013. Chinese investment increased substantially. China became the largest foreign investor in Malaysia in 2016—representing 14 percent of a diversified foreign direct investment outlook.[109] Though the definition of BRI projects is somewhat ambiguous, several major ventures in Malaysia are linked to the Chinese initiative. Infrastructure mega-projects have drawn most of the attention—and criticism. These include a planned, nearly 700-kilometer East Coast Railway Line, to be funded 85 percent through Chinese state loans. The railway was eagerly sought by Malaysian prime minister Najib Razak (2009–18) and seen by China as a key node in a regional, China-centric rail system. Malaysia also sought Chinese backing for rail terminals, housing developments, and port and industrial expansion. Chinese investment has expanded and diversified in other sectors too.[110]

However, several projects became embroiled in a corruption scandal of epic proportions when Prime Minister Najib was accused of laundering billions of dollars through 1MDB, Malaysia's state-controlled development entity. This included funds connected to several Chinese-backed projects,[111] which the political opposition argued risked a "debt trap." Criticism that Najib had sold Malaysia's autonomy vis-à-vis China helped oust the prime minister's Barisan

---

[105] Kuik, "How Do Weaker States Hedge?"
[106] Kuik, "Making Sense of Malaysia's China Policy," 451.
[107] Strating, "Small Power Hedging in an Era of Great-Power Politics."
[108] Despite moments of conflict, the case generally presents as Type 4 (1b, 2a, 3a).
[109] Yean, "Chinese Investment in Malaysia," 2.
[110] Yean, "The Belt and Road Initiative in Malaysia"; Blanchard, "Malaysia and China's MSRI," 105–7; Kuik, "Connectivity and Gaps," 459; Liu and Lim, "The Political Economy of a Rising China in Southeast Asia," 222–23.
[111] Pakiam, "Malaysia in 2018"; Blanchard, "Malaysia and China's MSRI," 107–8.

coalition in 2018.[112] Using the credible threat of domestic political rejection, the new government renegotiated elements of the projects with China to reduce Malaysia's debt exposure. It also gained trade commitments and concessions, especially for the palm oil industry, just as the European market enacted environmental restrictions.[113] Because many of the BRI-linked projects include a mix of state and private actors, Malaysia could encourage Chinese investment even while large state-backed projects were suspended or reduced. A Singapore-based think tank concluded in late 2019: "Malaysia's backing for the BRI demonstrates that through negotiations, it is possible to revise and make adjustments to previously unsatisfactory deals to achieve win-win outcomes."[114]

Malaysia's strategy has worked in part because it combined different elements of small-state power. The country manages its relations with ASEAN to act as a China-friendly, but not China-dependent, power. This has allowed it to steer some of ASEAN's collective power to its ends, shielding it from direct Chinese pressure. Bilaterally, Malaysia has taken advantage of its position in planned infrastructure developments to exercise particular-intrinsic influence. Malaysia's approach to hedging has produced economic benefits even in an increasingly contentious environment.

Failure: Myanmar and the Belt and Road Initiative

Over the last decade, Myanmar's economic relationship with China has followed the course of a boomerang. For decades, China was one of Myanmar's few international partners. Around 2010, Myanmar attempted an alternative path. It suspended China-backed projects where these seemed unfavorable, and it sought a greater diversity of international economic partners. By 2019, those efforts had fallen flat. Myanmar accepted China's favored projects even where they had been previously rejected. International partners backed away. This happened even as Myanmar partially liberalized—at least until an early 2021 coup replaced liberalization with intense repression. Before the coup, however, there had been increasing public scrutiny of Chinese economic influence. Why this failure of diversification and uncritical adherence to the BRI? In 2017, Myanmar's mass expulsion and repression of its Rohingya minority spurred international opprobrium. Using economic and political levers, China took advantage of Myanmar's renewed isolation to reinforce its pre-eminent position in its neighbor's economy. The coup has reinforced these dynamics.

---

[112] Because of intracoalitional disputes, the opposition government fell in early 2020.
[113] Gunn, "China's Globalization and the Belt and Road Project."
[114] Fook, "China-Malaysia Relations Back on Track?"

Like Malaysia, Myanmar is not a prototypical small state. Its population exceeds fifty million; however, poverty, state weakness, and juxtaposition between China and India mean that Myanmar's international position is defined by asymmetry. Despite its strategic position and abundant natural wealth, Myanmar is the poorest country in Southeast Asia (roughly $1,300 GDP per capita). Poverty and isolation increased dependence on China, one of the few countries willing to engage deeply with its repressive military regime from the late 1980s until about 2010.

Shortly before Myanmar's transition to a decade of partial civilian rule began in earnest, China and Myanmar agreed on major projects in hydropower, pipelines, railways, ports, and special economic zones.[115] These were complemented by "liberal economic assistance, cheap loans, trade, investment, energy deals, military, and diplomatic support."[116] Myanmar sits between China's southwestern province of Yunnan and the Bay of Bengal. Overland transit—railways and pipelines—through Myanmar would enhance western China's export potential and energy security. Chinese-controlled ports in Myanmar would facilitate China's naval projection in the Indian Ocean. "Myanmar is not only a crucial link between China and the Indian Ocean but also the corridor leading to South Asia."[117] Because of this geostrategic significance, Myanmar has seen increased attention and funding from China under the BRI, reinvigorating earlier projects.

Divergence between Myanmar's preferences and China's policy began to emerge in 2009,[118] as Myanmar sought to increase its international diversification. Initially, China broadened its engagement with Myanmar's new government and nonmilitary sectors.[119] Myanmar's location enhances its importance for China's BRI plans; the decades of subordinated relations helped cement policy preferences in Beijing.[120] China tolerated the Myitsone Dam cancellation to protect its investments and role in Myanmar from Western intrusion.[121] Myanmar tried to leverage greater international support to enhance its economic policy autonomy. China's attention to Myanmar increased and its preferences cohered in favor of expansive BRI projects.

Initially, Chinese attention and investment found a welcome audience in Myanmar. However, rather suddenly, Myanmar appeared to embark on a different trajectory. A partial democratic opening led to the election in 2015 of an

[115] Gong, "The Belt & Road Initiative and China's Influence in Southeast Asia."
[116] Malik, "Myanmar's Role in China's Maritime Silk Road Initiative," 134.
[117] Han, "Myanmar's Internal Ethnic Conflicts and Their Implications for China's Regional Grand Strategy," 473.
[118] This makes the case an inauspicious Type 1 (1a, 2a, 3a).
[119] Lanteigne, "'The Rock That Can't Be Moved.'"
[120] Han, "Myanmar's Internal Ethnic Conflicts and Their Implications for China's Regional Grand Strategy," 471.
[121] Han, "Myanmar's Internal Ethnic Conflicts and Their Implications for China's Regional Grand Strategy," 470.

opposition-led coalition led by Nobel Peace Prize laureate Aung San Suu Kyi. The country's foreign relations seemed poised to shift too. In 2011, the government cancelled an enormous Chinese-backed hydropower project, the Myitsone Dam, amid civil society and local protest. "This bold unilateral action on Myanmar's part caught China by surprise."[122] This set the stage for a "red" case. China considered the dam a high priority; construction had started two years earlier. But the project had awakened civil society opposition just as political space was increasing.[123] At the same time, an announced plan for a $20 billion railway, meant to connect western China with the Bay of Bengal, also failed to develop. Pausing China-backed projects ameliorated domestic opposition and fit with the opportunity created by growing interest from other international actors.

When the elected government took power in early 2016—to considerable applause from the United States, Western Europe, and Japan—it seemed Myanmar would deepen its turn away from China.[124] Initially, Suu Kyi's preference for a nonaligned foreign policy[125] coincided with reservations that China-Myanmar Economic Corridor (CMEC) projects would leave Myanmar with unmanageable debts. Myanmar never made a complete shift—China-backed oil and gas pipelines went ahead, for example—but the suspension of China's two highest-profile projects in Myanmar signaled an intention to decrease reliance on China. But whereas the pipelines generated revenue for the government,[126] the railway project was "not a major transit-infrastructure development priority in Myanmar."[127] Some officials even considered the railway a threat to national security, suggesting that China was using its mediation in Myanmar's ethnic conflicts to promote BRI projects.[128] Chinese actors had long occupied dominant roles in Myanmar's economy; the reforms "called into question the future role of Myanmar's preeminent neighbour" in the face of new international attention.[129]

Instead, the opposite took place. In November 2018, Myanmar agreed to a host of initiatives under the BRI-linked CMEC, which connects Western China with a China-backed port and economic zone on Myanmar's coast. In late 2019, shelved plans for a cross-country railway were dusted off and greenlighted; a port and economic zone planned since 2015 were fast-tracked. Suu Kyi's government plowed ahead "despite both security concerns and questions about debt and

---

[122] Kyaw, "Sinophobia in Myanmar and the Belt and Road Initiative," 3.
[123] Chan, "Asymmetric Bargaining between Myanmar and China in the Myitsone Dam Controversy."
[124] Malik, "Myanmar's Role in China's Maritime Silk Road Initiative," 134.
[125] Lanteigne, " 'The Rock That Can't Be Moved,' " 46.
[126] Malik, "Myanmar's Role in China's Maritime Silk Road Initiative," 139.
[127] Oh, "Power Asymmetry and Threat Points," 547.
[128] Gong, "The Belt & Road Initiative and China's Influence in Southeast Asia," 646; Han, "Myanmar's Internal Ethnic Conflicts and Their Implications for China's Regional Grand Strategy," 481.
[129] Lanteigne, " 'The Rock That Can't Be Moved,' " 39.

shared costs."[130] She signed onto some three dozen BRI projects in April 2019, which were advanced during Xi Jinping's visit to Myanmar in January 2020.[131] Though Myanmar has created a review committee to ensure the viability of BRI projects, the process has been marked by limited transparency.[132]

Why such a dramatic reversal? The civilian government's inability or unwillingness to restrain state violence against the Rohingya undermined U.S., European, and Japanese support and led to economic sanctions. Myanmar lost alternative economic partners and depended on China to block UN Security Council resolutions condemning its treatment of the Rohingya. Many Chinese investments are centered on Rakhine state—the epicenter of the Rohingya violence—leading China to support those operations.[133] "China has played interference on behalf of Myanmar at the UN Security Council and will expect concessions on its Rakhine infrastructure in exchange for continuing to shelter Myanmar from the much-deserved international opprobrium."[134] Hard pressed to deliver economic results to sustain its fledging popular legitimacy, Myanmar's new government hoped to "bandwagon for profit" and gain diplomatic cover.[135] This represented a return to patterns of foreign relations during military rule. As Enze Han notes, "The movement of the [previous Myanmar] government to distance Myanmar from economic domination by China seems to have been mostly reversed."[136] In doing so, Myanmar sacrificed greater control over its economic trajectory.

Europe

The global financial crisis exploded in the United States in 2008 before sending economic aftershocks across much of the globe. In Europe, the financial crisis created a deep secondary problem by bringing to light latent contradictions within the European Monetary Union (EMU), putting the fate of the single currency, the euro, at risk. It shook confidence in the debt of EMU members, setting off economic catastrophes across Southern Europe.[137]

---

[130] Lanteigne, " 'The Rock That Can't Be Moved,' " 41–42.

[131] Zin, "Myanmar in 2019," 141–42.

[132] Tritto, "The Belt and Road Initiative as a Catalyst for Institutional Development"; Myint, "Myanmar's Experience with China."

[133] Fink, "Myanmar in 2018," 180–83; Fair, "Rohingya: Victims of a Great Game East," esp. 72; Han, "Myanmar's Internal Ethnic Conflicts and Their Implications for China's Regional Grand Strategy," 468, 485–86.

[134] Fair, "Rohingya: Victims of a Great Game East," 72.

[135] The phrase comes from Schweller, "Bandwagoning for Profit."

[136] Han, "Myanmar's Internal Ethnic Conflicts and Their Implications for China's Regional Grand Strategy," 469, 487.

[137] Morlino and Sottilotta, *The Politics of the Eurozone Crisis in Southern Europe.*

At the start of the crisis, Greece and Portugal were similar on several relevant factors, with a shared currency, mounting debts, and similar-sized populations and economies. (In fact, Greece had the larger economy and higher per capita income.) Public debt and recurring deficits had generated concern even before the crisis. Though Greece touched off the regional crisis in the closing days of 2009, Portugal's own austerity politics were not far behind. Both countries were involved in highly asymmetric negotiations and bailouts in which "the Troika"— a grouping of the European Commission, the European Central Bank, and the IMF—was the more powerful counterpart. The following sections examine how Portugal and Greece managed these negotiations and bailouts. Both suffered recessions, but Portugal managed the crisis and its creditors more successfully than Greece.

Success: Portugal leans into the euro crisis

The global financial crisis arrived late in Portugal. Its banks were not heavily exposed to subprime debt, nor were property prices inflated. The country seemed insulated from the worst effects. After a year of warning signs, the spillover hit in 2010.[138] An early, expansionist response to the crisis helped drive the budget deficit above 10 percent. Investors demanded higher risk premiums on Portuguese debt—a problem for a country that had not produced a budget surplus since its transition to democracy. Higher borrowing expenses fed fears about repayment, boosting costs further.[139] Those warning signs combined with the Greek crisis and broader eurozone panic. Soon credit became unaffordable. After months of looking for other options, Portugal requested European financial assistance on April 6, 2011, following the path Greece had started a year earlier.

Situated on the western edge of the Iberian Peninsula, Portugal has been on the periphery of Western European integration. The country received a significant boost from democratization and inclusion in the European project, with strong economic growth throughout the 1990s. However, by the beginning of the crisis, Portugal's population of 10.5 million was experiencing stagnant economic growth, low productivity, and growing indebtedness.[140] Portugal's situation was complicated by a 2011 political deadlock that left a caretaker government to negotiate with the Troika. These were not auspicious signs.

Though the crisis inflicted serious economic and social pain, Portugal avoided the depths of Greece's decline in part due to better international management.

---

[138] Baer, Dias, and Duarte, "The Economy of Portugal and the European Union."
[139] Pereira and Wemans, "Portugal and the Global Financial Crisis."
[140] Baer, Dias, and Duarte, "The Economy of Portugal and the European Union"; Rocha and Stoleroff, "The Challenges of the Crisis and the External Intervention in Portugal."

Portugal's request for a bailout thrust it to the center of the Troika's priorities. Responses to the Greek crisis, and European preparations for possible contagion, had solidified the Troika's increasingly cohesive preferences. However, Portugal was more closely aligned with Troika (and German) economic policy priorities.[141] Under generally "green" relational conditions, Portuguese governments effectively performed that alignment, which meant the country's salience declined over time. This granted Portugal additional space in its implementation of bailout conditionality under increasingly noncrisis, "white" case conditions.

For decades, Portuguese politics were marked by pro-European consensus across major political parties and in the population. Portugal readily coordinated its responses to the global financial crisis with European institutions. Following European guidance, Portugal responded to the U.S. crisis with stimulus spending in 2009. In 2010, European concerns turned to debt sustainability, and Portugal's Socialist government implemented cuts with a clear aim of avoiding a bailout and reassuring private credit markets. Throughout early 2011, Prime Minister José Sócrates insisted Portugal must avoid a rescue package because it would come at the cost of policy autonomy. Meanwhile, his government "exploited a window of opportunity to pass a series of reforms it deemed necessary."[142] Sócrates made painful cuts in consultation with European institutions, but he sought to make them on his own terms, allowing Portugal "to gain some bargaining influence at important EU meetings ahead."[143]

Amid expanding doubts about eurozone debt, the cuts were not enough. Sensing an electoral opportunity, Portugal's center-right party opposed the austerity budget in March 2011, forcing new elections and making "the request for external financial assistance inevitable," as commercial borrowing was unviable.[144] Portugal faced an election even as it urgently negotiated an unprecedented bailout.[145]

Given the caretaker status of the government, all major parties engaged in the negotiations. Portuguese Socialists maintained several red lines, including shielding pensions and wages for lower-income sectors. Portuguese parties used conditionality to create external impetus for politically difficult domestic priorities. One Socialist official told researchers, "The majority of the Troika's memorandum are things the government wanted to do, the vast majority."[146] For conservatives, the bailout agreement was "an opportunity for budgetary consolidation and the liberalisation of the Portuguese economy."[147] On May 17,

---

[141] This would make the case Type 4 (1b, 2a, 3a) on the typology, though priority declined gradually over time, moving the case toward Type 7 (1b, 2b, 3a).

[142] Moury and Standring, " 'Going beyond the Troika,' " 674.

[143] Pereira and Wemans, "Portugal and the Global Financial Crisis," 248.

[144] Sousa and Gaspar, "Portugal, a União Europeia e a Crise," 80.

[145] Magalhães, "The Elections of the Great Recession in Portugal."

[146] Qtd. in Moury and Standring, " 'Going beyond the Troika,' " 669.

[147] Sousa and Gaspar, "Portugal, a União Europeia e a Crise," 80.

2011, the Troika and Portugal's major parties signed the memorandum of understanding (MOU) on the bailout conditions. During the electoral campaign, the conservative opposition made its approval clear—despite its earlier vote against the austerity budget. Incoming prime minister Pedro Passos Coelho told the press he would "go beyond the requirements of the rescue agreement."[148] Indeed, his government sought to do just that.

In fact, the government used the international rescue package to limit the scope for political debate. International conditions provided ready justification for difficult policies—even when those policies were not strictly demanded by the lenders.[149] The conservative government, elected in June 2011, held strong pro-reform and austerity preferences, and it inserted these preferences into revised MOUs to buttress its goals.[150] Another official said, "The programme was not imposed by the Troika. The Troika was the way to do what was needed."[151] To the extent the Troika pushed the Portuguese government, it was pushing an open door. Avoiding a second bailout became a national priority; the Greek case strongly suggested additional bailouts would be accompanied by decreasing autonomy and more international supervision. This fear helped the government maintain opposition support for its program, while also achieving agreements with labor and employer organizations. Portugal signaled its commitments to fiscal responsibility at the European level by giving strong support to deepening economic and fiscal integration, while advancing its priorities through those agreements.[152] Though there were several large protests and general strikes in the face of austerity, the only major institutional constraint was Portugal's Constitutional Court. The judiciary found several austerity measures unconstitutional and forced adjustments; because Europeans were loath to undercut judicial autonomy, the court curtailed European pressure.

Court decisions and improving fiscal conditions allowed some flexibilization of austerity by 2014—even as Greece's crisis reached its nadir. Portugal successfully completed its conditionality in May 2014, allowing it to exit special supervision. It made an advance payment on its IMF debts in February 2014. In a further sign of relative success, Portugal's major parties survived the crisis, and the Socialists—voted out in the moment of greatest uncertainty in early 2011— returned to power in late 2015. Under this new left government, "The most visible 'austerity' measures of the past were reversed, and still commitments with Brussels were met."[153] There are two further elements to Portugal's relative

---

[148] Qtd. in Moury and Standring, "'Going beyond the Troika,'" 672.
[149] Pi Ferrer and Rautajoki, "Navigating Coercion in Political Rhetoric"; Fonseca and Ferreira, "Through 'Seas Never before Sailed.'"
[150] Moury and Standring, "'Going beyond the Troika,'" 671.
[151] Qtd. in Hardiman et al., "Tangling with the Troika," 1272.
[152] Lisi and Ramalhete, "Challenges and Opportunities under Conditionality: Portugal," 191.
[153] Fernandes, Magalhães, and Santana-Pereira, "Portugal's Leftist Government," 519.

success in managing the Troika. First, at least in the broad outlines, the national governments' priorities were compatible with Troika calls for economic reform. Portugal assessed the situation and leaned into the reform program to shape it to its advantage. By doing so, Portuguese parties used international constraints to achieve domestic priorities, not only surviving the crisis but also exiting it with improved European standing.[154]

Failure: The eurozone's Greek tragedy

The global financial crisis hit Greece in earnest in late 2009. The result has been lasting and catastrophic. A decade after the crisis, Greece's GDP remained more than 20 percent below its precrisis level. Unemployment and poverty are stubbornly high, and Greece remains as deeply indebted as ever.[155] The country accepted unprecedented intrusions into its domestic economic policy. Several countries were hard-hit by the eurozone crisis, but none sank so deeply, has been so slow to rise, or lost as much policy autonomy as Greece.

Between 2010 and 2015, negotiations between Greece and its international creditors were nearly constant. There were three major rescue packages, in which Greece accepted harsh austerity and oversight in exchange for bailout loans. The bailouts achieved all parties' minimal shared objective of avoiding a messy Greek default and keeping Greece in the eurozone. However, in most other ways, each successive agreement was further from the preferences enunciated by Greek governments. Whether judged against the government's stated preferences or against standards of economic performance, Greece did very poorly.[156]

When Greece joined the eurozone in 2001, the country of eleven million already had substantial accumulated debt, though Greece's robust growth made it appear manageable. EMU membership reduced borrowing costs, and during the early 2000s, Greek governments took advantage to increase spending while avoiding politically difficult reforms.[157] When the U.S. financial crisis exploded, Greece's latent weaknesses surfaced. In October 2009, a newly elected Greek government revised its predecessor's calculations, doubling the budget deficit to 12 percent of GDP. Panic erupted. Greek's deficit climbed just as credit markets tightened. With Greece largely unable to access private debt markets, the Troika

---

[154] Lisi and Ramalhete, "Challenges and Opportunities under Conditionality: Portugal," 188–91; Moury and Standring, "'Going beyond the Troika.'"

[155] GDP in constant euros, World Bank national accounts data.

[156] Lim, Moutselos, and McKenna, "Puzzled Out?"; Tsebelis, "Lessons from the Greek Crisis"; Zahariadis, "Bargaining Power and Negotiation Strategy."

[157] Featherstone and Papadimitriou, "Greece: A Crisis in Two-Level Governance," 234–37.

became the central interlocutor. Behind the European Commission and the European Central Bank, France and especially Germany played decisive roles.

The Greek crisis remained salient for all parties, spurring multiple rounds of intensive, high-level negotiations and drawing breathless global coverage. There was a baseline agreement among most actors on avoiding default and keeping Greece in the eurozone but disagreement on much else. The status quo policies of the Troika—and Germany—differed greatly from Greek preferences, and this gap expanded in 2015 with the election of an anti-austerity government in Greece. Troika preference cohesion experienced a greater change between 2010 and 2015. The first talks were marked by uncertainty about how to understand and approach the situation, and over what responses were feasible and appropriate.[158] While most accounts highlight July 2015 as Greece's most spectacular fiasco—rarely has a government asked so much, so publicly, and gotten so little—perhaps Greece's more meaningful failure came in May 2010.

The first bailout emerged in a context of great uncertainty. In six months, Greece went from borrowing at low rates to being effectively shut off from credit.[159] European institutions lacked formal authority to bail out member economies, muddying their response. Germany resisted extending public funds but feared contagion and eurozone collapse. The Greek government was unsure about whether to seek European or IMF intervention. Wild market swings created daily stress and time pressure, pushing all parties to negotiate an unprecedented rescue package under "orange" crisis conditions.[160] Greece got a €110 billion loan to stave off default in May 2010. The deal imposed numerical targets for budget reductions that would have been difficult to meet in good times but were impossible in a deep global recession.[161] Harsh cuts deepened Greece's recession in a global climate where few options for near-term growth existed. The deal set deadlines for Greece's return to private credit markets that were unreasonable in a global financial freeze.[162]

Creditors praised Greece's initial efforts at hitting targets and making reforms,[163] but the package's infeasibility was quickly evident. The depth of the Greek recession—much worse than forecast—put targets out of reach. International assessments of Greek debt slid as private creditors were pressured to write off billions of dollars of loans. Greek leaders accepted further cuts in exchange for a new round of rescue loans, but social unrest grew, forcing out Prime Minister George A. Papandreou in late 2011. A technocratic national

---

[158] In 2010, the situation is understood as Type 2 (1a, 2a, 3b); in 2015, Type 1 (1a, 2a, 3a).

[159] Ardagna and Caselli, "The Political Economy of the Greek Debt Crisis," 293.

[160] Zahariadis, "Bargaining Power and Negotiation Strategy," 293.

[161] Moschella, "When Some Are More Equal Than Others," 259; Featherstone, "The Greek Sovereign Debt Crisis and EMU," 202–4.

[162] Ardagna and Caselli, "The Political Economy of the Greek Debt Crisis."

[163] Featherstone, "The Greek Sovereign Debt Crisis and EMU," 207.

unity government followed, installed largely to implement a second bailout of
€130 billion, negotiated in July 2011 but not fully agreed upon until February
2012. Amid political gridlock, austerity continued without Greece making much
progress on hitting creditors' targets.

Austerity, recession, and perceived national humiliation boiled over in the
January 2015 elections, with the victory of an anti-establishment, anti-austerity
coalition led by the radical left party, SYRIZA. The new government's goals were
clear: in addition to keeping Greece in the eurozone, it sought a restructuring
and reduction of Greek debt, "elimination of primary surpluses as a condition
for financial assistance, the curtailment of planned privatizations, a renegotiation of pension system reforms and exceptional spending on the country's
'humanitarian crisis'"—in short, a rewrite of the conditionality of previous
bailouts.[164] Once he took office, new prime minister Alexis Tsipras "unilaterally rescinded many reforms and austerity measures, ousted the much-disliked
Troika supervisors and, most importantly, called for a renegotiation of the current programme."[165]

The Troika responded by withholding the next installment of the bailout
and demanding tougher conditions for future assistance as "hard bargaining
led to harder bargaining by the other side."[166] Disagreement, salience, and increasingly cohesive preferences created "red" conditions. In February, Tsipras
agreed on a four-month extension of the European program, without substantive gains. The piecemeal concessions that Tsipras offered on taxes and pensions
were deemed insufficient and his goals of restructuring unrealistic.[167] Creditors
grew frustrated with the tactics deployed by Tsipras and his finance minister,
Yanis Varoufakis, a "media-savvy academic economist" and "celebrity game-
theorist."[168] When the February extension expired in late June 2015, the break
had harsh repercussions: Greek banks were shuttered for weeks and capital
controls imposed—including a prohibition on overseas transfers and a daily cash
withdrawal limit of €60.[169]

Amid the negotiation breakdown, Tsipras called a snap referendum on the
latest European offer—an idea that had been proposed and rejected in 2012.
Tsipras campaigned against the package on offer in his own referendum—leading
European leaders to see the Greek government as bad-faith negotiators.[170] As

[164] Lim, Moutselos, and McKenna, "Puzzled Out?," 336.
[165] Wolf, "Debt, Dignity, and Defiance: Why Greece Went to the Brink," 832.
[166] Zahariadis, "Bargaining Power and Negotiation Strategy," 689.
[167] Lim, Moutselos, and McKenna, "Puzzled Out?," 338.
[168] Featherstone, "Greece: When Populism Fails."
[169] "Greek debt crisis," June 28, 2015, BBC News, https://www.bbc.co.uk/news/world-europe-33305019.
[170] Zahariadis, "Bargaining Power and Negotiation Strategy," 689; Lim, Moutselos, and McKenna, "Puzzled Out?," 338; Tsebelis, "Lessons from the Greek Crisis," 31.

Tsipras hoped, Greeks rejected the European proposal by a sixty-one-to-thirty-nine margin. Tsipras believed the vote would strengthen his hand at the negotiating table. It did not. Tsipras's insistence on his mandate and on creditors' need to respect Greek democracy found no audience with exhausted negotiators who considered Greek desires both to avoid default and to minimize austerity as incoherent. The prime minister confused gaining a domestic mandate with having a credible domestic constraint.

The SYRIZA government apparently believed it could stare down Germany in a game of "chicken," with both actors threatened with unacceptable harm. Instead, in June 2015, the Troika explained the steps that had been and would be taken to insulate banks and the euro from a Greek default. "For the first time since the crisis began, the nuclear button of Grexit seemed about to be pressed."[171] However, destruction was no longer mutually assured. Days after the referendum, Tsipras agreed to a package that he "declared unfair and as blackmail, since the alternative was the economic destruction of Greece."[172] The €86 billion rescue package obligated him to swallow demands for harsher austerity, wider privatization, and deeper intrusion into domestic decision-making.[173] Where Greece achieved concessions, including some debt reduction, these emerged from IMF insistence on ameliorating what it considered an unsustainable deal, not from Greek negotiating "wins."[174]

Could there have been a better approach? Two economists conclude that policy options were available in 2010 and 2012 that would have left everyone better off. Instead, Greece was forced into "unrealistic goals."[175] Though better than default, bailout conditions inflicted economic damage and political turmoil. The public, highly political, and protracted process pressured leaders to stick to announced positions couched in a moralized discourse instead of locating effective compromises.[176] The point is not that Greece could have forced or bluffed its creditors into generosity, but that in early 2010, Greece might have advanced a longer-term outlook with greater concern for the feasibility of cuts and reforms. The task was less one of hard bargaining than of persuasion during a period of incoherent preferences.[177] With the benefit of hindsight, "giving Greece more time to reduce the deficit before returning to borrowing on private markets might have increased the chances of success of the stabilization program, at no large increase in the political or financial cost borne by the lenders."[178] In 2015, Tsipras tried to

---

[171] Featherstone and Papadimitriou, "Greece: A Crisis in Two-Level Governance," 246.
[172] Tsebelis, "Lessons from the Greek Crisis," 25.
[173] Hennessy, "Good Samaritans vs. Hardliners," 757.
[174] Lim, Moutselos, and McKenna, "Puzzled Out?," 338.
[175] That is, outcomes were Pareto suboptimal. Ardagna and Caselli, "The Political Economy of the Greek Debt Crisis."
[176] Featherstone and Papadimitriou, "Greece: A Crisis in Two-Level Governance," 243.
[177] For a discussion, see Grobe, "The Power of Words."
[178] Ardagna and Caselli, "The Political Economy of the Greek Debt Crisis," 313.

take a different approach but misread the situation. His hard bargaining failed to bring the Troika's position closer to Greek goals, instead solidifying unity among European counterparts and removing the possibility of crafting alliances with countries that may have harbored sympathy for Greece's plight.

Conclusions

The global economy provides many opportunities for small states, but it is not a level playing field. While small states' greater reliance on external capital and markets can produce sustainable prosperity, it entails political and economic vulnerabilities. Larger, wealthier states can withhold assistance, loans, or investment. That said, interdependence can be astutely managed. Policy space can be retained even in highly asymmetric economic relationships. Leaders in Rwanda and Bolivia asserted their interests by selectively deploying sovereign prerogatives in combination with narratives of fairness and recompense. Both Malaysia and Portugal adopted broad policies of alignment, but they did so in ways that let them shape the nature of investments, in Malaysia's case, and loans and reforms, in Portugal's. In all four successful cases, economic gains were achieved, as compared to realistic alternatives. Policy space was retained or enhanced. Of course, that is not always the case. Zambian leaders lacked cohesive plans for advancing their own goals, so were overwhelmed by the demands of creditors and donors. Greek leaders missed an opportunity for persuasion and then later misplayed their hand. Despite its internal unity, the authoritarian Paraguayan government missed potentially massive long-term economic benefits in the creation of the world's largest hydroelectric facility. In different ways, all these cases show how cultivating external options can help maintain international economic policy autonomy, but nowhere is that clearer than in Myanmar's abandonment of its quest for greater economic balance. There is no silver bullet for achieving economic objectives, but having robust and well-supported plans, maintaining multiple partners, and advancing a persuasive narrative allowed four of the states here to achieve significant wins.

7

Institutions, Law, and Norms

Beyond bilateral relationships, highlighted in the preceding two chapters, small states have sought to reshape international society by engaging with international institutions, strengthening international law, and promoting favorable norms. As Chapter 2 emphasizes, a world with more robust institutions, law, and norms is generally preferable for small states. The insight is not a new one: Keohane and Nye noted four decades ago that "International organizations are frequently congenial institutions for weak states."[1] That view remains widely held and finds support in this book, despite the acknowledgment that international institutions and law are not neutral. They crystallize constellations of power and ensconce advantages for powerful states—a big reason great powers often sponsor their creation. In international institutions, law, and norms, asymmetries remain— though sometimes they become less visible.[2]

And yet, small states generally support international institutions, law, and norms. The explanation for this contrast emerges from the dynamics of asymmetry, which lead small and large powers to approach the world in different ways. Institutions help large states manage their broad spectrum of interests. Institutional constraints—which can usually be broken in extreme cases—are worth the legitimacy they produce and the low-cost extension of influence they facilitate. Small states recognize these limitations, but they value institutions, law, and norms for their own reasons. In Womack's terms, institutions create an appearance of "mutual respect."[3] Beyond that, institutions, law, and norms provide opportunities for small states to participate in "big" conversations—that is, global discussions about central issues of international order—in an environment that avoids direct confrontation. Working through institutions, law, and norms allows non–great powers the possibility of gaining lasting, if diffuse, changes to international politics.

To consider these forms of diffuse change, this chapter examines the broader constellations of international relationships that underpin institutions, law, and norms. This allows consideration of issues that quickly spill outside the bounds

---

[1] Keohane and Nye, *Power and Interdependence*, 36.
[2] From very different vantage points, see Mearsheimer, "The False Promise of International Institutions"; Anghie, *Imperialism, Sovereignty and the Making of International Law*.
[3] Womack, *Asymmetry and International Relationships*, 51–55.

A Small State's Guide to Influence in World Politics. Tom Long, Oxford University Press. © Oxford University Press 2022. DOI: 10.1093/oso/9780190926205.003.0007

of the bilateral: climate and the environment, the international promotion of human rights, regional international organizations, and global public health. These sections provide more general overviews of small states' international engagement in these issue areas, with reference to specific examples. Doing so allows this chapter to capture aspects of small states' international affairs that might be rendered invisible by the country- and policy-specific approach to the security and international political economy cases.

Case 1: Climate and environment

Clad in scuba gear and several meters underwater, the president of the Maldives gripped a waterproof pencil and declared an "SOS from the frontline" of a global environmental catastrophe. By convening "the world's first underwater Cabinet meeting," the Maldives hoped to capture the world's attention and shape the direction of the upcoming 2009 Copenhagen global climate summit.[4] As the publicity stunt suggested, on the matter of small states and climate change, the consequences are dire, the rhetoric and theatrics dramatic. The very existence of several small island states—at least in their current form—will be eroded by the effects of climate change within decades. In response, some of the world's smallest states by territory and population have adopted large strategies for highlighting life-or-death consequences, existential threat, and dire costs of inaction.

The role of small states in global environmental, and especially climate, negotiations can be framed as a stunning success or an abysmal failure. Compared to their slight size, small island developing states (SIDS) have scored tremendous successes during three decades of international climate negotiations. But when compared to the scale of the problem, and its consequences for these same states, those victories appear Pyrrhic. In this section, we examine how small states achieved significant influence in shaping the agenda, institutions, and agreements at the heart of the global climate change regime, as well as how this influence has fallen short.

SIDS are often described as the frontline of climate change, or the "canaries in the coalmine."[5] Though they emit little carbon dioxide and other greenhouse gases, SIDS will be among the first and most affected states by the consequences of climate change. The risks are most pronounced for low-lying atoll states, which will be submerged as sea levels rise; however, many island and coastal states face pronounced threats from flooding, extreme weather events, and salination of

---

[4] The President's Office, Republic of the Maldives, "Maldives Holds World's First Underwater Cabinet Meeting," October 17, 2009, https://presidency.gov.mv/Press/Article/633.

[5] Benwell, "The Canaries in the Coalmine."

freshwater sources.[6] Economic dependence on agriculture, tourism, and fish-eries, all subject to environmental risks, creates further vulnerabilities. Yet there is little that small states can do on their own to offset the problem. Even drastic reductions to the small states' emissions are symbolic on a global scale. The costs of adaptation are, in some cases, estimated to be several times higher than a state's gross domestic product (GDP). Even whether submerged states continue to exist as internationally recognized, legal entities will rest largely in the hands of other states.[7] The problems of small states and climate change are deeply embedded in asymmetries, both historical and contemporary.[8]

Climate change emerged on the international political scene in the late 1980s, though scientific concern started decades before. Small states, particularly is-lands, were engaged in international climate negotiations from the beginning. SIDS recognized and emphasized the risks they faced, and they helped place and maintain climate change on the international agenda—albeit with un-even commitment from large states. In the late 1980s and early 1990s, special-ized forums and summits where small islands were well represented, such as the Commonwealth and Pacific Islands Forum, helped small states coordinate positions and develop strategies.[9] A global framework emerged at the 1992 Rio de Janeiro Earth Summit, taking the form of the UN Framework Convention on Climate Change (UNFCCC). Ultimately incorporating nearly two hundred state-parties, the UNFCCC created an overwhelming negotiating environ-ment. A multitude of varied actors possess divergent preferences regarding the broad array of issues on the table. The forum operates, nominally, by consensus. While this format creates opportunities for SIDS, "the very same UNFCCC de-sign features that provide small island states with a much needed voice in the negotiation process also spell trouble for negotiation when extended to all other UNFCCC members."[10]

The combination of climate change's ruinous consequences and SIDS's dimin-utive stature has put the discourse of "vulnerability" at the heart of these states' engagement in global climate negotiations. Prime Minister Bikenibeu Paeniu of Tuvalu, with a population of less than ten thousand, gained international at-tention by warning about existential threats of sea-level rise. He began lobbying large powers and seeking to shape the agenda.[11] Strategically deploying this

---

[6] Campbell and Barnett, *Climate Change and Small Island States*, chap. 1; Nurse et al., "Small Islands."

[7] Costi and Ross, "The Ongoing Legal Status of Low-Lying States in the Climate-Changed Future."

[8] Sealey-Huggins, "'1.5° C to Stay Alive,'" 2445.

[9] Ashe, Van Lierop, and Cherian, "The Role of the Alliance of Small Island States (AOSIS) in the Negotiation of the United Nations Framework Convention on Climate Change (UNFCCC)."

[10] Bagozzi, "The Multifaceted Nature of Global Climate Change Negotiations," 442, 444. Also Carter, "Multilateral Consensus Decision Making."

[11] Campbell and Barnett, *Climate Change and Small Island States*, 87.

vulnerability and related moral clarion calls, small states gained surprising influence in global climate negotiations. Smallness had been an asset, according to some, allowing SIDS to depoliticize climate issues by making scientific and moral claims. "It is the vulnerability of small states that sets them apart from political wrangling and gives them a natural leadership role."[12] The combination of vulnerability and a lack of historic fault for emissions has allowed SIDS to act as the "conscience" of the UNFCCC.[13] Island states "turn morality into their main asset and core leadership strategy ... to delegitimize and shame other states with different discourses, positions, and interests."[14]

There is something ironic about the prominence of SIDS's "vulnerability": its salience emerges in part from the agency, adaptability, effectiveness, and resilience of the same states whose condition the narrative describes. While vulnerability recognizes aspects of these states' challenges, a near-exclusive focus on weaknesses overlooks how these states can adapt and engage internationally. As Barnett and Campbell note, many small island states have faced recurring shocks, from colonization to storms to world wars. "Pacific Island communities have historically been capable of adapting to change, but these capabilities are rarely recognized in outsiders' representations of the region."[15] The focus on vulnerability can underestimate resilience domestically and regionally, while also overlooking the sources of power these small states retain.[16] Most prominently, small states have developed collective power through groupings with other small states and alliances with larger states and nonstate actors. In addition, small states have at times shed the discourse of vulnerability to employ overlooked bases of particular-intrinsic power.

Nearly as soon as they sought to put climate change and rising sea levels on the international agenda, small islands states realized they could gain strength in numbers that exceeded their individual weight. This insight led to the creation of the Alliance of Small Island States (AOSIS) in 1990. Many of the most notable small-state achievements in climate negotiations have been connected to this grouping,[17] which fomented cross-regional ties between organizations of island states in the Pacific and Caribbean and served as a platform to attract, develop, and deploy assistance from foundations and nongovernmental organizations (NGOs). AOSIS mattered not just for its moral claims, but because it facilitated

---

[12] Benwell, "The Canaries in the Coalmine," 207.

[13] Carter, "Multilateral Consensus Decision Making," 3; Corbett, Xu, and Weller, "Norm Entrepreneurship and Diffusion 'from below' in International Organisations."

[14] de Águeda Corneloup and Mol, "Small Island Developing States and International Climate Change Negotiations," 292.

[15] Campbell and Barnett, *Climate Change and Small Island States*, 17.

[16] Barnett and Waters, "Rethinking the Vulnerability of Small Island States"; McGregor and Yerbury, "Politics of Rising Tides," 121.

[17] Betzold, "'Borrowing' Power to Influence International Negotiations"; Carter, "Multilateral Consensus Decision Making."

unity on core goals and messages. "A coalition such as AOSIS strengthens small states' voice in the political arena: it makes a difference for other governments and the broader population whether an issue is raised by a single state or by 40 of them."[18] AOSIS scored notable achievements as a "first-mover" during the early 1990s consolidation of the UN climate regime.[19] Perhaps the most lasting was recognition of SIDS as a category that suffered special effects and deserved greater inclusion.[20] Starting in Rio in 1992, AOSIS would be a visible and consistent force pushing for more ambitious and binding commitments to reducing greenhouse gas emissions.[21]

Despite these early victories, progress was uneven. AOSIS depended on its ability to persuade larger polluters that they should take costly actions. Climate negotiations in the 1990s, and particularly the 1997 Kyoto Protocol, featured arguments from large, developing economies that their development should not be impeded because historic responsibility for emissions rested with wealthy countries. Mostly developing economies themselves, AOSIS members understood this argument but countered that without action by the likes of Brazil, China, and India, SIDS would suffer tremendously.[22] AOSIS sought, with little success, to gain greater financial commitments from wealthy states to help implement adaptations to living in a changing climate, though it did win mention of international assistance for adaptation in the Kyoto Protocol. The implementation of Kyoto was slow and mitigation disappointing. AOSIS struggled with the positions of emerging economies. Worse, its moral arguments had little purchase in the electoral politics of the United States, which turned against Kyoto in 2000, as they would turn against the Paris Accords in 2016.

In the intervening years, the scientific consensus around climate change and its deleterious effects for island and coastal states grew more robust and prominent. Along with determined advocacy, this increased the issue's salience in many large countries, in part within a discourse and international framework that AOSIS had played a hand in shaping. Large developing economies like the BRICS (Brazil, Russia, India, China, and South Africa) boomed after the signing of Kyoto—and so did their share of global emissions. More positively, the European Union grew serious about climate change, driving closer partnerships at a regional level and bilaterally between AOSIS and EU member states. These links have provided an additional source of funding, expertise, and diplomatic

---

[18] Jaschik, "Small States and International Politics," 287.
[19] Betzold, Castro, and Weiler, "AOSIS in the UNFCCC Negotiations," 594.
[20] Carter, "Multilateral Consensus Decision Making," 96–97; Rasheed, "Role of Small Islands in UN Climate Negotiations," 216.
[21] Campbell and Barnett, *Climate Change and Small Island States*, 102.
[22] Campbell and Barnett, *Climate Change and Small Island States*, 102–4.

support for shared goals—though AOSIS has pushed for even more ambitious targets than the European Union.

These conditions set the stage for the Fifteenth Conference of Parties (COP), the summit meeting for the UNFCCC, in Copenhagen in 2009. Though hopes were high for meaningful progress, "the final outcome, the Copenhagen Accord, was far from what SIDS had strived for."[23] The conference failed to achieve a consensual and binding agreement to reduce emissions—the overarching AOSIS goal. AOSIS failed to gain adherence to specific goals, such as a 1.5° Celsius limit to warming above preindustrial levels (2° Celsius was the generally accepted target). The progress on finance for adaptation to the effects of climate change was also a disappointment, both in the amount and the mechanisms created to administer those funds. Concrete achievements in Copenhagen were few. However, AOSIS did lay groundwork for greater progress, including getting some one hundred states to adopt its goal of the 1.5° Celsius limit to temperature increases. The final accord mentioned a global climate fund, which was adopted the following year.[24] Still, the summit's failure opened the eyes of many AOSIS leaders for the need for greater consultation with BRICS states.[25]

If Copenhagen was a visible failure followed by quiet successes, Paris was a triumph followed by frustration. The panorama for the 2015 Paris summit was more positive, largely because of an agreement between the two largest emitters, the United States and China, the previous year.[26] The European Union continued to push for strong reductions, with legal obligations, along with AOSIS and an increasing number of developing economies. AOSIS emphasized its 1.5° Celsius limit, with a publicity campaign around the slogan of "1.5° to stay alive."[27] SIDS also made a renewed push for the inclusion of loss and damages in the agreement—essentially legal liabilities for the catastrophes they expect climate change to incur. Given the potential costs, large states were largely united in opposition; even its nonbinding inclusion was considered something of a victory.[28] Though imperfect, AOSIS celebrated the final deal as including or acknowledging its major concerns.[29] After Paris, however, the opposition of U.S. president Donald Trump forced AOSIS members to find lower-profile approaches for pursuing their climate goals.

---

[23] de Águeda Corneloup and Mol, "Small Island Developing States and International Climate Change Negotiations," 290.

[24] de Águeda Corneloup and Mol, "Small Island Developing States and International Climate Change Negotiations"; Carter, "Multilateral Consensus Decision Making," 76–78.

[25] Bishop and Payne, "Climate Change and the Future of Caribbean Development," 1541.

[26] Dimitrov, "The Paris Agreement on Climate Change."

[27] Ourbak and Magnan, "The Paris Agreement and Climate Change Negotiations."

[28] Dimitrov, "The Paris Agreement on Climate Change," 4; Ourbak and Magnan, "The Paris Agreement and Climate Change Negotiations," 2203–4.

[29] Ourbak and Magnan, "The Paris Agreement and Climate Change Negotiations," 2204.

While the UNFCCC is the highest-profile venue for climate action, small states have tried to shape the global issue in other ways. One innovative strategy by European small states was unilateral action on carbon taxes, an early recommendation for incentivizing reduced emissions. Though one might expect these states to act as free riders in the climate regime, Finland, Sweden, Norway, and Denmark enacted carbon taxes even before the 1992 Rio Earth Summit.[30] These small states were "acting as climate mitigation pioneers [because] it was expected that other countries would follow their example, creating a more level playing field." Few large states did so.[31] In 1997, shortly after its emergence from the Soviet bloc, Slovenia became the first non-Nordic state to implement a carbon tax.[32] More recently other European small states have done so—Portugal, Iceland, Ireland, Croatia, Switzerland, and Estonia. These have echoes in Europe's ambitious plans for climate reduction, including through trade measures, announced in July 2021.

The early use of carbon taxes is one example of how small states emerged as climate policy innovators and entrepreneurs. Climate innovations extend beyond Europe. Barbados has created detailed climate action plans and become a regional leader in the production and use of efficient solar water heaters.[33] Some of the same Pacific islands most active in AOSIS, often depicted as small and vulnerable, have reconceptualized themselves as "large ocean states." Because many of these states include scattered islands, international law grants them maritime territory and exclusive economic zones (EEZs) many times larger than their "dry" territory. While maritime territory and EEZs were long seen as a source of income through the sale of fishing licenses, several states have set swaths of ocean aside as "no take" marine protected environments. This policy innovation serves a conservation purpose and demonstrates leadership in environment and climate, helping small states influence the international "ocean agenda." As in the evolution of AOSIS, small states have partnered with environmental foundations and NGOs to enhance their previously limited capacities, in this case to monitor and police their maritime territory, enhancing their "positive sovereignty."[34] These sorts of novel arrangements may even become important to arguing for the continuity of legal sovereignty if these states, or parts of them, become uninhabitable.[35]

A final, post–Paris Accord example of small-state leadership in climate change emerges from a largely overlooked corner of the UN system—the International

[30] Andersen, "The Politics of Carbon Taxation," 1084; Carter, Little, and Torney, "Climate Politics in Small European States."

[31] Andersen, "The Politics of Carbon Taxation," 1085.

[32] Andersen, "The Politics of Carbon Taxation," 1083.

[33] Bishop and Payne, "Climate Change and the Future of Caribbean Development," 1548–49.

[34] Chan, " 'Large Ocean States.' "

[35] Costi and Ross, "The Ongoing Legal Status of Low-Lying States in the Climate-Changed Future."

Maritime Organization (IMO). Like with the previous example, small states have exploited a form of particular-intrinsic power. In the IMO, states' influence is linked to the number of shipping companies on their registries. Numerous small states sell flag rights for shipping as a source of income,[36] putting them among the largest state registries in the IMO—Panama, Liberia, Marshall Islands, Singapore, Malta, and the Bahamas possess the six largest registries in the world. After Paris, a coalition of academics, NGOs, and small-state leaders hit on the idea of using the IMO to seek emissions cuts. The global shipping industry was responsible for about 2.8 percent of all emissions, and that share had grown. Marshall Islands foreign minister "[Tony] de Brum and his colleagues from RMI [Republic of the Marshall Islands] identified the IMO as a place where they could exert influence disproportionate to their size and push forward their interests."[37] Bucking routine, de Brum attended the IMO meetings himself. Further rupturing the cozy practice of sticking to "technical" matters, the minister pushed climate politics onto the agenda. Though his first efforts were rebuffed, his actions changed the dynamic; other states quickly responded in future meetings. His assertive leadership and unexpected choice of venue won a pledged 50 percent reduction in shipping company emissions. "These successes are remarkable for small states and would have been considered impossible only a few years earlier."[38]

The successes of small states in the context of international environmental politics are extraordinary when considering the context of asymmetry and entrenched interests. But as noted with the UNFCCC, even these impressive victories—shaping agendas and institutional frameworks, building coalitions, and reshaping discourses—are not enough to avoid severe consequences. Given almost certainly inadequate mitigation, small states will need to deploy similar strategies to push for dramatic climate adaptation. As two experts on Pacific Island states wrote a decade ago, "Adaptation is the only response open to the PICs [Pacific Island countries] given the global failure to mitigate climate change."[39]

Case 2: Human rights

Though it is rarely noted, small states have been prominent advocates for the internationalization of human rights. At the international level, human rights are closely bound up with institutions, law, and norms. And while large states have often considered the promotion of human rights bilaterally—targeting violations

[36] Cooper and Shaw, "The Diplomacies of Small States at the Start of the Twenty-First Century."
[37] Corbett et al., "Climate Governance, Policy Entrepreneurs and Small States," 832.
[38] Corbett et al., "Climate Governance, Policy Entrepreneurs and Small States," 837.
[39] Campbell and Barnett, *Climate Change and Small Island States*, 110.

of rights in a specific (often small) state with shame and sanctions—small states often focus on the international infrastructure of rights promotion. Small-state advocacy of human rights is associated with wealthy Northern European states, but small states from around the world have made rights a prominent feature of their diplomacies. This section explores how small states have advocated human rights in their foreign policies, the contributions they have made, and the progress achieved.

Key moments in the history of international human rights owe a great deal to small states. As Kathryn Sikkink has shown, Latin Americans played outsize roles in the formulation of international human rights agreements immediately after World War II, despite their exclusion from the inner sanctum of global order making. The victorious great powers were often ambivalent or opposed to formalizing human rights commitments, but many less powerful states insisted that rights be included in the new UN structure. The framers of the Universal Declaration of Human Rights drew heavily on the preparations for the American Declaration of the Rights and Duties of Man. Influential advocates came from small states: Alejandro Álvarez of Chile, Ricardo Alfaro of Panama, Minerva Bernadino of the Dominican Republic, Antoine Fragulis of Greece, Charles Malik of Lebanon, and Dardo Regules of Uruguay all made signal contributions to UN and regional human rights frameworks.[40] Small states continued their contributions to international human rights and humanitarianism, shaping the Helsinki Accords, backing protections for civilians in conflicts, animating campaigns against apartheid and landmines, and supporting the International Criminal Court.[41]

Why do many small states pursue human rights, even though they are more likely to find themselves targeted by large states in the name of humanitarian concerns? Human rights allow small states to make claims about central elements of international society and state behavior—including core security concerns— in venues that are more favorable to small-state influence. While the prioritization of human rights often corresponds to domestic political identity, it also furthers international goals—gaining a seat at the table, emerging as a regional representative, or demonstrating greater status. Advocacy of the internationalization of human rights coincides with general support for a more institutionalized, more juridically robust, and more egalitarian international system that is amenable to small states.

Doing so is not without risk or cost. Stronger human rights institutions can generate intense scrutiny of internal practices—indeed, that is the point—and

---

[40] Sikkink, *Evidence for Hope*, chaps. 2–3; Waltz, "Universalizing Human Rights."
[41] Deitelhoff and Wallbott, "Beyond Soft Balancing"; Brysk, *Global Good Samaritans*, 3; Bower, "Norms without the Great Powers"; Mantilla, "Social Pressure and the Making of Wartime Civilian Protection Rules."

small states can find themselves subject to that criticism. Small states' leaders may promote human rights for domestic reasons, with the hope that international scrutiny might constrain their successors and encourage lasting democratic transitions.[42] But the promotion of human rights in foreign policy can expose small states to conflicts with, and sanction from, large powers, as critics of Chinese human rights practices or friends of the Dalai Lama can attest.[43]

The classic examples of small states' international promotion of human rights come from northern Europe. In the 1980s, Norwegian scholar-turned-policy-maker Jan Egeland called for the northern European states to draw on their traditions of social democracy and internationalism to become "potent small states" in the area of human rights.[44] Since 1979, the Netherlands has declared human rights an "essential element" of its foreign policy—for which Egeland dubbed it "probably the most effective human rights advocate today."[45] Dutch commitments emerged from a belief in the value of international "legal machinery" for a small, trading state that "stood to benefit from international rules and institutions to enforce them vis-à-vis the larger countries."[46] In her comparative study of human rights foreign policies, Alison Brysk refers to Sweden as "the gold standard" for its considerable funding, broad advocacy, and relative welcome to asylum seekers.[47] All these states possess significant wealth and deep levels of internationalization. Though small in population, they often have seats and voice at the global table. They draw on material and relational resources to cultivate humanitarianism as a component of their foreign policies through commitments in funding and participation in human rights bodies, peacekeeping, and conflict resolution.[48] Human rights allows them to gain additional influence and to shape events well beyond the more limited geographical scope traditionally attributed to small states' foreign policies.

These small states have made human rights an important piece of their foreign policies, and even their national identities. Norway defines itself as a "peace state," capitalizing on its role as host of the Nobel Peace Prize to project a favorable state identity.[49] They employ bilateral and multilateral channels, including high levels of foreign development assistance with strong human rights components. Bilaterally, they undertake public criticism and private, diplomatic suasion. Their targets have included allies and important commercial partners.

---

[42] Moravcsik, "The Origins of Human Rights Regimes"; Hafner-Burton, Mansfield, and Pevehouse, "Human Rights Institutions, Sovereignty Costs and Democratization."
[43] Fuchs and Klann, "Paying a Visit."
[44] Egeland, "Ineffective Big States, Potent Small States."
[45] Baehr, Castermans-Holleman, and Grünfeld, "Human Rights in the Foreign Policy of the Netherlands."
[46] Oomen, Rights for Others, 9–10.
[47] Brysk, Global Good Samaritans, 42.
[48] Jakobsen, Nordic Approaches to Peace Operations, 159–60.
[49] Johnsen, "Gifts Favour the Giver."

Sweden criticized the United States in the Vietnam War and the war on terror; it continues to criticize numerous states for their use of the death penalty. China and Israel have been targets of critical statements and reports.[50] In addition to its expansive bilateral programs, Sweden funds and participates heavily in UN and European human rights, humanitarian, and peacekeeping initiatives. Dutch bilateral criticism is perceived as more selective and conditioned by commercial considerations, but nonetheless it has provoked reprisals from China and Indonesia. The Netherlands has worked to shape the EU stance on human rights to gain greater weight for its positions and to "hide behind the broad back of the European Union."[51]

These Northern European countries are the best-known examples of small states' human rights policies. Given their wealth and privileged international positions, they are rightly seen as exceptions. However, human rights are an important element of foreign policy for states well beyond Northern Europe. Small states that have experienced transitions from authoritarianism to democracy can make human rights central to their international engagement. Chile and the Czech Republic are two illustrative cases. During the Cold War, both states were prominent targets of human rights criticism; in fact, today's transnational human rights movement emerged in its current form partially in response to the 1973 Chilean coup d'état.[52] Since transitioning to democracy in the early 1990s, both countries have become prominent advocates of human rights and democratization. The international pursuit of these issues served domestic purposes and buttressed the identities of new governments. Despite continued military clout in its transitional government, democratic Chile immediately joined a wide array of international agreements and institutions on human rights, with strong support for enforcement mechanisms, the responsibility to protect, and the International Criminal Court (ICC). "Chile's conception of its new international role was driven by the need to enhance legitimacy in accordance with the use of human rights as authoritative norms in world politics," argues Claudia Fuentes-Julio.[53] Chilean diplomats learned to deploy collective power in cooperation with established human rights promoters like the Netherlands to enhance its voice in multilateral institutions.

Though less internationally recognized, the Czech Republic also focused its foreign policy on human rights and transitions to democracy after it emerged from the 1993 "velvet divorce" as an independent state. During the 1990s, the new country sought to reshape its position in European and UN bodies from a

[50] Brysk, *Global Good Samaritans*, 44–53.
[51] Baehr, Castermans-Holleman, and Grünfeld, "Human Rights in the Foreign Policy of the Netherlands," 1001.
[52] Kelly, *Sovereign Emergencies*.
[53] Fuentes-Julio, "Norm Entrepreneurs in Foreign Policy," 263–64.

recipient of human rights assistance to an active participant in the international protection of human rights. It capitalized on its own transitional experience and the prominent leadership of Václav Havel to establish its credentials. That approach also created limitations, with reliance on Havel's stature lessening the urgency of institutionalizing human rights policies. In the 2000s, Czech integration into the European Union provided new tools for addressing human rights concerns, but it also left the country's efforts overshadowed by its new peers.[54]

Outside the North Atlantic core of the liberal international order, other democracies have enhanced their international status through human rights foreign policies. From nearly opposite points of the globe, New Zealand and Costa Rica offer examples. The Central American republic has promoted regional human rights and democracy protections since the 1960s, and more recently has advocated international commitments on rights for the disabled and indigenous people, favored deeper multilateral institutionalization of human rights mechanisms, and argued to expand the role of the ICC. Costa Rica's promotion of human rights emerged as a central part of its response to regional conflicts in the 1980s, allowing it to project itself as "an island of peace in Central America."[55] As a country without armed forces since 1948, Costa Rica advocates demilitarization and assists in police reform in Latin America.[56] Its close association with democracy, peace, and human rights granted greater autonomy from the United States during the Cold War and beyond and helps attract investment and tourism.[57]

New Zealand has employed human rights advocacy—along with its nonnuclear status—to escape the shadow of its larger neighbor, Australia. Consciously adopting a role as a small state at a global level, New Zealand "seeks to win respect from peer [UN] member states . . . by being a good international citizen in carrying out peacekeeping roles and promoting international and human rights law."[58] This has helped New Zealand cultivate a reputation as a benign regional presence in the Pacific, focused on "conflict avoidance and resolution, humanitarian assistance, human rights, and environmental defense."[59]

The 1998 signature of the Rome Statute and the 2002 founding of the ICC represented a major shift in the international institutionalization of human rights. Unlike most international law, which centers on states, the court's design would allow international prosecution of individuals responsible for grave rights violations. Middle powers and small states in Africa, Europe, and Latin America

[54] Zemanová, "When Could New 'Potent Small States' Emerge?"
[55] Brysk, *Global Good Samaritans*, 115.
[56] Brysk, *Global Good Samaritans*, 96–103.
[57] Longley, *The Sparrow and the Hawk*; Brysk, *Global Good Samaritans*, 115.
[58] Devetak and True, "Diplomatic Divergence in the Antipodes," 248.
[59] Buchanan, "Lilliputian in Fluid Times," 276.

all played a significant role in driving a process that inspired great-power am-bivalence.[60] Not all states had the resources or will to participate equally in the negotiations for the court's creation,[61] but there was considerable and growing engagement from small states.

In the two decades since its founding, the ICC has been subject to increasing political contestation, with the United States refusing to join and pressuring small states to accept bilateral exemptions to shield U.S. citizens from prosecu-tion.[62] Many African small states emerged first as champions of the ICC before growing more critical.[63] Today, the ICC faces a crisis in its relations with the African Union (AU); the near-exclusive focus on investigations and prosecutions in Africa has fueled concerns about bias and double standards, interference, and a lack of customary immunity for heads of state.[64] However, the deeper reasons that some African states and the AU have fallen out with the ICC are sugges-tive. One analysis of the initial ICC negotiations concludes that the court's later practices contrasted with the vision many African states had for an aspirational court that "embodied and sought to build a fairer international system that could provide a check on the major powers." In short, many African states sought a court that would ameliorate international asymmetries and not just one that curtailed leaders' impunity.[65] Though the AU and numerous African states have threatened a rupture with the ICC, Botswana has been "an outspoken ICC-sup-porter" and criticized threats of an African exodus from the ICC. Botswana's leaders even insisted they would arrest Sudanese then-president Omar al-Bashir, who had been indicted by the ICC.[66]

Have small states' human rights policies been successful? The goals of a human rights policy are not always straightforward, particularly beyond the bi-lateral level. States pursue changes in other states' repressive behaviors, but they have other goals as well. There is substantial debate about the effectiveness of human rights promotion generally; by its collective nature, attributing credit for systemic shifts is impractical. But the expansion of human rights has deep-ened the institutionalization and legalization of the international system in ways broadly beneficial to small states. For many, human rights foreign policies allow for an expression of state identity and facilitate international legitimacy for do-mestic democratization. Small states from Scandinavia to Central America have

[60] Behringer, "Middle Power Leadership on the Human Security Agenda"; Panke, "Small States in Multilateral Negotiations"; Deitelhoff and Wallbott, "Beyond Soft Balancing"; Chatoor, "The Role of Small States in International Diplomacy."

[61] Iommi, "Al-Bashir Didn't Start the Fire."

[62] Bosco, Rough Justice.

[63] Gissel, "A Different Kind of Court." Senegal became the first country in the world to ratify the Rome Statute.

[64] Gissel, "A Different Kind of Court," 728–29.

[65] Gissel, "A Different Kind of Court," 744.

[66] Mills and Bloomfield, "African Resistance to the International Criminal Court," 121.

gained enhanced international and regional status, moral leadership, and public diplomatic benefits from their human rights advocacy.

Case 3: Regional organizations

Despite the power disparities they often reflect, international organizations are preferred environments for small states. Outside of Europe, most attention has been on small states' participation in organizations at the global level, like the United Nations or the World Trade Organization. But small states' actions suggest that less emphasized regional organizations are just as important. Smaller memberships, proximity, and, sometimes, greater linguistic and cultural commonalities can make regional organizations friendlier settings for small states. Scholars count roughly eighty multipurpose regional organizations, which encompass an array of issues and functions.[67] Regional organizations work for the promotion of economic goals, like trade integration, as well as collective security, technical assistance, and cooperation on shared transnational challenges. While some regional organizations are asymmetric, with a major power at their core, in other cases, even very small states have formed regional organizations. The largest member of the Organization of Eastern Caribbean States is St. Lucia, with a population of 175,000.

Regional organizations are not neutral forums, nor are they uniformly beneficial for small states. Instead, "it is typically the powerful states who become champions of regionalism," using regional organizations to assert their leadership, including through coercion.[68] Grouping states into a regional international organization does not eliminate the pre-existing power asymmetries between small states and their larger neighbors. However, regional organizations often serve as venues where consensus and cordiality are prized. In these environments, asymmetries can be softened—and this can be useful to small and large states alike. Even hegemonic regional organizations require the participation and acceptance of small states to gain a degree of legitimacy.[69]

Small states pursue a variety of goals in and through asymmetrical regional organizations. Economic goals are salient. Regional organizations that include large states can enhance small states' exports by providing greater market access and certainty about the rules governing trade, even though the gains from trade may disproportionately benefit the larger partner.[70] Joining regional

[67] Panke, "Regional Cooperation through the Lenses of States"; Jetschke et al., "Patterns of (Dis) Similarity in the Design of Regional Organizations." There are also a multitude of narrower economic agreements, especially plurilateral trade agreements.
[68] Panke, "Regional Cooperation through the Lenses of States," 477.
[69] Acharya, "Regionalism in the Evolving World Order."
[70] Schiff, *Regional Integration and Development in Small States.*

organizations with large states may grant entry to preferred schemes for migration, infrastructure investment, or development assistance, or other forms of "shelter" from security threats and economic vulnerabilities.[71] Asymmetrical regional organizations provide opportunities for voice and pressure with large states, sometimes in more informal and consensus-based environments than those great powers accept at the global level.[72] In fact, the international legal structures that allow regional organizations as part of global security and economic governance emerged from pressure by small and medium Latin American states. Those states had found Pan American regional organizations helpful for navigating asymmetry with the United States before World War II.[73]

On the other hand, small states may form more symmetrical regional organizations without the participation of great powers. These too can have a variety of purposes. Some more symmetrical organizations are explicitly "counterhegemonic," using the force of numbers to offset material power advantages and resist great-power projects.[74] Others seek to "enmesh" great powers in regional institutions through more cooperative engagement.[75] Perhaps the greatest successes of symmetrical regional organizations are in helping small states develop complementary advantages and strategies. Some coordinate diplomatic capacities and representation to overcome their members' material constraints. The regional Pacific Islands Forum and Caribbean Community serve as platforms for addressing climate change because they allow small states to pursue common interests. Small states–based organizations integrate small markets to gain efficiencies, innovate in shared government administration, and seek common positions in international negotiations.

The study of small states in regional organizations remains heavily focused on the institutions of the European Union. The European Union's dense institutional environment provides security for small states, as well as myriad economic advantages. These possibilities encouraged three small states, Belgium, the Netherlands, and Luxembourg, to participate in founding the first post–World War II European institutions.[76] As European institutions expanded and became increasingly supranational, they retained their attraction for many small states: "more secure access to markets, reliable sources of supply, participation in decision-making institutions, a more effective role in the management of external affairs, and enhancement of opportunities to deal with fundamental social, economic, environmental and security challenges."[77] Given the importance

---

[71] Thorhallsson, "European Integration: Genuine or False Shelter."
[72] Hurrell, "One World? Many Worlds?"
[73] Long, "Historical Antecedents and Post-World War II Regionalism in the Americas."
[74] Saltalamacchia Ziccardi, "Regional Multilateralism in Latin America."
[75] Goh, "Great Powers and Hierarchical Order in Southeast Asia."
[76] Thorhallsson, "Small States in the UNSC and the EU," 38; Hey, "Luxembourg: Where Small Works (and Wealthy Doesn't Hurt)."
[77] Pace, "Malta and EU Membership," 33.

of the European market, most small states have decided that a seat at the table and access to greater information are worth the tradeoffs.

Most EU members are small by population, but power asymmetries remain a defining feature of the organization. These manifest in different respects, including a formal "qualified majority voting" structure that gives greater weight to large states—though small states are overrepresented on a per capita basis— and informal mechanisms that favor France, Germany, and other bigger states. Though military coercion is off the table in the European Union, economic clout still shapes bargaining. In addition, small states face a major challenge in keeping up with the expanding EU agenda, with ever-more committees and bureaucratic specialization. Most small European states lack the administrative capacity to prepare for, or even attend, all relevant meetings. This makes prioritization of key issues a must for small states, allowing them to deploy persuasive, technical arguments that shape the EU policies that matter most to them.[78] "To overcome their structural weaknesses, small states need to acknowledge their limitations, have the political will to try to exert influence, set priorities, develop diplomatic skills and knowledge, develop a positive image, build coalitions, take initiative and exploit the special characteristics of their small public administrations."[79]

Small states also gain diplomatic benefits from EU membership. While member states, especially large ones, have resisted giving up control in foreign policy, the European Union has expanded its capacities through diplomacy and aid. The growth of the European Union's diplomatic presence abroad provides small states a channel in foreign capitals where they cannot afford to maintain their own embassies.[80] The European Union has also emerged as an important actor in foreign aid, humanitarian relief, and peacekeeping operations. By participating in these ventures, active small states can shape the exercise of much greater resources than they could individually deploy.[81] It is true that big states will usually exercise more influence, but in the case of the European Union, the package of advantages has shaped an environment that provides greater security and opportunities for influence than small states enjoy elsewhere.

The European Union is unusual in many respects, but Europe is not the only region where small states turn to regional organizations. While some scholars perceive a U.S.-led model of regionalism, emphasizing economic integration with minimal supranational structures, the Americas include a variety of regional organizations. In South America, Mercosur emerged to manage relations between a democratizing Argentina and Brazil. Small states Paraguay and Uruguay were founding members, but they are often treated as afterthoughts.

---

[78] Panke, "Small States in EU Negotiations"; Panke, "Small States in EU Decision-Making."
[79] Thorhallsson, "Small States in the UNSC and the EU," 35.
[80] Bátora, "Small If Needed, Big If Necessary," 73.
[81] Jakobsen, "Small States, Big Influence."

However, Uruguay has found regional economic institutions to be valuable—even though much of its trade goes outside the region—because of regional dispute settlement mechanisms that help offset Argentine and Brazilian material advantages and diplomatic muscle.[82]

Small Caribbean states participate in both asymmetrical and symmetrical regional organizations to improve their international projection, manage relations with the United States, and enhance their national capabilities. Such goals led to the 1973 creation of the Caribbean Community (CARICOM), which was deepened in 2006 with the agreement of a single market to "attempt to move away from a reliance on preferential trading arrangements with the United States, Canada and Europe."[83] Though leading scholars like Jacqueline Braveboy-Wagner criticize Caribbean states for "highly nationalistic and idiosyncratic" foreign policies and inconsistent commitments to regionalism, Caribbean organizations have scored important successes nonetheless.[84]

One recent example comes from the negotiation for the UN Arms Trade Treaty (ATT). Rising rates of gun violence, often connected to illicit trafficking and loose rules on gun sales in the United States, plague much of the region. As a response, CARICOM states have sought to curtail small arms trade and trafficking. Drawing on support from likeminded states and NGOs, Caribbean governments coordinated positions, strategies, and even delegation selection through prior consultations and preparatory workshops. "By speaking with one voice and acting in concert at the Conference, CARICOM Member States enhanced their bargaining capacity and strengthened their competitive advantage and negotiating leverage."[85] Doing so partially offset budgetary restrictions and the states' small delegations. Caribbean states made common cause with Europe, lending weight due to their numbers and the negative social effects they suffer from arms trafficking. Though somewhat frustrated by the United States' domestic political resistance—a powerful U.S. lobby, the National Rifle Association, is a major treaty opponent—Caribbean states managed to insert their preferred language into important sections of the treaty. In the absence of full consensus, the UN General Assembly passed the ATT in 2013 with 156 votes in favor and 3 opposed.

In Southeast Asia, small and medium states have tried to navigate the rise of a regionally assertive China through the Association of Southeast Asian Nations (ASEAN) and associated groupings. Initially formed as an anti-communist

[82] Gómez-Mera and Molinari, "Overlapping Institutions, Learning, and Dispute Initiation in Regional Trade Agreements," 272; González and Romero, "El MERCOSUR y la Inserción Externa de Uruguay y Paraguay, 1994–2015."

[83] Braveboy-Wagner, "The Diplomacy of Caribbean Community States," 100.

[84] Braveboy-Wagner, Small States in Global Affairs, 203.

[85] Joseph, "Reflections from the Arms Trade Treaty," 100.

alliance in 1967, ASEAN expanded its membership and mandate after the Cold War, seeking to position itself and its members at the center of regional dynamics. The goal was, to an extent, to manage great-power rivalries and retain an agenda-setting role through "distinctive opportunities for agency to shape the larger strategic environment in which large powers operate."[86] After receiving extensive praise for its development of regional collective identity and practices of fluid dialogue,[87] assessments of ASEAN have grown increasingly critical, with opinions varying so much that a prominent scholar recently referred to "the great ASEAN Rorschach test."[88] Chinese pressure has exposed divisions within the grouping; meanwhile, its emphasis on nonintervention and public avoidance of conflict have left both security and environmental challenges unsolved.[89] Facing Chinese claims in its immediate neighborhood, two critics declaim that ASEAN "demonstrated impotence rather than collective strength."[90]

However, to judge ASEAN's effectiveness as a cohesive proponent of collective action or a common front vis-à-vis great powers is different than asking whether small states have found ASEAN useful. Small states have used ASEAN to gain a more influential voice with China, the United States, Japan, and other powers, even when they have not been able to fully restrain them or agree on uniform preferences. ASEAN's small states have created institutions to make their environment more stable and predictable, albeit imperfectly, facilitating economic growth while still prioritizing state autonomy.[91] A retrospective on the membership of Brunei, one of ASEAN's smallest members, is instructive. The small sultanate joined immediately upon its independence, looking to gain diplomatic experience and international insertion. Brunei valued ASEAN's low-key, largely nonbinding approach for its ability to open doors to "wider margin of involvement" through economic and regional forums with big powers.[92] ASEAN matters for its members beyond the thorny—though crucially important—issue of U.S.-China relations. It provides a platform for engaging with nonmembers like New Zealand on security and shared priorities in maritime, fisheries, and disaster response issues.[93] ASEAN puts small members on the map; for others, like Singapore, it allows a degree of regional agenda setting that amplifies their voices.[94]

---

[86] Ba, "Multilateralism and East Asian Transitions," 262; Goh, "Great Powers and Hierarchical Order in Southeast Asia."

[87] Acharya, *Constructing a Security Community in Southeast Asia*.

[88] Beeson, "The Great ASEAN Rorschach Test."

[89] Jones and Jenne, "Weak States' Regionalism"; Beeson, "The Great ASEAN Rorschach Test."

[90] Jones and Jenne, "Weak States' Regionalism," 229.

[91] Tang, *Small States and Hegemonic Competition in Southeast Asia*, 5, 27.

[92] Thambipillai, "Brunei Darussalam and ASEAN," 91.

[93] Rolls, "Like-Minded States."

[94] Chong, "Small State Soft Power Strategies," 400–402.

Regional organizations have also proliferated in Africa, usually with strong small-state support. The continental AU recognizes eight subregional groupings. Many of these are nominally economic but also shape peace and security. Whereas the fifty-four-member AU can overwhelm the voices of smaller members or stagnate amid disagreements, subregional organizations are characterized by more frequent and fluid high-level diplomacy.[95] The Economic Community of West African States (ECOWAS) has been particularly important. Though described mostly as a Nigeria-led bloc, smaller ECOWAS members often prefer working through the organization instead of at the AU or global level.[96] ECOWAS helped stabilize national unity governments in the region amid domestic turmoil, playing a significant role in Togo from 2006 to 2010.[97] In East Africa, Djibouti has worked to internationalize its security engagement through regional organizations (see Chapter 5).[98] Regional organizations serve as interlocutors for African small states' engagements with powerful international financial institutions, external powers, and donor states.

Regional organizations are not always friendly to small states' interests, of course, and they may serve to isolate small states.[99] In June 2017, a major crisis split the Gulf Cooperation Council (GCC), a six-member organization in the Persian Gulf. After years of building tensions, several states led by Saudi Arabia launched a diplomatic and economic blockade against fellow member Qatar. For years, Qatar had deployed wealth, international investments, transit hubs, and its Al Jazeera television network to enhance its international status.[100] Qatar's prominent and independent (of the Saudis) international stature provoked retaliation, especially its open relations with Iran and the Muslim Brotherhood.[101] The Saudis viewed both entities as threatening; perceiving Qatari deference to be insufficient, Saudi Arabia launched a "media offensive," followed by a diplomatic campaign and an attempt to cut off air and sea transit links to isolate Qatar. The blockade was meant to demonstrate that "in spite of its wealth and concomitant political weight, [Qatar] remains a geographically small entity depending on its neighbours to thrive."[102] Qatar managed to offset the worst effects of the blockade through extra-GCC links, as well as greater toleration from members

---

[95] Warner, "Beyond the Collective," 66–71.

[96] Momodu, "Nationalism Underpinned by Pan-Regionalism," 109.

[97] Noyes, "The Role of African Regional Organizations in Post-Election Governments of National Unity," 87.

[98] Le Gouriellec, "Djibouti's Foreign Policy in International Institutions," 391.

[99] One salient example is the isolation of Cuba from many asymmetrical regional organizations in the Americas.

[100] Kamrava, *Qatar: Small State, Big Politics*; Mohammadzadeh, "Status and Foreign Policy Change in Small States."

[101] Milton-Edwards, "The Blockade on Qatar"; Bianco and Stansfield, "The Intra-GCC Crises."

[102] Bianco and Stansfield, "The Intra-GCC Crises," 315.

Kuwait and Oman. However, mediation through the GCC failed to spur more than perfunctory dialogues about the stalemate.

Regional organizations can provide venues and instruments for directly engaging with larger powers or to gain greater stature collectively, though they provide no guarantee of small-state influence. However, when small states identify and prioritize certain objectives, regional bodies can provide a boost through the facilitation of voice opportunities, provision of information, construction of coalitions, and the amplification of favored agenda items.

Case 4: Global public health

Over the course of February and March 2020, the rapid global spread and devastating effects of the novel coronavirus became clear. On one level, it seemed the size of nations was irrelevant—or perhaps that smallness was even beneficial—as large countries like Brazil, China, Russia, the United Kingdom, and the United States experienced some of the gravest outbreaks that year. But large countries also leveraged their size. The United States, in particular, was accused of bullying suppliers and hoarding vital medical supplies during the pandemic's first months.[103] The Trump administration's turn against the World Health Organization (WHO) threatened international expertise and cooperation just as many small states badly needed them.[104] After its own industrial reopening, China launched vigorous "mask diplomacy," closely related to the One China Policy, in which it gifted medical supplies to garner favor with small states.[105] But China also used its clout to push aside calls for transparency about the emergence and early handling of the pandemic.[106] While a virus might not care about size, material power, or borders, the international response to the virus has been profoundly shaped by those very factors. Is global public health—despite frequent rhetoric of humanitarianism and cooperation—just one more venue of power politics where small states are bound to suffer?[107]

In normal times, it does not seem so. Small states' resilience and adaptability are evident in approaches to public health. The populations of the world's very small states are generally healthy compared to global averages, with longer life

---

[103] Nahal Toosi, "US Cast as Culprit in Global Scrum over Coronavirus Supplies," April 4, 2020, Politico, https://www.politico.eu/article/coronavirus-united-states-cast-as-culprit-in-global-scrum-over-supplies/.

[104] Reich and Dombrowski, "The Consequence of COVID-19."

[105] Telias and Urdinez, "China's Foreign Aid Determinants."

[106] "China Rejects WHO Plan for Second Phase of Virus Origin Probe," July 23, 2021, BBC News, https://www.bbc.co.uk/news/world-asia-china-57926368.

[107] Pedi and Wivel, "Small State Diplomacy after the Corona Crisis."

expectancy and better performance on many indicators.[108] However, small states do face recurring public health challenges, especially states with the smallest populations and island states. Small population makes it difficult to support a full range of medical specialties or to develop adequate expertise in the diagnosis and treatment of rare diseases. This lower degree of specialization can affect every level of health services of very small states. As one study notes:

> Some Directors of Health in small Pacific states may spend mornings or after-noons in the operating theatre or general medical clinic, and may be on call at night and weekends for emergency cases, while also attending to the admin-istration of the health service, compiling epidemiological and health service statistics, and interacting with international and aid agencies.[109]

In addition to limitations on specialization and administrative capacity, small markets create asymmetries when negotiating the purchase of medicines and health supplies. This translates into higher prices. As seen in response to COVID-19, asymmetry can make small states a low priority in overwhelmed supply chains. Challenges also arise at the level of management and training, with limited abilities to maintain research or epidemiological bureaucracies. The smallest states struggle to maintain nursing schools; wealthier and more populous small states may have medical schools but cannot support specialized training. Retaining skilled workers is an additional hurdle, given robust global demand for workers in the highly skilled health sector.[110] As one health expert notes, "Small health services are not just scaled-down versions of large health services; they are qualitatively different."[111]

The contrast between these challenges and small states' above-average health outcomes suggests that many small states have managed to overcome the limita-tions of size. While many small-state health adaptations are rooted in domestic social policies, from an International Relations perspective, what is interesting is how these limitations have encouraged small states to develop international strategies to improve health systems and outcomes. Many small states' interna-tional adaptations in the health sector recognize and respond to international asymmetries by turning to bilateral relationships and emphasizing multilateral

---

[108] Studies show this using the Commonwealth and World Bank population limit of 1.5 million. Azzopardi-Muscat and Camilleri, "Challenges and Opportunities for the Health Sector in Small States," 447–48.

[109] Taylor, "The Tyranny of Size," 70.

[110] These challenges are repeatedly noted by public heath scholars and national and international administrators. For example, Briguglio and Azzopardi Muscat, "The Vulnerability and Resilience Framework Applied to the Public Health System"; World Health Organization, "Building Resilience"; Taylor, "The Tyranny of Size"; Cameron, Nuzzo, and Bell, "Global Health Security Index," 49.

[111] Taylor, "The Tyranny of Size," 65.

international organizations. Small states often augment the capabilities of their health systems through bilateral agreements with large states—usually neighbors or former colonial metropoles. "Small countries tend to rely on larger countries for training and recruiting professionals from a wide range of disciplines and for the provision and procurement of certain services and products," a recent WHO report noted.[112] Malta developed its domestic health capabilities over decades through arrangements with the United Kingdom; these have included sending students abroad, bringing visiting specialists to Malta for procedures and to impart training, and creating compatible accreditation. More recently, Malta has supplemented UK links with deeper EU engagement.[113] While training students abroad is common, the high-technology and specialization-rich medical environments of large countries may create mismatches in skills and practices when graduates return to small states, where flexibility and generalization are in more immediate need.

Many Pacific and Indian Ocean island states face intense challenges in maintaining health systems beyond the level of nursing and primary care, especially across archipelagos. Several small states have fashioned bilateral agreements for publicly supported travel to larger states for certain health services. In other situations, they bring in visiting doctors. Such arrangements provide access to specialized care that would otherwise be unavailable. Careful management is required, public health experts stress, to control costs and ensure that these arrangements enhance domestic capacities where feasible instead of diverting resources from providing services at home.[114]

Global and regional international organizations play an important role in small states' health strategies. Globally, the WHO provides expertise and capabilities that supplement those of small states with limited domestic research, epidemiological, and health information capabilities. In the context of the global sustainable development goals, the WHO has increased its attention to small states through the creation of the Small Countries Initiative, organized from the European Office. In doing so, it follows the model of organizations like the Commonwealth and international financial institutions like the World Bank. The WHO initiative creates a forum for European small states, at times joined by non-European states, to share experiences and build capacity.[115] The creation of the initiative reflects the relatively strong voice of small states within the WHO, a result of favorable voting structures, the predominance of regional offices where

---

[112] World Health Organization, "Building Resilience," 42.
[113] World Health Organization, "Building Resilience," 40–53.
[114] Suzana et al., "Achieving Universal Health Coverage in Small Island States"; Taylor, "The Tyranny of Size," 71.
[115] Zambon and Nemer, "The WHO Regional Office for Europe Small Countries Initiative."

small states have greater voice, and the advocacy of policy entrepreneurs in small states.[116]

Regional multilateral cooperation is most deeply institutionalized through the European Union, which provides a form of "shelter" to small states' health sectors through access to medical goods and services.[117] European accession spurred health sector reforms in new members, often trumping entrenched veto players in the medical sector.[118] Regional health bodies are sometimes more attuned to small states' specific needs. Beyond Europe, Caribbean states activated regional mechanisms—designed and developed largely in response to extreme weather events—to take preparations for the global COVID-19 pandemic in early 2020. Regional bodies like the CARICOM and the Pan American Health Organization facilitated a regional response that included earlier restrictions on travel, better-enforced stay-at-home orders, and regional information sharing.[119] The Caribbean states benefitted from previous efforts to institutionalize a regional health infrastructure through the Caribbean Regional Public Health Agency (CARPHA). During the onset of the pandemic, CARPHA helped coordinate the sharing of laboratory facilities and assisted with training and information sharing. The region's small states also drew on a joint development bank and extensive connections with other international organizations.[120] These were helpful in the crucial early days of the pandemic, though eventually, viral waves crashed on nearly all shores.

While smallness shapes small states' public health needs, the dynamics of asymmetry also create opportunities. As a New Zealand–based author noted, the realities of transborder disease transmission mean that larger states in the Pacific have an "enlightened self-interest" in improving health preparations and resilience in their small neighbors.[121] This realization, combined with humanitarian impulses and strategic concerns, means that there is often international aid available to small states' health sectors. Health is also an issue area in which tremendous nongovernmental and foundational resources are available. These are not unalloyed benefits—reporting and grant application requirements of international organizations and NGOs can be overwhelming for small states' health care bureaucracies[122]—but the careful deployment of narratives of vulnerability

[116] Corbett, Yi-Chong, and Weller, "Small States and the 'Throughput' Legitimacy of International Organisations," 193–95; Hanrieder, *International Organization in Time.*
[117] Thorhallsson, "European Integration: Genuine or False Shelter."
[118] Azzopardi-Muscat et al., "Policy Challenges and Reforms in Small EU Member State Health Systems."
[119] Hambleton, Jeyaseelan, and Murphy, "COVID-19 in the Caribbean Small Island Developing States."
[120] Parthenay, "Uniting (Regionally) against Covid-19: Sica and Caricom," 411–15.
[121] Boyd et al., "The 2019 GHSI and Its Implications for New Zealand and Pacific Regional Health Security," 89. See also Ratuva, "New Zealand Development Assistance in the Pacific."
[122] Azzopardi-Muscat et al., "Health Information Systems in Small Countries of the WHO European Region."

and resilience can spur attention and attract resources.[123] The range of outcomes in response to HIV/AIDS is suggestive; whereas Botswana managed incoming flows to reduce a severe crisis and (eventually) strengthen its own health system, other small states saw their primary health systems strained and disrupted by inflows of resources and domineering international aid responses.[124]

As the first months of the COVID-19 pandemic demonstrated, there are severe limitations to these strategies in times of global crisis.[125] Before the pandemic, one report presciently noted: "in a pandemic, demand for resources likely would exceed available surge capacity, making it even more difficult for small nations to procure needed drugs, vaccines, therapeutics, or other resources."[126] This did happen at times, as large and powerful states scrambled for medical equipment. It was even more pronounced regarding vaccines. Many non-European small states (and nearly all of Sub-Saharan Africa) struggled for doses during 2021, as these were monopolized by the European Union and a few large states. Even as vaccine surpluses emerged in parts of the Global North, the virus raged in the Global South. Few small states can launch their own vaccine research and production initiatives, so self-sufficiency was not an option. International partnerships provided greater access for several small states. Having purchased aggressively, Israel managed perhaps the world's most effective early vaccination campaign. Bhutan benefited from its special ties to India to obtain doses and then vaccinated most of its population in two weeks. Chile drew on its domestic research capacity and active diplomacy to access vaccines faster than larger neighbors; it then distributed them rapidly. By mid-2021, many world leaders in vaccination per capita were small states, including Malta, Iceland, Seychelles, and the United Arab Emirates—but these were still the privileged few.[127]

In comparative terms, small states fared relatively well during the eighteen months of the pandemic, though the effects were severe almost everywhere.[128] By September 2020, it appeared that there was no correlation between a country's population and its rate of COVID-19 infections or mortality. Testing rates appeared to be higher in small states. In some states, smallness seemed to

[123] For related arguments, see Corbett, Xu, and Weller, "Norm Entrepreneurship and Diffusion 'from below' in International Organisations."
[124] Renwick, "Global Society's Response to HIV/AIDS"; Biesma et al., "The Effects of Global Health Initiatives on Country Health Systems."
[125] See, especially, the special sections of *Small States and Territories* and *The Round Table*, respectively. Högenauer, Sarapuu, and Trimikliniotis, "Small States and the 'Corona Crisis'"; McDougall and Ong, "Introduction: COVID-19 and Commonwealth Countries."
[126] Cameron, Nuzzo, and Bell, "Global Health Security Index," 49.
[127] Dorji and Tamang, "Bhutan's Experience with COVID-19 Vaccination in 2021"; Kirby, "How Chile Built One of the World's Most Successful Vaccination Campaigns"; Balicer and Ohana, "Israel's COVID-19 Endgame." Comparative vaccination data from Our World in Data, https://ourworldind ata.org/covid-vaccinations.
[128] Pedi and Wivel, "Small State Diplomacy after the Corona Crisis."

promote greater social adherence to restrictions, attentive disease surveillance, and faster, flexible responses to changing conditions and scientific evidence.[129] Difficulties of specialization remained highly relevant, though. In a WHO briefing, experts noted that small states often had few hospitals and could not designate COVID-only response areas or teams.[130]

The demands and challenges of restarting small, internationally dependent economies shaped the course of the pandemic and inflicted social suffering. Small states that have thrived through openness and global connections face a deep threat to their economic models. Nowhere is that more evident than in many small states' tourism-centric economies.[131] Commonwealth secretary general Patricia Scotland noted that the economic effects on tourism and remittances had weakened Caribbean island economies just as hurricane season was starting. "The reality is that COVID-19 profoundly compounds the ongoing risks they already face on a daily basis."[132] These challenges have led the Commonwealth, along with many individual states, to initiate calls for post-COVID debt relief focused on SIDS.

The pandemic threw into relief the benefits and challenges of small states' international engagement in public health. On the one hand, multilateral and bilateral international relationships are invaluable for small states, helping them ameliorate the limitations imposed by small populations and markets. The international sphere can provide financial and scientific resources that would be out of reach, and international cooperation can help those benefits reach broader portions of the population. On the other hand, while there are risks of these connections—the emigration of skilled workers, the transmission of communicable diseases—eliminating those risks is not feasible for most small states. Robust international engagement, then, drawing first on regional and global multilateral frameworks, and supplemented with bilateral agreements and assistance, remains the better bet for small states in a post-COVID world.

Conclusions

For small states, building a more robust structure of international institutions, law, and norms is sometimes seen as an end in itself. These facets of international society provide a more stable environment in which the threat of force recedes. Institutions, law, and norms are also crucial tools that small states use to pursue

[129] Högenauer, Sarapuu, and Trimikliniotis, "Small States and the 'Corona Crisis.'"
[130] Briguglio and Azzopardi-Muscat, "Small States and COVID-19."
[131] Sheller, "Reconstructing Tourism in the Caribbean"; Connell and Taulealo, "Island Tourism and COVID-19 in Vanuatu and Samoa."
[132] Scotland, "COVID-19 Debt Relief Must Consider the Vulnerabilities of Small States."

specific goals. Drawing on a wide range of examples, this chapter has examined several issue areas in which these are particularly important. For many small island and coastal states today, curtailing the devastating effects of climate change is an overriding diplomatic priority. In cooperation with other small states, the Marshall Islands and fellow SIDS recast climate norms and institutions through agenda setting and moral claims for action. Small states have drawn on their identities and historical experiences to emerge as advocates for the internationalization of human rights, enhancing their status in the process. Regional organizations, often seen as the domains of large powers, are also valued forums for small states to coordinate and manage asymmetrical relationships. Finally, recourse to institutions and appeals to humanitarian norms have allowed small states to achieve robust health outcomes for their citizens—or manage the threat of a global pandemic. Though these issues are sometimes relegated to international politics' third division—below security and economy—this chapter suggests two things. First, for small states, such issues are central and may assume greater immediacy than "traditional" concerns. In this sense, small states are at the leading edge of trends of global politics, where formerly overlooked "soft" issues like the environment now fill the crucible of global affairs. Second, small states use institutions, law, and norms to shape core security and economic issues while avoiding confrontation and playing to their strengths.

8

Conclusion

Small states do not automatically march to tunes called by great powers. However, International Relations' (IR) explanations of the relationships between large and small states often have that implicit assumption. Small allies are treated as clients,[1] bandwagoners,[2] or subordinates.[3] When small states strike visibly independent foreign policies, often they are derided as merely symbolic. Other times, small states are lauded for demonstrating a degree of domestic or international autonomy, whether or not this achieves policy successes.[4] Pessimistic perspectives on small states are countered by agency-focused accounts, until recently concentrated on Europe. These studies are cognizant of external constraints but often emphasize the more favorable international environment and demonstrate the individuality, adaptability, resilience, and creativity of small states.[5]

This book has offered a different conceptualization, perspective, and explanation of small states in global politics. It has located small states in their relationships with great powers and explored the constraints and opportunities those relationships create. Though their agency is often overlooked in discussions of great powers, small states are crucial partners in those relationships; their actions can determine the nature of the relationship as much as those of the great power. Great powers' positions in the world are constituted in large measure by their relationships with small states, and they devote much of their attention to them. Therefore, a serious analysis of small states is fundamental to understanding how all states, large and small, partake in and shape international politics. As we discuss later, this affects fundamental aspects of IR theory, such as

---

[1] Shoemaker and Spanier, *Patron-Client State Relationships*; more recently, with attention to small-state agency, Wong, "Managing Small Allies Amidst Patron–Adversary Rapprochement."

[2] Schweller, "Bandwagoning for Profit"; Little, *The Balance of Power in International Relations.*

[3] Lake, *Hierarchy in International Relations.*

[4] Russell and Tokatlian, "From Antagonistic Autonomy to Relational Autonomy"; for a discussion of domestic-international autonomy tradeoffs, see Tetreault, "Autonomy, Necessity, and the Small State." Others see tradeoffs between autonomy and influence, notably within the European Union. See Wivel, "The Security Challenge of Small EU Member States"; Haugevik and Rieker, "Autonomy or Integration?" In Asia, see Tang, *Small States and Hegemonic Competition in Southeast Asia.*

[5] Ingebritsen, "Norm Entrepreneurs"; Panke, "Small States in EU Negotiations"; Archer, Bailes, and Wivel, *Small States and International Security*; Wivel and Crandall, "Punching Above Their Weight, but Why?"

A Small State's Guide to Influence in World Politics. Tom Long, Oxford University Press. © Oxford University Press 2022. DOI: 10.1093/oso/9780190926205.003.0008

whether we understand international politics as fundamentally anarchical, hierarchical, or heterodox.

This concluding chapter sums up the insights, benefits, and limitations of our relational and asymmetrical approach to small states. It also allows for additional comparative analysis across the book's relational case studies and issue-area surveys. First, we will expand comparison within the framework of our typological theory. This book's cases included a wide variety of issues, regions, small states, and great powers. In the following section, we draw out lessons from a comparison of those cases by type, with reference to our typology and associated strategies. By doing so, we address how the different combinations of relational conditions—captured in our approach as distinct "types"—shape small states' strategies and outcomes. We then consider how strategies and outcomes vary by issue area, including both our economic and security cases and the surveys of climate change, human rights, regional organizations, and public health included in Chapter 7. Finally, we will underscore the implications of our work for policymakers and its contributions for broader understandings of asymmetry and small states in IR theory.

Comparing types and cases

Our approach suggests that relational conditions with salient great powers have primary, near-term importance in shaping small states' international engagement. When small states seek changes to the policies of great powers, their foreign policy possibilities are conditioned by the degree of policy divergence, the level of issue salience, and preference cohesion within the great power. Those conditions interact to present more or less auspicious situations for small states (see Appendix, Table A1 for a summary of the typology, strategies, and cases). Our case studies were not selected randomly, nor are they a representative sample of the broader universe of cases, so we cannot make claims about how all possible cases would be distributed across the types we highlight; instead, we examine the processes that characterize each type of case.

As expected, many of the cases where small states failed to achieve their goals match the conditions of "red" cases (Type 1): high policy divergence, issue salience, and preference cohesion in the great power. Small states were unable to prompt near-term change in great powers' policies when they faced those circumstances. In the economic sphere, negotiations were often deadlocked; in moments of crisis this created intense pressure on the small states to accept their partners' terms. The dramatic retreat in the Greek negotiating position in 2015 is a clear example: an anti-austerity government accepted bailout conditions it had publicly rejected days earlier. In the security sphere, this combination of conditions has entrenched divergence between Bhutan and China over their disputed border; Indian pressure further limits Bhutan's room for concessions by reinforcing policy divergence and blocking issue linkages. Small states may curtail their interests or persevere against great-power resistance, but attempts to overturn the situation in the immediate term are risky. In 1989, Nepal sought to break its deadlock over its unequal security relations with India by making arms purchases from China. But facing "red" relational conditions with India, the attempt drew a sharp rebuke and punishing countermeasures. Even when these situations do not threaten a small state's physical survival, they can have deleterious effects for ruling governments and regimes, as the Nepalese monarchy discovered. Such a deadlock between the Moldovan government and Russia over the small country's security alignment in the early 1990s and again in 2004–2005 exacerbated Moldovan insecurity and sustained a breakaway de facto state within its borders.

Each of these cases has dramatic differences in geography, the nature of the issue, and the great power involved. However, the typology of relational conditions underscores important similarities in the situations faced by the small state. It is these inauspicious conditions that limit small states' possibilities for success in "red" cases and often mean that the small states may have to persevere against an unfavorable environment. These sorts of cases have captured a great deal of the attention in IR studies of small states' relationships with great powers. They are marked by divergence and conflict; material asymmetries are evident and linked to the possibility or exercise of coercion.

It may seem like this is case closed for small states. If a great power cares, it will enforce its will over the small state's resistance. In the extreme, that may be true (though a great power's ability to achieve the changes it seeks can be more limited). However, a nuanced approach to asymmetry, going beyond simple divergence in material capabilities, suggests that great powers usually will not exercise this type of determined, coherent opposition for two broad reasons. First, divergence is not the rule. Though conflict receives most of the attention in IR, small states' interests may be compatible with those of a great power. This can occur due to a genuine, exogenous coincidence of interests, or it may happen because asymmetry gradually redirects a small state's interests.[6] An economically powerful neighbor can exercise coercion, but its market may present opportunities that small states pursue voluntarily. Second, great powers cannot care about all small states and all issues or maintain cohesive preferences all the time. Asymmetries of capabilities tend to produce inverse asymmetries of attention.

---

[6] Abdelal and Kirshner, "Strategy, Economic Relations, and the Definition of National Interests"; Kat, "Subordinate-State Agency and US Hegemony."

The small state focuses intensively on the great power, while the great power divides its attention among many states and issues.[7]

On the other end of the spectrum, in a sense, are "green" cases (Type 4), which are characterized by low divergence but high salience and preference cohesion. The low divergence means the cases often relate to "problem-solving" negotiations, where the large and small state have compatible preferences.[8] That overlap means that significant policy change is not necessary, though adjustments or new approaches might be valued by the small state. An emblematic case is Portugal's negotiations with the European Union and international lenders during the eurozone crisis, in which the government's goals for domestic reforms often aligned with the types of policies sought by the creditors. Here, there was something of an exogenous or long-term coincidence of reform interests and a shared acceptance of economic policy paradigms. Somewhat differently, when Rwanda became a major issue for donors in 1994, it succeeded in shifting the terms of aid relationships and asserting the new government's centrality to the management of that aid. In both cases, the small state used alignment and attention strategically to maximize support while retaining considerable policy autonomy. Key to achieving this is a small state's ability to persuasively present policy adjustments as providing mutual benefits. Rwanda provides donors with a postconflict development success story, so long as they excuse troubling aspects of the government's anti-democratic behavior. Portugal showed that Troika reforms could be embraced by a broad political coalition and offer greater stability than in Greece.

Some of the cases that best highlight small states' creative agency relate to strategies of agenda setting and the promotion of alternative policy options or interpretations. In different ways, "orange," "yellow," "blue," and "violet" cases (Types 2, 3, 5, and 6, respectively) describe situations where such ideational and diplomatic space exists for small states to achieve meaningful influence, but in which success is less certain. In "orange" cases, a great power's status quo policies are challenged by changing circumstances—a flashing warning of risks and rewards for the small state. Shocks within or exogenous to the relationship create opportunities for small states to shape emerging policy understandings and options. In Bolivia, social turmoil followed by the landmark election of Evo Morales as first indigenous president challenged Brazil's status quo support for its state oil company's anti-reform position. Changing circumstances caused a rift in preference cohesion. Bolivia drew on strong domestic backing to exploit that rift; it offered some deference to Brazil's regional leadership ambitions

---

[7] Womack, *Asymmetry and International Relationships.*

[8] Elgström and Jönsson, "Negotiation in the European Union"; Hopmann, "Two Paradigms of Negotiation."

while taking bold steps to renegotiate the terms of foreign participation in its oil and gas sector. The result increased state revenues dramatically. In a very different context, newly independent Estonia responded to intense Russian pressure by making itself an attractive North Atlantic Treaty Organization (NATO) partner. In a moment of great geopolitical change, the small state played a part in reshaping U.S. and NATO status quo policy on Baltic expansion and achieved its major security goals—the withdrawal of Russian forces and an alignment with the West. However, "orange" cases are certainly not uniform successes. Despite major preference fragmentation among its donors, Zambia failed to enunciate and defend its own position on donor relations and national development. Longstanding colonial asymmetries and recurring economic crises curtailed the country's ability to reset the terms of its aid policy relationships.

"Yellow," "blue," and "violet" cases (Types 3, 5, and 6, respectively) present different opportunities for creative agency. If the opportunity in "orange" cases emerges from changing circumstances, in "blue" cases (Type 5), it emerges from divergent understandings. The change in the nature of the Rwanda case over a longer period is instructive. The small country's salience for great powers' policymakers declined after the Rwandan conflict and genocide gave way to relative stability in the late 1990s. When the country's salience for U.S. and UK policymakers fell, the Rwandan government, under the Rwandan Patriotic Force (RPF), succeeded in enunciating certain representations of the conflict in which the RPF's own role for maintaining peace and stability took on great weight. Over two decades, the RPF proactively mitigated potential policy divergence with U.S. and UK policymakers, while remaining a development-agency priority and encouraging preference cohesion in those countries through "extraversion" strategies. In "violet" cases (Type 6), a small state must try to achieve greater relational salience to gain the high-level attention needed to change status quo policies. For Bhutan, for example, the nature of its historic treaty relationship with India meant that high-level attention was necessary to change that treaty. Given the more limited aspirations of the Bhutanese monarchy—it did not seek a total break from India and desired Indian support in many sectors—gaining high-level attention created fewer risks. In another instance, Djibouti's place in France's strategic priorities declined during the 1990s, and so the small state turned to new international partners to achieve its goal of security diversification. Gabon could not manage the same feat given the more cohesive nature of French preferences in maintaining security predominance there in the 2000s. Across these cases, the broad similarities in the relational context shaped the nature of small states' policy space, as well as the strategies they adopted. Those differences do not emerge from similarities in the characteristics of the small states themselves: Bhutan, Djibouti, and Rwanda are surely very different countries, but we can compare the cases due to similarities in the relational conditions.

Finally, we turn to "white" and "grey" cases (Types 7 and 8, respectively), in which status quo policies tend to remain dominant, though they may be subject to drift or haggling over benefits. Honduras's and El Salvador's negotiations of military bases possess significant similarities in the country-level characteristics and relational histories of the two countries. Lasting asymmetries have shaped the nature of each state and the definition of its interests. Like Bhutan, neither Central American state has sought a radical break with its place in the great power–led regional security hierarchy. Both El Salvador and Honduras have been supportive of status quo policies on U.S. basing arrangements; substantial deference to U.S. wishes on security issues has been the rule. Within that context, however, El Salvador's diplomatic recognition of China struck some in the United States as a challenge. Though neither country seeks to overturn the status quo on basing, El Salvador has managed to maintain (comparatively) greater autonomy and derive similar benefits compared to its next-door neighbor. Honduras has seen its policy space erode, and its professions of deference have grown more extreme. The subtle difference between growing fragmentation in U.S. preferences in the Salvadoran relationship versus the cohesive preferences regarding Honduras suggest why this has occurred, despite the notable similarities in background conditions. The divergent strategies and state projects of the two countries' foreign policies also shaped the outcomes.

Looking across the cases, our typology offers insights that comparisons on country-level characteristics like material capacities, ideological position, or regime type do not. First, some interactions of relational factors offer more propitious possibilities—and these allow for creative agency in situations of both coinciding and conflicting interests. Second, relational conditions matter for small states' foreign policy success and strategies in systematic ways that are amenable to analysis, comparison, and theory building. This is the theoretical payoff of the move to a relational approach. Bringing this theory to the forefront is important in the study of small states in IR, given that comparison, theory, and dialogue with broader currents of IR theory have often been cited as obstacles. Finally, the typology offers tools for policymakers to diagnose the conditions of their own states' relational situations. It is not a full-fledged recipe for achieving all goals, but a starting point and guide to reflect on different strategies as responses to policy challenges. We will return to those lessons later.

Comparing issue areas

Before we turn to some concluding lessons for theory and policy, this section will consider what can be learned from comparing the issue areas of security, political economy, and institutions, law, and norms. In IR more broadly, it is often assumed that security and economic issues have different characteristics. In this book, those cases (in Chapter 5 and 6) are both examined in a narrower bilateral sense. Are small states more disadvantaged in their relationships in the security sphere? As earlier, it should be noted that we make no claims to have a representative sample of cases, so our attention here will be on dynamics and processes that recur across cases—not general or probabilistic covering laws.

The conventional wisdom is that security issues are characterized by zero-sum logics or relative gains, while economic issues may emphasize positive-sum logics or absolute gains. If so, security issues should be subject to the sort of distributional bargaining that disadvantages small states. There are examples of such dynamics in our case studies: for example, Nepal's attempt to balance its security dependence on India with arms purchases from China was perceived in zero-sum terms by Indian policymakers. However, the conventional wisdom did not play out uniformly across our cases. In the core—and often contentious—issue of military basing, Djibouti advanced positive-sum solutions that helped it achieve greater security diversification. The move from zero-sum to positive-sum issue framings did not always produce positive results for small states, though. Brazil recast its security-related boundary dispute with Paraguay into the positive-sum economic issue of energy production. The resulting Itaipú hydroelectric project grew the pie, but Brazil ate the lion's share.

In short, security issues were sometimes successfully recast as positive sum, while economic issues could be understood as zero sum. Such lines are not clear-cut; instead, they are the product of divergent perceptions and attempts at (re)framing issues. As basing negotiations sometimes demonstrate, supposedly zero-sum security issues can generate direct and ancillary benefits for small states,[9] while supposedly positive-sum commercial arrangements can slide into mercantilist trade disputes. One recurring pattern across both chapters is that "red" cases (Type 1) often were understood by the involved actors as zero sum; that can complicate small states' efforts to achieve positive policy change. As a result of such a zero-sum framing, in the 2015 debt negotiations, the Greek government was perceived to have "lost," even though the same understanding did not apply to Portugal's 2011 austerity-inducing deal with the same economic powers.

There are some notable distinctions between the issues surveyed in Chapter 7 and the studies of security and economic cases in Chapters 5 and 6, especially differences in the extent to which the small state can choose the forum for policy action. Because the policy issues considered in Chapter 7 drew on a plethora of relationships instead of bilateral ties, they were more amenable to venue selection by the small state. Shaping the choice of venue allowed the small state greater latitude over narratives and forms of actions. For example, states that favored the

---

[9] Cooley and Nexon, "'The Empire Will Compensate You.'"

international promotion of human rights could develop unilateral programs to advance those aims and apply those in different relationships as they found most beneficial. They could emphasize different rights and preferred mechanisms for ensuring them. Small states also could turn to multilateral forums like the United Nations or promote their preferred norms at the regional level. Because the small states' goal was often to advance a certain identity and enhance their international status, multiple venues allowed them to reach diverse audiences and amplify their messages.

Not all issues allowed such broad choice of venue for the small state. When the ultimate objective requires a change of behavior from a specific larger partner, the impact of relational conditions is more immediately felt. The more narrowly bilateral a policy goal, the less venue choice a small state will possess. Appeals to third parties could still be instrumental, such as when small states turn to the World Trade Organization to resolve a dispute with a larger trading partner.[10] When Malaysia sought to improve the terms and reduce the debt burden of its Belt and Road Initiative projects with China, it could not choose a different venue—the road to policy change ran through Beijing. Having a range of investment partners may have provided leverage with China—conversely, the disappearance of such external options curtailed Myanmar's quest for diversification—but it could not shift the ultimate venue of decision.

At the other end of the spectrum, small states looking to improve their capacities in public health provision can appeal to a wide array of actors, including states, international organizations, nongovernmental organizations, and well-heeled foundations. Even in the most venue-restricted issue discussed in Chapter 7—climate change, where the UN Framework Convention on Climate Change (UNFCCC) is the dominant forum—small states can expand their policy space through creating alternative groupings like Alliance of Small Island States (AOSIS) or pursuing their goals in nontraditional sites like the International Maritime Organization. This important difference may arise from the nature of the issue; however, in many cases, the same issue may be addressed in narrow bilateral channels or diffusely. Often, then, the difference relates to the immediacy of small states' goals: shifting human rights norms and building regional international organizations are generally longer-term projects. They will have more immediate focal points, such as particular climate summits, for example, but the goal is to ensure a broader behavioral change. The more immediate and the more narrowly bilateral an issue, the less scope the small state has to select, shop for, or create its favored venue.

***

[10] For an example regarding Antigua and Barbuda against the United States, see Jackson, "Small States and Compliance Bargaining in the WTO."

Policy applications

For policymakers, the overarching implication of the book, and particularly the comparisons earlier, is that there is no single recipe for small states' foreign policy success. Instead, the key for policymakers is to diagnose the relational conditions they face, assess the possibilities for success, and then tailor their strategies to those conditions and their own bases of power. The corollary of this implication is that for the small state, a deep understanding of the politics of the relevant great power is essential. Without that, diagnosing the great power's status quo policy, one's own relational salience, and especially the degree and nature of preference cohesion will be difficult. It is understandable that small states, especially those afflicted by conflictual relations with a great power, may overestimate both their own salience and the cohesion of preferences within their larger counterpart. The underpinning theory of asymmetry, however, suggests that great powers' attention to small states is likely to experience cycles of fixation and inattention at high levels, helping shape opportunities for small states to change the status quo.

Of course, not all situations will favor the small state. In inauspicious circumstances, policymakers may do best to go beyond the bilateral relationship. As noted previously, "red" cases leave few immediate options within the asymmetrical relationship. Small states may turn to international institutions and norms, for example, to prepare the groundwork for later changes while managing domestic discontent.[11] As noted earlier, stepping outside the bilateral relationship allows the small state greater choice of venue. Even when near-term changes are unlikely, this can increase pressure on the great power and serve as testing ground for alternative policy proposals and framings.

In other situations, there is more ambiguity in both diagnosis and strategic choice. While an issue may be understood as a crisis for a small state, in seeking policy change, it is more important to assess whether the great power also perceives it as such. That will affect whether the small state should prioritize agenda setting to increase salience or focus on presenting favorable alternatives. Depending on the level of divergence between small states' preferences and the status quo, such agenda setting may be achieved through lobbying (in proximate relationships) or appeals to external institutions and states (in less proximate relationships). Appeals within the relationship are most effective when there is a general overlap in policy paradigms, though that may disguise substantial uncertainty over the type of policy required for "problem-solving." Here, the need for solutions can open opportunities to improve upon unsatisfactory status quo policies. When those status quo policies remain entrenched, perhaps due to

---

[11] As an example, the strategy of appealing to the UN Security Council helped Panama overcome entrenched opposition in the United States to renegotiating the canal treaties. Long, "Putting the Canal on the Map."

bureaucratic support, the task for the small state is more challenging because a higher level of policy attention will be required to change them.

Once small states' policymakers have assessed and "diagnosed" their relational situations, they must identify strategies that take advantage of their own strengths and respond to the context. Here, we recall the discussion about particular-intrinsic, derivative, and collective sources of power in Chapter 4. Barring situations of extreme state weakness, all states have some capacities to enunciate and advance their goals. In addition to responding to the relational context, a strategy must marry the small state's goals with its resources—that is, its material, ideational, and relational bases of power. Such bases are often applicable for different policy pursuits. Strategic location can lend itself to security diversification or to greater influence on matters of international commerce. International recognition can assist in the promotion of human rights or help achieve influence within international organizations. Centrality in relational networks may help a small state derive power to gain advantage in regional conflicts or allow it to act as a bridge for negotiations. Small states have these capacities in different levels and combinations, but to gain influence, they must identify and employ them creatively.

Findings and implications

An argument that runs through this book is that the study of small states and their relationships must be more thoroughly integrated into the larger corpus on IR theory. Here, we emphasize some lessons for the study of small states and for IR more broadly, before suggesting where research at this intersection might turn in the future.

Compared to a relational approach, structuralist IR theories have limited insights into the conditions of small states. They struggle to incorporate the diverse contexts, and, perhaps most importantly, their assumptions regarding the goals that small states pursue miss the mark. Our theoretical approach suggests, and our case studies confirm, that small states express and pursue a wide variety of foreign policy goals. Even when these goals are (relatively) autonomously determined, small states' interests will not always entail conflict with great powers. Cases of coinciding interests are also important objects of study. Exploring small states' goals should be an empirical starting point, displacing analysts' assumptions about what it is that small states seek. This starting point counters an ingrained assumption in IR that the lack of autonomy is such a recurring feature of small states that it essentially defines them.[12] Just as realist IR theory long assumed power to be the overriding goal of great powers, scholars have assumed autonomy to be the overriding goal of small states. Too often,

---

[12] Goetschel, "The Foreign and Security Policy Interests of Small States in Today's Europe," 19.

autonomy was conflated with taking actions that visibly diverged from great powers' preferences. Instead of implicitly favoring conflict-producing forms of autonomy, framing the study of small states' foreign policy in terms of the ability to achieve the goals enunciated by small states' leaders themselves allows us to consider how small states might better achieve their goals through orientations that range from confrontation to cooperation.[13]

This book's emphasis on asymmetrical relationships suggests new approaches to the conceptualization of small states and the challenges they face. Most intuitively, this approach allows for comparison and theory building about relationships at the dyadic level, explaining how certain relationships and sets of conditions may be favorable (or not) to the influence of small states. However, the largely dyadic approach in Chapters 5 and 6 is just one compatible line of research; an asymmetrical and relational approach also facilitates comparison and theory building based in the positionality of small states or could underpin more formalized network analyses of small states in the world.

On this latter point, there is a clear opportunity for dialogue with core IR theory concerning the expanding agenda of research on hierarchy in international politics. Although IR theory long emphasized the centrality of anarchy—the lack of a recognized, central governing authority over sovereign states—during the last decade hierarchy has emerged as one of IR's hottest topics. While anarchy and hierarchy were long considered opposites, the "new hierarchy" research agenda has emphasized the existence of forms of hierarchy that do not imply a central governing authority.[14] The shift from anarchy to hierarchy, or the recognition of the heterodox nature of international relationships, has facilitated investigations into the role of status concerns in international relations.[15] This is another area in which the study of small states has already suggested new directions of research.[16] Though many of the early contributions on both hierarchy and status were dedicated to great powers, the two growing research agendas provide important opportunities to better integrate the study of small states with mainstream conversations in IR theory.

As we note in Chapter 1, the very category of small states emerged through hierarchical diplomatic practice and still implies the existence of distributional hierarchies of capabilities. Foregrounding small states in the hierarchy research agenda is crucial to avoid replicating the distortions of earlier generations of great power–centric theory; these distortions are evident in accounts of

---

[13]   Kat, "Subordinate-State Agency and US Hegemony."
[14]   Mattern and Zarakol, "Hierarchies in World Politics"; Donnelly, "Sovereign Inequalities and Hierarchy in Anarchy"; Hobson and Sharman, "The Enduring Place of Hierarchy in World Politics"; Mcconaughey, Musgrave, and Nexon, "Beyond Anarchy."
[15]   Paul, Larson, and Wohlforth, *Status in World Politics.*
[16]   de Carvalho and Neumann, *Small State Status Seeking*; Baxter, Jordan, and Rubin, "How Small States Acquire Status"; Long and Urdinez, "Status at the Margins."

hierarchy that assume small states' submissiveness but do not investigate small states' interests and agency.[17] However, international hierarchy might relate simply to ranking states along certain dimensions, without implying a recognition of authority.[18] Broader approaches to hierarchy leave that question open. As we emphasize in our discussion of the international system, networks of international relationships also reflect asymmetries of power—including forms of hierarchy. Whether international hierarchies reduce small states' room to maneuver depends on the nature of those hierarchies, and the nature of those hierarchies is also shaped by small states' actions. While relationalist work on hierarchy by Daniel Nexon and coauthors is compatible with our understanding of small states and their place in world politics,[19] the literature on hierarchy has so far paid limited attention to the agency of small states.

In broad terms, this book has argued that to understand great powers' positions, roles, and actions in the world, we need to understand small states.[20] We do not mean simply understanding what great powers *do to* small states—on that, there are library shelves filled with studies of imperialism and hegemony in IR and History. Power disparities have been a part of international politics from the very beginning. Realist-inspired IR emphasized that power disparities left little space for the weak to pursue their own priorities. If small states had little autonomy, then their decisions and actions were not particularly interesting on their own. With that implicit logic, IR's major paradigms and great debates granted ontological preference to relations among the great powers as opposed to between the great and small. This missed at least half the story: great powers are not "great" in relation to one another, but when compared to the smaller members of international society. Great powers are only leaders to the extent that they convince small states to follow.[21] Small states do not always comply; when they do, it is often in part in pursuit of their own goals, or as the result of bargaining and accommodation. Dynamic, asymmetrical relationships change actors on both sides of the continuum of size and power, though in different ways.[22] Small states' interests, actions, and ideas must be given greater weight for their part in constituting great powers' international positions, shaping the web of international relationships, and making up much of the content of international politics.

[17] E.g., Lake, *Hierarchy in International Relations*, which emphasizes the actions and rationales of the larger state.
[18] Musgrave, "Asymmetry, Hierarchy, and the Ecclesiastes Trap."
[19] Mcconaughey, Musgrave, and Nexon, "Beyond Anarchy"; Jackson and Nexon, "Reclaiming the Social."
[20] As Musgrave notes, the growing attention to the dynamics of asymmetry strongly suggests "measurable and systematic great-power underperformance." Musgrave, "Asymmetry, Hierarchy, and the Ecclesiastes Trap," 15.
[21] Schirm, "Leaders in Need of Followers"; Williams, Lobell, and Jesse, *Beyond Great Powers and Hegemons*.
[22] Musgrave, "Asymmetry, Hierarchy, and the Ecclesiastes Trap."

Appendix

Table A1 Combined typological theory

	Policy divergence (1)	Relational issue salience (2)	Preference cohesion (3)
High (a)			
Low (b)			

Type	Color code	Combination of conditions	Description	Degree of opportunity for small state's goal seeking	Small state strategy	Bilateral cases
1	Red	1a, 2a, 3a	Conflict/gridlocked distributional negotiations	Lowest opportunity	Perseverance, underimplementation, foot-dragging	Mali/France (Ch. 5); Moldova/Russia (Ch. 5); Estonia-Russia (Ch. 5); Nepal-India, 1989 (Ch. 5) Bhutan/China border (Ch. 5); Greece/Troika, 2015 (Ch. 6); Myanmar/China (Ch. 6); Bolivia/Brazil, 2003–2006 (Ch. 6)
2	Orange	1a, 2a, 3b	Crisis or political shift that overturns understanding of a situation or policy paradigm	Medium opportunity	Problem redefinition	Estonia/NATO (Ch. 5); Rwanda/UK-U.S., 1994 (Ch. 6) Bolivia/Brazil, 2006 (Ch. 6); Zambia/donors (Ch. 6)
3	Yellow	1a, 2b, 3b	Status quo policy without vested interests	High opportunity	Agenda setting for salience	Djibouti/France (Ch. 5); Bhutan/India (Ch. 5)

Table A1 *Continued*

Type	Color code	Combination of conditions	Description	Degree of opportunity for small state's goal seeking	Small state strategy	Bilateral cases
4	Green	1b, 2a, 3a	Problem-solving negotiations within shared problem understanding	Most likely	Finding mutual benefits	Portugal/Troika 2011 (Ch. 6); Malaysia/China (Ch. 6)
5	Blue	1b, 2a, 3b	Problem-solving negotiations, but divergent problem understandings	Medium opportunity	"Extraversion"	Rwanda–U.S./UK, post-2000 (Ch. 6); Greece/Troika 2010 (Ch. 6)
6	Violet	1a, 2b, 3a	Status quo policy supported by vested interests	Low opportunity	Agenda setting and new alternatives	Gabon/France (Ch. 5)
7	White	1b, 2b, 3a	Status quo policy supported by both countries (but with potential bargaining over benefits)	Status quo likely to be maintained	Maintain status quo and seek additional benefits	Honduras/U.S. (Ch. 5); Paraguay/Brazil (Ch. 6)
8	Grey	1b, 2b, 3b	Status quo policy subject to drift	Change unlikely to be sought	Maintain status quo while seeking additional benefits amid policy incoherence	El Salvador/U.S. (Ch. 5)

Bibliography

Abdelal, Rawi, and Jonathan Kirshner. "Strategy, Economic Relations, and the Definition of National Interests." *Security Studies* 9, nos. 1–2 (1999): 119–56.

Abente, Diego. "The War of the Triple Alliance: Three Explanatory Models." *Latin American Research Review* 22, no. 2 (1987): 47–69.

Acharya, Amitav. *Constructing a Security Community in Southeast Asia: ASEAN and the Problem of Regional Order*. 3rd ed. New York: Routledge, 2014.

Acharya, Amitav. *The End of American World Order*. New York: John Wiley & Sons, 2014.

Acharya, Amitav. "Regionalism in the Evolving World Order: Power, Leadership, and the Provision of Public Goods." In *21st Century Cooperation: Regional Public Goods, Global Governance, and Sustainable Development*, edited by Antoni Estevadeordal and Louis Goodman, 39–54. New York: Routledge, 2017.

Acharya, Amitav. *Singapore's Foreign Policy: The Search for Regional Order*. Singapore: World Scientific, 2008.

Acharya, Amitav, and Barry Buzan. *The Making of Global International Relations*. New York: Cambridge University Press, 2019.

Adams, Roy D., and Ken McCormick. "Private Goods, Club Goods, and Public Goods as a Continuum." *Review of Social Economy* 45, no. 2 (1987): 192–99.

Adhikari, Dhruba Raj. "A Small State between Two Major Powers: Nepal's Foreign Policy since 1816." *Journal of International Affairs* 2, no. 1 (2018): 43–74.

Águeda Corneloup, Inés de, and Arthur P. J. Mol. "Small Island Developing States and International Climate Change Negotiations: The Power of Moral 'Leadership.'" *International Environmental Agreements: Politics, Law and Economics* 14, no. 3 (2014): 281–97.

Alden, Chris. "China in Africa." *Survival* 47, no. 3 (2005): 147–64.

Alesina, Alberto, and Enrico Spolaore. *The Size of Nations*. Cambridge, MA: MIT Press, 2003.

Alves, Ana Cristina. "China and Gabon: A Growing Resource Partnership." African Perspectives, Global Insights. Johannesburg, South Africa: South African Institute of International Affairs, 2008. https://www.saiia.org.za/wp-content/uploads/2008/04/chap_rep_04_alves_200805.pdf.

Anckar, Dag. "Homogeneity and Smallness: Dahl and Tufte Revisited." *Scandinavian Political Studies* 22, no. 1 (1999): 29–44.

Andersen, Mikael Skou. "The Politics of Carbon Taxation: How Varieties of Policy Style Matter." *Environmental Politics* 28, no. 6 (September 19, 2019): 1084–104. https://doi.org/10.1080/09644016.2019.1625134.

Anghie, Antony. *Imperialism, Sovereignty and the Making of International Law*. New York: Cambridge University Press, 2007.

Angstrom, Jan, and Magnus Petersson. "Weak Party Escalation: An Underestimated Strategy for Small States?" *Journal of Strategic Studies* 42, no. 2 (2019): 282–300.

Archer, Clive. "The Nordic States and Security." In *Small States and International Security: Europe and Beyond*, edited by Clive Archer, Alyson J.K. Bailes, Anders Wivel, 121–38. Abingdon: Routledge, 2014.

Archer, Clive, Alyson J. K. Bailes, and Anders Wivel, eds. *Small States and International Security: Europe and Beyond*. Abingdon: Routledge, 2014.

Ardagna, Silvia, and Francesco Caselli. "The Political Economy of the Greek Debt Crisis: A Tale of Two Bailouts." *American Economic Journal: Macroeconomics* 6, no. 4 (2014): 291–323.

Aresti, María Lasa. "Oil and Gas Revenue Sharing in Bolivia." Natural Resource Governance Institute, 2016.

Arieff, Alexis. "Senegal: Background and US Relations." Washington, DC: Congressional Research Service, 2011.

Armstrong, Harvey W., and Robert Read. "The Phantom of Liberty?: Economic Growth and the Vulnerability of Small States." *Journal of International Development* 14, no. 4 (2002): 435–58.

Arrarás, Astrid, and Grace Deheza. "Referéndum del Gas En Bolivia 2004: Mucho Más Que un Referéndum." *Revista de Ciencia Política* 25, no. 2 (2005): 161–72.

Arreguin-Toft, Ivan. "How the Weak Win Wars: A Theory of Asymmetric Conflict." *International Security* 26, no. 1 (2001): 93–128.

Ashe, John W., Robert Van Lierop, and Anilla Cherian. "The Role of the Alliance of Small Island States (AOSIS) in the Negotiation of the United Nations Framework Convention on Climate Change (UNFCCC)," *National Resource Forum* 23, no. 3 (August 1999): 209–20.

Axelrod, Robert, and Robert O. Keohane. "Achieving Cooperation under Anarchy: Strategies and Institutions." *World Politics* 38, no. 1 (1985): 226–54.

Azzopardi-Muscat, Natasha, and Carl Camilleri. "Challenges and Opportunities for the Health Sector in Small States." In *Handbook of Small States: Economic, Social, and Environmental Issues,* edited by Lino Briguglio, 445–74. Abingdon: Routledge, 2018. https://doi.org/10.4324/9781351181846-24.

Azzopardi-Muscat, Natasha, Tjede Funk, Sandra C. Buttigieg, Kenneth E. Grech, and Helmut Brand. "Policy Challenges and Reforms in Small EU Member State Health Systems: A Narrative Literature Review." *European Journal of Public Health* 26, no. 6 (December 1, 2016): 916–22. https://doi.org/10.1093/eurpub/ckw091.

Azzopardi-Muscat, Natasha, Pauline Vassallo, Neville Calleja, Alena Usava, Francesco Zambon, and Claudia Stein. "Health Information Systems in Small Countries of the WHO European Region: Report from the Small Countries Health Information Network." *Public Health Panorama* 2, no. 3 (2016): 279–84.

Ba, Alice D. "Multilateralism and East Asian Transitions: The English School, Diplomacy, and a Networking Regional Order." *International Politics* 57, no. 2 (April 1, 2020): 259–77. https://doi.org/10.1057/s41311-019-00202-x.

Baehr, Peter R., Monique C. Castermans-Holleman, and Fred Grünfeld. "Human Rights in the Foreign Policy of the Netherlands." *Human Rights Quarterly* 24, no. 4 (2002): 992–1010.

Baer, Werner, Daniel A. Dias, and Joao B. Duarte. "The Economy of Portugal and the European Union: From High Growth Prospects to the Debt Crisis." *Quarterly Review of Economics and Finance* 53, no. 4 (2013): 345–52.

Bagozzi, Benjamin E. "The Multifaceted Nature of Global Climate Change Negotiations." *Review of International Organizations* 10, no. 4 (2015): 439–64.

Bailes, Alyson J. K., Jean-Marc Rickli, and Baldur Thorhallsson. "Small States, Survival and Strategy." In *Small States and International Security*, edited by Clive Archer, Alyson J. K. Bailes, and Anders Wivel, 52–71. Abingdon: Routledge, 2014.

Baldacchino, Godfrey. *Island Enclaves: Offshoring Strategies, Creative Governance, and Subnational Island Jurisdictions*. Toronto: McGill Queen's University Press, 2010.

Baldacchino, Godfrey. "Mainstreaming the Study of Small States and Territories." *Small States & Territories* 1, no. 1 (2018): 3–16.

Baldacchino, Godfrey. "Small States: Challenges of Political Economy." In *Handbook on the Politics of Small States*, edited by Godfrey Baldacchino and Anders Wivel, 70–82. Cheltenham: Edward Elgar Publishing, 2020. https://www.elgaronline.com/view/edc oll/9781788112925/9781788112925.00011.xml.

Baldacchino, Godfrey. "Thucydides or Kissinger? A Critical Review of Smaller State Diplomacy." In *The Diplomacies of Small States: Between Vulnerability and Resilience*, edited by Andrew F. Cooper and Timothy M. Shaw, 21–40. New York: Palgrave Macmillan, 2009.

Baldacchino, Godfrey, and Anders Wivel, eds. *Handbook on the Politics of Small States*. Cheltenham: Edward Elgar Publishing, 2020.

Baldacchino, Godfrey, and Anders Wivel. "Small States: Concepts and Theories." In *Handbook on the Politics of Small States*, edited by Godfrey Baldacchino and Anders Wivel, 2–19. Cheltenham: Edward Elgar Publishing, 2020.

Balding, Christopher. "Why Democracies Are Turning against Belt and Road." *Foreign Affairs* 24 (2018). https://www.foreignaffairs.com/articles/china/2018-10-24/why-democracies-are-turning-against-belt-and-road

Baldwin, David A. *Power and International Relations: A Conceptual Approach*. Princeton, NJ: Princeton University Press, 2016.

Balicer, Ran D., and Reut Ohana. "Israel's COVID-19 Endgame." *Science* 372, no. 6543 (2021): 663.

Ball, Christopher P., Claude Lopez, and Javier Reyes. "Remittances, Inflation and Exchange Rate Regimes in Small Open Economies." *World Economy* 36, no. 4 (2013): 487–507.

Balmaceda, Margarita M. "Privatization and Elite Defection in de Facto States: The Case of Transnistria, 1991–2012." *Communist and Post-Communist Studies* 46, no. 4 (2013): 445–54.

Barnett, Jon, and Elissa Waters. "Rethinking the Vulnerability of Small Island States: Climate Change and Development in the Pacific Islands." In *The Palgrave Handbook of International Development*, edited by Jean Grugel and Daniel Hammett, 731–48. London: Springer, 2016.

Barnett, Michael, and Raymond Duvall. "Power in International Politics." *International Organization* 59, no. 1 (2005): 39–75.

Barnett, Thomas P. M. *The Pentagon's New Map: War and Peace in the Twenty-First Century*. New York: Penguin, 2005.

Bartmann, Barry. "Meeting the Needs of Microstate Security." *Round Table* 91, no. 365 (2002): 361–74.

Bátora, Jozef. "Reinvigorating the Rotating Presidency: Slovakia and Agenda-Setting in the EU's External Relations." *Global Affairs* 3, no. 3 (2017): 251–63.

Bátora, Jozef. "Small If Needed, Big If Necessary: Small Member States and the EU's Diplomatic System in Kiev." In *Small States in the Modern World: Vulnerabilities and Opportunities*, edited by Harald Baldersheim and Michael Keating, 73–90. Cheltenham: Edward Elgar Publishing, 2015. https://doi.org/10.4337/9781784711 443.00015.

Baumgartner, Frank R. "Ideas and Policy Change." *Governance* 26, no. 2 (2013): 239–58.

Baumgartner, Frank R., and Bryan D. Jones. *Agendas and Instability in American Politics.* Chicago: University of Chicago Press, 1993.

Baxter, Phil, Jenna Jordan, and Lawrence Rubin. "How Small States Acquire Status: A Social Network Analysis." *International Area Studies Review* 21, no. 3 (2018): 191–213.

Beeson, Mark. "The Great ASEAN Rorschach Test." *Pacific Review* 33, nos. 3–4 (2020): 574–81.

Behringer, Ronald M. "Middle Power Leadership on the Human Security Agenda." *Cooperation and Conflict* 40, no. 3 (2005): 305–42.

Benabdallah, Lina. "Contesting the International Order by Integrating It: The Case of China's Belt and Road Initiative." *Third World Quarterly* 40, no. 1 (2019): 92–108.

Bennett, Andrew, and Colin Elman. "Case Study Methods in the International Relations Subfield." *Comparative Political Studies* 40, no. 2 (2007): 170–95.

Bennett, Andrew, and Colin Elman. "Qualitative Research: Recent Developments in Case Study Methods." *Annual Review of Political Science* 9 (2006): 455–76.

Benwell, Richard. "The Canaries in the Coalmine: Small States as Climate Change Champions." *Round Table* 100, no. 413 (2011): 199–211.

Bereketeab, Redie. "The Intergovernmental Authority on Development: Internal Culture of Foreign Policymaking and Sources of Weaknesses." In *African Foreign Policies in International Institutions*, edited by Jason Warner and Timothy M. Shaw, 113–25. New York: Palgrave Macmillan, 2018.

Berg, Eiki, and Kristel Vits. "Quest for Survival and Recognition: Insights into the Foreign Policy Endeavours of the Post-Soviet de Facto States." *Ethnopolitics* 17, no. 4 (2018): 390–407.

Bergamaschi, Isaline. "The Fall of a Donor Darling: The Role of Aid in Mali's Crisis." *Journal of Modern African Studies* 52, no. 3 (2014): 347–78.

Bergamaschi, Isaline. "Mali: Patterns and Limits of Donor-Driven Ownership." In *The New Politics of Aid: African Strategies for Dealing with Donors*, edited by Lindsay Whitfield, 217–45. New York: Oxford University Press, 2009.

Beswick, Danielle. "Aiding State Building and Sacrificing Peace Building? The Rwanda–UK Relationship 1994–2011." *Third World Quarterly* 32, no. 10 (2011): 1911–30.

Beswick, Danielle. "From Weak State to Savvy International Player? Rwanda's Multi-Level Strategy for Maximising Agency." In *African Agency in International Politics*, edited by William Brown and Sophie Harman, 172–88. Abingdon: Routledge, 2013.

Betts, Richard K. "The Soft Underbelly of American Primacy: Tactical Advantages of Terror." *Political Science Quarterly* 117, no. 1 (2002): 19–36. https://doi.org/10.2307/798092.

Betzold, Carola. "'Borrowing' Power to Influence International Negotiations: AOSIS in the Climate Change Regime, 1990–1997." *Politics* 30, no. 3 (2010): 131–48.

Betzold, Carola, Paula Castro, and Florian Weiler. "AOSIS in the UNFCCC Negotiations: From Unity to Fragmentation?" *Climate Policy* 12, no. 5 (September 1, 2012): 591–613. https://doi.org/10.1080/14693062.2012.692205.

Bhal, John de. "Never Thaw That Coming! Latin American Regional Integration and the US–Cuba Thaw." *Third World Quarterly* 40, no. 5 (2019): 855–69.

Bianco, Cinzia, and Gareth Stansfield. "The Intra-GCC Crises: Mapping GCC Fragmentation after 2011." *International Affairs* 94, no. 3 (2018): 613–35.

Biesma, Regien G., Ruairí Brugha, Andrew Harmer, Aisling Walsh, Neil Spicer, and Gill Walt. "The Effects of Global Health Initiatives on Country Health Systems: A Review of the Evidence from HIV/AIDS Control." *Health Policy and Planning* 24, no. 4 (July 1, 2009): 239–52. https://doi.org/10.1093/heapol/czp025.

Bishop, Matthew Louis. "The Political Economy of Small States: Enduring Vulnerability?" *Review of International Political Economy* 19, no. 5 (2012): 942–60.

Bishop, Matthew Louis, and Anthony Payne. "Climate Change and the Future of Caribbean Development." *Journal of Development Studies* 48, no. 10 (2012): 1536–53.

Bisht, Medha. "Bhutan–India Power Cooperation: Benefits Beyond Bilateralism." *Strategic Analysis* 36, no. 5 (September 1, 2012): 787–803. https://doi.org/10.1080/09700161.2012.712390.

Bisht, Medha. "Bhutan's Foreign Policy Determinants: An Assessment." *Strategic Analysis* 36, no. 1 (January 1, 2012): 57–72. https://doi.org/10.1080/09700161.2012.628481.

Bisht, Medha. "India–Bhutan Relations: From Developmental Cooperation to Strategic Partnership," *Strategic Analysis* 34, no. 3 (2010): 350–53.

Bisht, Medha. "The Rupee Crunch and India-Bhutan Economic Engagement." Issue Brief. New Delhi: Institute for Defence Studies & Analyses, 2012. https://idsa.in/issuebrief/TheRupeeCrunchandIndiaBhutanEconomicEngagement_MedhaBisht_160712.

Bisht, Medha. "Sino-Bhutan Boundary Negotiations: Complexities of the 'Package Deal.'" New Delhi: Institute for Defence Studies and Analyses, January 19, 2010. https://idsa.in/idsacomments/Sino-BhutanBoundaryNegotiations_mbisht_190110.

Bitar, Sebastian E. *US Military Bases, Quasi-Bases, and Domestic Politics in Latin America*. Palgrave Macmillan, 2015.

Björkdahl, Annika. "Norm Advocacy: A Small State Strategy to Influence the EU." *Journal of European Public Policy* 15, no. 1 (2008): 135–54.

Blanchard, Jean-Marc F. "Malaysia and China's MSRI: The Road to China Was Taken Before the (Maritime Silk) Road Was Built." In *China's Maritime Silk Road Initiative and Southeast Asia*, edited by Jean-Marc F. Blanchard, 95–131. Singapore: Palgrave Macmillan, 2019.

Bleck, Jaimie, and Kristin Michelitch. "The 2012 Crisis in Mali: Ongoing Empirical State Failure." *African Affairs* 114, no. 457 (2015): 598–623.

Blight, James G., and Philip Brenner. *Sad and Luminous Days: Cuba's Struggle with the Superpowers after the Missile Crisis*. Lanham, MD: Rowman & Littlefield Publishers, 2002.

Bodian, Mamadou, and Catherine Lena Kelly. "Senegalese Foreign Policy: Leadership Through Soft Power from Senghor to Sall." In *African Foreign Policies in International Institutions*, edited by Jason Warner and Timothy M. Shaw, 327–51. New York: Palgrave Macmillan, 2018. https://doi.org/10.1057/978-1-137-57574-6_21.

Bosco, David L. *Rough Justice: The International Criminal Court in a World of Power Politics*. New York: Oxford University Press, 2014.

Bourantonis, Dimitris. *The History and Politics of UN Security Council Reform*. London: Routledge, 2004.

Bow, Brian. *The Politics of Linkage: Power, Interdependence, and Ideas in Canada-US Relations*. Vancouver: UBC Press, 2010.

Bower, Adam. "Norms without the Great Powers: International Law, Nested Social Structures, and the Ban on Antipersonnel Mines." *International Studies Review* 17, no. 3 (2015): 347–73.

Boyd, Matt, Michael G. Baker, Cassidy Nelson, and Nick Wilson. "The 2019 Global Health Security Index (GHSI) and Its Implications for New Zealand and Pacific Regional Health Security." *New Zealand Medical Journal* 133, no. 1516 (2020): 83–92.

Brady, Anne-Marie. *Small States and the Changing Global Order: New Zealand Faces the Future*. Cham: Springer, 2019.

Branch, Jordan. *The Cartographic State: Maps, Territory, and the Origins of Sovereignty*. New York: Cambridge University Press, 2013.

Branch, Jordan. "'Colonial Reflection' and Territoriality: The Peripheral Origins of Sovereign Statehood." *European Journal of International Relations* 18, no. 2 (2012): 277–97.

Brands, Hal. *Latin America's Cold War*. Cambridge, MA: Harvard University Press, 2010.

Brautigam, Deborah. *The Dragon's Gift: The Real Story of China in Africa*. New York: Oxford University Press, 2009.

Braveboy-Wagner, Jacqueline A. "The Diplomacy of Caribbean Community States: Searching for Resilience." In *The Diplomacies of Small States*, edited by Andrew F. Cooper and Timothy M. Shaw, 96–115. New York: Palgrave Macmillan, 2009.

Braveboy-Wagner, Jacqueline A., ed. *The Foreign Policies of the Global South: Rethinking Conceptual Frameworks*. Boulder, CO: Lynee Rienner, 2003.

Braveboy-Wagner, Jacqueline A. "Opportunities and Limitations of the Exercise of Foreign Policy Power by a Very Small State: The Case of Trinidad and Tobago." *Cambridge Review of International Affairs* 23, no. 3 (September 1, 2010): 407–27. https://doi.org/10.1080/09557571.2010.484049.

Braveboy-Wagner, Jacqueline A. *Small States in Global Affairs: The Foreign Policies of the Caribbean Community*. New York: Palgrave Macmillan, 2008.

Brazys, Samuel, and Diana Panke. "Why Do States Change Positions in the United Nations General Assembly?" *International Political Science Review* 38, no. 1 (2017): 70–84.

Brenner, Philip, and Soraya Castro. "David and Gulliver: Fifty Years of Competing Metaphors in the Cuban-United States Relationship." *Diplomacy & Statecraft* 20, no. 2 (2009): 236–57.

Brenner, Philip, and Peter Eisner. *Cuba Libre: A 500-Year Quest for Independence*. New York: Rowman & Littlefield, 2017.

Brezzo, Liliana M. "La Guerra de La Triple Alianza En Los Límites de La Ortodoxia: Mitos y Tabúes." *Universum (Talca)* 19, no. 1 (2004): 10–27.

Briguglio, Lino., Gordon Cordina, and Eliawony J. Kisanga, eds. *Building the Economic Resilience of Small States*, Malta: Formatek Publishing, 2008.

Briguglio, Lino. "Small Island Developing States and Their Economic Vulnerabilities." *World Development* 23, no. 9 (1995): 1615–32.

Briguglio, Lino, Gordon Cordina, Stephanie Vella, and Constance Vigilance. *Profiling Vulnerability and Resilience: A Manual for Small States*. London: Commonwealth Secretariat, 2010.

Briguglio, Lino, and Natasha Azzopardi-Muscat. "Small States and COVID-19." Webinar presented at the Collaborating Centre on Health Systems and Policies in Small States, University of Malta, September 2, 2020.

Briguglio, Lino, and Natasha Azzopardi Muscat. "The Vulnerability and Resilience Framework Applied to the Public Health System." Presented at the High-Level Meeting of the European Small Countries, Monaco, October 11, 2016.

Brooks, Stephen G. "The Globalization of Production and the Changing Benefits of Conquest." *Journal of Conflict Resolution* 43, no. 5 (1999): 646–70.

Brooks, Stephen G., and William C. Wohlforth. "The Rise and Fall of the Great Powers in the Twenty-First Century: China's Rise and the Fate of America's Global Position." *International Security* 40, no. 3 (2016): 7–53.

Broome, André. "Negotiating Crisis: The IMF and Disaster Capitalism in Small States." *Round Table* 100, no. 413 (2011): 155–67.

Browning, Christopher S. "Small, Smart and Salient? Rethinking Identity in the Small States Literature." *Cambridge Review of International Affairs* 19, no. 4 (December 1, 2006): 669–84. https://doi.org/10.1080/09557570601003536.

Brysk, Alison. *Global Good Samaritans: Human Rights as Foreign Policy.* Oxford: Oxford University Press, 2009.

Buchanan, Paul G. "Lilliputian in Fluid Times: New Zealand Foreign Policy after the Cold War." *Political Science Quarterly* 125, no. 2 (2010): 255–79.

Bueger, Christian, and Anders Wivel. "How Do Small Island States Maximize Influence? Creole Diplomacy and the Smart State Foreign Policy of the Seychelles." *Journal of the Indian Ocean Region* 14, no. 2 (May 4, 2018): 170–88. https://doi.org/10.1080/19480 881.2018.1471122.

Burges, Sean W. *Brazil in the World: The International Relations of a South American Giant.* Manchester: Manchester University Press, 2017.

Burges, Sean W. "Revisiting Consensual Hegemony: Brazilian Regional Leadership in Question." *International Politics* 52, no. 2 (2015): 193–207.

Buszynski, Leszek. "Small States, China and the South China Sea." In *Handbook on the Politics of Small States*, edited by Godfrey Baldacchino and Anders Wivel, 329–42. Cheltenham: Edward Elgar Publishing, 2020.

Büthe, Tim. "Taking Temporality Seriously: Modeling History and the Use of Narratives as Evidence." *American Political Science Review* 96, no. 3 (2002): 481–93.

Buzan, Barry. "Universal Sovereignty." In *The Globalization of International Society*, edited by Tim Dunne and Christian Reus-Smit, 227–47. Oxford: Oxford University Press, 2017.

Cameron, Elizabeth E., Jennifer B. Nuzzo, and Jessica A. Bell. "Global Health Security Index: Building Collective Action and Accountability." Baltimore, MD: Johns Hopkins University, 2019. https://www.ghsindex.org/wp-content/uploads/2020/04/2019-Glo bal-Health-Security-Index.pdf.

Campbell, John, and Jon Barnett. *Climate Change and Small Island States: Power, Knowledge and the South Pacific.* Abingdon: Routledge, 2010.

Canese, Ricardo. *La recuperación de la soberanía hidroeléctrica del Paraguay: en el marco de Políticas de Estado de energía.* Asunción, Paraguay: CINERGIAS, Centro de Investigación de Energía, Ambiente y Sociedad, 2006.

Cantir, Cristian, and Ryan Kennedy. "Balancing on the Shoulders of Giants: Moldova's Foreign Policy toward Russia and the European Union." *Foreign Policy Analysis* 11, no. 4 (2015): 397–416.

Cardoso, Guilherme R. "A Energia dos Vizinhos: uma análise da Política Externa do governo Lula na 'nacionalização' do gás boliviano e nas alterações do Tratado de Itaipu." MA thesis, Instituto de Relações Internacionais da PUC-Rio, 2010. https://www.maxw ell.vrac.puc-rio.br/colecao.php?strSecao=ocorrencia&nrSeq=17837@1&nrseqoco= 61065.

Carney, Christopher P. "International Patron-Client Relationships: A Conceptual Framework." *Studies in Comparative International Development* 24, no. 2 (1989): 42–55.

Carrillo Reveles, Veremundo. "México en la Unión de las Repúblicas Americanas: El Panamericanismo y la Política Exterior Mexicana, 1889–1942." PhD diss. El Colegio de México, 2018.

Carson, Austin, and Alexander Thompson. "The Power in Opacity: Rethinking Information in International Organizations." In *International Institutions and Power Politics: Bridging the Divide*, edited by Anders Wivel and T. V. Paul, 101–16. Washington, DC: Georgetown University Press, 2019.

Carter, George Joseph. "Multilateral Consensus Decision Making: How Pacific Island States Build and Reach Consensus in Climate Change Negotiations." PhD diss., Australian National University, 2018.

Carter, Miguel. "Itaipú: La Riqueza Energética Perdida Del Paraguay." Presented at the Asociación Paraguaya de Profesionales Graduados en los EE.UU., Asunción, Paraguay, March 22, 2018. http://www.ccpa.edu.py/userfiles/files/Carter_Itaipu_PY.pdf.

Carter, Neil, Conor Little, and Diarmuid Torney. "Climate Politics in Small European States." *Environmental Politics* 28, no. 16 (2019): 981–96.

Carvalho, Benjamin de, and Iver B. Neumann. *Small State Status Seeking: Norway's Quest for International Standing*. Abingdon: Routledge, 2014.

Castro Mariño, Soraya, and Ronald W. Pruessen. *Fifty Years of Revolution: Perspectives on Cuba, the United States, and the World*. Gainesville, FL: University Press of Florida, 2012.

Cha, Taesuh. "The Formation of American Exceptional Identities: A Three-Tier Model of the 'Standard of Civilization' in US Foreign Policy." *European Journal of International Relations* 21, no. 4 (2015): 743–67.

Cha, Victor D. "Abandonment, Entrapment, and Neoclassical Realism in Asia: The United States, Japan, and Korea." *International Studies Quarterly* 44, no. 2 (2000): 261–91.

Chafer, Tony. "Chirac and 'La Francafrique': No Longer a Family Affair." *Modern & Contemporary France* 13, no. 1 (2005): 7–23.

Chafer, Tony. "France and Senegal: The End of the Affair?" *SAIS Review* 23, no. 2 (2003): 155–67.

Chafer, Tony. "Franco-African Relations: Still Exceptional?" In *The Palgrave Handbook of African Colonial and Postcolonial History*, edited by Martin S. Shanguhyia and Toyin Falola, 801–19. New York: Palgrave Macmillan, 2018. https://doi.org/10.1057/978-1-137-59426-6_32.

Chan, Debby Sze Wan. "Asymmetric Bargaining between Myanmar and China in the Myitsone Dam Controversy: Social Opposition Akin to David's Stone against Goliath." *Pacific Review* 30, no. 5 (September 3, 2017): 674–91. https://doi.org/10.1080/09512748.2017.1293714.

Chan, Nicholas. "'Large Ocean States': Sovereignty, Small Islands, and Marine Protected Areas in Global Oceans Governance." *Global Governance: A Review of Multilateralism and International Organizations* 24, no. 4 (December 10, 2018): 537–55. https://doi.org/10.1163/19426720-02404005.

Chand, Bibek, and Lukas K. Danner. "Implications of the Dragon's Rise for South Asia: Assessing China's Nepal Policy." *Strategic Analysis* 40, no. 1 (2016): 26–40.

Chatoor, Delia. "The Role of Small States in International Diplomacy: CARICOM's Experience in the Negotiations on the Rome Statute of the International Criminal Court." *Journal of International Peacekeeping* 7, no. 1 (2001): 295–310.

Chen, Shaofeng. "Regional Responses to China's Maritime Silk Road Initiative in Southeast Asia." *Journal of Contemporary China* 27, no. 111 (2018): 344–61.

Chew, Tai Soo. "A History of the Forum of Small States." In *50 Years of Singapore and the United Nations*, edited by Tommy Koh, Li Lin Chang, and Joanna Koh, 35–38. Singapore: World Scientific, 2015.

Chisala, Victoria. "Foreign Aid Dependency: The Case of Zambia." PhD diss., School of Oriental and African Studies, 2006.

Chollet, Derek, and James Goldgeier. *America between the Wars, 11/9 to 9/11: The Misunderstood Years between the Fall of the Berlin Wall and the Start of the War on Terror*. New York: PublicAffairs, 2008.

Chong, Alan. "Small State Security in Asia: Political and Temporal Constructions of Vulnerability." In *Small States and International Security*, edited by Clive Archer, Alyson J. K. Bailes, and Anders Wivel, 52–71. Abingdon: Routledge, 2014.

Chong, Alan. "Small State Soft Power Strategies: Virtual Enlargement in the Cases of the Vatican City State and Singapore." *Cambridge Review of International Affairs* 23, no. 3 (2010): 383–405.

Chong, Alan, and Matthias Maass. "Introduction: The Foreign Policy Power of Small States." *Cambridge Review of International Affairs* 23, no. 3 (September 1, 2010): 381–82. https://doi.org/10.1080/09557571.2010.505131.

Choudhury, T. K. Roy. "The India–Bhutan Relationship: Some New Trends." *World Today* 37, no. 12 (1981): 476–81.

Clark, Paul Coe. *The United States and Somoza, 1933–1956: A Revisionist Look*. Westport, CT: Praeger, 1992.

Clegg, Peter. "Banana Splits and Policy Challenges: The ACP Caribbean and the Fragmentation of Interest Coalitions." *Revista Europea de Estudios Latinoamericanos y Del Caribe/European Review of Latin American and Caribbean Studies*, no. 79 (2005): 27–45.

Coggins, Bridget. *Power Politics and State Formation in the Twentieth Century: The Dynamics of Recognition*. Cambridge: Cambridge University Press, 2014.

Connell, John, and Tautalaaso Taulealo. "Island Tourism and COVID-19 in Vanuatu and Samoa: An Unfolding Crisis." *Small States & Territories* 4, no. 1 (2021): 105–24.

Conniff, Michael L., and Gene E. Bigler. *Modern Panama: From Occupation to Crossroads of the Americas*. Cambridge University Press, 2019.

Contessi, Nicola P. "Prospects for the Accommodation of a Resurgent Russia." In *Accommodating Rising Powers: Past, Present, and Future*, edited by T. V. Paul, 268–92. New York: Cambridge University Press, 2016.

Cooley, Alexander. *Great Games, Local Rules: The New Great Power Contest in Central Asia*. New York: Oxford University Press, 2014.

Cooley, Alexander, and Daniel Nexon. *Exit from Hegemony: The Unraveling of the American Global Order*. New York: Oxford University Press, 2020.

Cooley, Alexander, and Daniel H. Nexon. "'The Empire Will Compensate You': The Structural Dynamics of the US Overseas Basing Network." *Perspectives on Politics* 11, no. 4 (2013): 1034–50.

Cooper, Andrew F. "The G20 and Contested Global Governance: BRICS, Middle Powers and Small States." *Caribbean Journal of International Relations and Diplomacy* 2, no. 3 (2014): 87–109.

Cooper, Andrew F. "Niche Diplomacy: A Conceptual Overview." In *Niche Diplomacy: Middle Powers after the Cold War*, edited by Andrew F. Cooper, 1–24. London: Palgrave Macmillan, 1997.

Cooper, Andrew F., and Timothy M. Shaw. "The Diplomacies of Small States at the Start of the Twenty-First Century: How Vulnerable? How Resilient?" In *The Diplomacies of Small States: Between Vulnerability and Resilience*, edited by Andrew F. Cooper and Timothy M. Shaw, 1–25. New York: Palgrave Macmillan, 2009.

Cooper, Andrew F., and Timothy M. Shaw, eds. *The Diplomacies of Small States: Between Vulnerability and Resilience*. New York: Palgrave Macmillan, 2009.

Corbett, Jack. "Territory, Islandness, and the Secessionist Imaginary: Why Do Very Small Communities Favour Autonomy Over Integration?" *Nations and Nationalism* 26, no. 4 (2020): 1087–103.

Corbett, Jack, Mélodie Ruwet, Yi-Chong Xu, and Patrick Weller. "Climate Governance, Policy Entrepreneurs and Small States: Explaining Policy Change at the International Maritime Organisation." *Environmental Politics* 29, no. 5 (2020): 825–44.

Corbett, Jack, and Wouter Veenendaal. *Democracy in Small States: Persisting against All Odds*. Oxford: Oxford University Press, 2018.

Corbett, Jack, and Wouter Veenendaal. "Why Small States Are Beautiful." *Political Insight* 10, no. 1 (2019): 4–8.

Corbett, Jack, Yi-chong Xu, and Patrick Weller. "Norm Entrepreneurship and Diffusion 'from below' in International Organisations: How the Competent Performance of Vulnerability Generates Benefits for Small States." *Review of International Studies* 45, no. 4 (2019): 647–68. https://doi.org/10.1017/S0260210519000068.

Corbett, Jack, Xu Yi-Chong, and Patrick Weller. "Climate Change and the Active Participation of Small States in International Organisations." *Round Table* 107, no. 1 (2018): 103–5.

Corbett, Jack, Xu Yi-Chong, and Patrick Weller. "Small States and the 'Throughput' Legitimacy of International Organisations." *Cambridge Review of International Affairs* 31, no. 2 (2018): 183–202.

Costi, Alberto, and Nathan Jon Ross. "The Ongoing Legal Status of Low-Lying States in the Climate-Changed Future." In *Small States in a Legal World*, edited by Petra Butler and Caroline Morris, 101–38. Cham: Springer International Publishing, 2017. https://doi.org/10.1007/978-3-319-39366-7_6.

"Country/Territory Report - Mali." *Mali Country Monitor*, January 2020, 1–48.

Crandall, Matthew. "Hierarchy in Moldova-Russia Relations: The Transnistrian Effect." *Studies of Transition States and Societies* 4, no. 1 (2012): 3–15.

Crandall, Matthew. "Soft Security Threats and Small States: The Case of Estonia." *Defence Studies* 14, no. 1 (2014): 30–55.

Crandall, Russell. *The Salvador Option*. Cambridge University Press, 2016.

Cumming, Gordon D. "Nicolas Sarkozy's Africa Policy: Change, Continuity or Confusion?" *French Politics* 11, no. 1 (2013): 24–47.

Curtis, Devon E. A. "Development Assistance and the Lasting Legacies of Rebellion in Burundi and Rwanda." *Third World Quarterly* 36, no. 7 (2015): 1365–81.

Dabhade, Manish, and Harsh V Pant. "Coping with Challenges to Sovereignty: Sino-Indian Rivalry and Nepal's Foreign Policy." *Contemporary South Asia* 13, no. 2 (2004): 157–69.

Dahl, Robert A. "The Concept of Power." *Behavioral Science* 2, no. 3 (1957): 201–15.

Dahl, Robert Alan, and Edward R Tufte. *Size and Democracy*. Vol. 2. Stanford University Press, 1973.

Darius, Reginald, Travis Mitchell, Sanjana Zaman, and Charumathi Raja. "The Fiscal Consequences of Natural Disasters: Does Country Size Matter?" In *Handbook of Small States*, edited by Lino Briguglio, 550–72. Abingdon: Routledge, 2018.

Darnton, Christopher. "Asymmetry and Agenda-Setting in US-Latin American Relations: Rethinking the Origins of the Alliance for Progress." *Journal of Cold War Studies* 14, no. 4 (2012): 55–92.

Darnton, Christopher. *Rivalry and Alliance Politics in Cold War Latin America.* Baltimore, MD: Johns Hopkins University Press, 2014.

De Waal, Thomas. *Uncertain Ground: Engaging with Europe's de Facto States and Breakaway Territories.* Brussels: Carnegie Europe, 2018.

Deitelhoff, Nicole, and Linda Wallbott. "Beyond Soft Balancing: Small States and Coalition-Building in the ICC and Climate Negotiations." *Cambridge Review of International Affairs* 25, no. 3 (2012): 345–66.

Delgado, Ana Carolina T., and Clayton M. Cunha Filho. "Bolivia-Brazil: Internal Dynamics, Sovereignty Drive, and Integrationist Ideology." In *Foreign Policy Responses to the Rise of Brazil: Balancing Power in Emerging States*, edited by Gian Luca Gardini and Maria Hermínia Tavares de Almeida, 129–44. New York: Palgrave Macmillan, 2016.

DeMeritt, Jacqueline H. R. "International Organizations and Government Killing: Does Naming and Shaming Save Lives?" *International Interactions* 38, no. 5 (2012): 597–621.

Demirdirek, Hülya. "In the Minority in Moldova: (Dis)Empowerment through Territorial Conflict." In *Europe's Last Frontier?: Belarus, Moldova, and Ukraine between Russia and the European Union*, edited by Oliver Schmidtke and Serhy Yekelchyk, 115–31. New York: Palgrave Macmillan, 2008.

Desrosiers, Marie-Eve, and Haley J. Swedlund. "Rwanda's Post-Genocide Foreign Aid Relations: Revisiting Notions of Exceptionalism." *African Affairs* 118, no. 472 (2019): 435–62.

Deudney, Daniel, and G. John Ikenberry. "The Nature and Sources of Liberal International Order." *Review of International Studies* 25, no. 02 (1999): 179–96.

Deutsch, Karl W., and J. David Singer. "Multipolar Power Systems and International Stability." *World Politics* 16, no. 3 (1964): 390–406.

Devetak, Richard, and Jacqui True. "Diplomatic Divergence in the Antipodes: Globalisation, Foreign Policy and State Identity in Australia and New Zealand." *Australian Journal of Political Science* 41, no. 2 (2006): 241–56.

Dias, Vanda Amaro. "The EU's Post-Liberal Approach to Peace: Framing EUBAM's Contribution to the Moldova–Transnistria Conflict Transformation." *European Security* 22, no. 3 (2013): 338–54.

Didier, Laurent. "Economic Diplomacy: The 'One–China Policy' Effect on Trade." *China Economic Review* 28, (April 2018): 223–43.

Dimitrov, Radoslav S. "The Paris Agreement on Climate Change: Behind Closed Doors." *Global Environmental Politics* 16, no. 3 (2016): 1–11.

Donnelly, Jack. "The Discourse of Anarchy in IR." *International Theory* 7, no. 3 (2015): 393–425.

Donnelly, Jack. "Sovereign Inequalities and Hierarchy in Anarchy: American Power and International Society." *European Journal of International Relations* 12, no. 2 (2006): 139–70.

Dorji, Thinley, and Saran Tenzin Tamang. "Bhutan's Experience with COVID-19 Vaccination in 2021." *BMJ Global Health* 6, no. 5 (May 1, 2021): e005977. https://doi.org/10.1136/bmjgh-2021-005977.

Dudley, Steven. "Honduras Elites and Organized Crime." Washington, DC: InSight Crime, 2016. https://idl-bnc-idrc.dspacedirect.org/bitstream/handle/10625/55848/IDL-55848.pdf?sequence=1.

Dunne, Timothy, and Christian Reus-Smit. *The Globalization of International Society.* Oxford University Press, 2017.

Duque, Marina G. "Recognizing International Status: A Relational Approach." *International Studies Quarterly* 62, no. 3 (2018): 577–92.

Durant, Robert F., and Paul F. Diehl. "Agendas, Alternatives, and Public Policy: Lessons from the U.S. Foreign Policy Arena." *Journal of Public Policy* 9, no. 2 (1989): 179–205.

East, Maurice A. "Size and Foreign Policy Behavior: A Test of Two Models." *World Politics* 25, no. 4 (1973): 556–76. https://doi.org/10.2307/2009952.

Easterly, William, and Aart Kraay. "Small States, Small Problems? Income, Growth, and Volatility in Small States." *World Development* 28, no. 11 (2000): 2013–27. https://doi.org/10.1016/S0305-750X(00)00068-1.

Eckstein, Harry. "Case Study and Theory in Political Science." In *Case Study Method: Key Issues, Key Texts*, edited by Roger Gomm, Martyn Hammersley, and Peter Foster, 119–64. London; Thousand Oaks, CA: SAGE Publications, 2000.

Efremova, Ksenia. "Small States in Great Power Politics: Understanding the 'Buffer Effect.'" *Central European Journal of International & Security Studies* 13, no. 1 (2019): 100–21.

Egeland, Jan. "Focus On: Human Rights—Ineffective Big States, Potent Small States." *Journal of Peace Research* 21, no. 3 (September 1, 1984): 207–13. https://doi.org/10.1177/002234338402100301.

Elgström, Ole, and Christer Jönsson. "Negotiation in the European Union: Bargaining or Problem-Solving?" *Journal of European Public Policy* 7, no. 5 (2000): 684–704.

Elman, Colin. "Explanatory Typologies in Qualitative Studies of International Politics." *International Organization* 59, no. 2 (2005): 293–326.

Elman, Miriam Fendius. "The Foreign Policies of Small States: Challenging Neorealism in Its Own Backyard." *British Journal of Political Science* 25, no. 2 (1995): 171.

Emerson, R. Guy. "Radical Neglect? The 'War on Terror' and Latin America." *Latin American Politics and Society* 52, no. 1 (2010): 33–62.

Engel, Jeffrey A. "A Better World . . . but Don't Get Carried Away: The Foreign Policy of George H. W. Bush Twenty Years On." *Diplomatic History* 34, no. 1 (January 6, 2010): 25–46. https://doi.org/10.1111/j.1467-7709.2009.00831.x.

Estevadeordal, Antoni, and Louis W. Goodman, eds. *21st Century Cooperation: Regional Public Goods, Global Governance, and Sustainable Development*. New York: Routledge, 2017.

Evans, Peter B., Harold Karan Jacobson, and Robert D. Putnam, eds. *Double-Edged Diplomacy: International Bargaining and Domestic Politics*. Berkeley: University of California Press, 1993.

Fair, C. Christine. "Rohingya: Victims of a Great Game East." *Washington Quarterly* 41, no. 3 (2018): 63–85.

Fané, Zoumana. "La Politique Étrangère Du Mali: 1960–2008: Permanences, Ajustements et Perspectives: Action Extérieure d'un Etat Sahélien Enclavé," 2008.

Fazal, Tanisha M. *State Death: The Politics and Geography of Conquest, Occupation, and Annexation*. Princeton, NJ: Princeton University Press, 2011.

Fearon, James D. "Bargaining, Enforcement, and International Cooperation." *International Organization* 52, no. 2 (1998): 269–305.

Featherstone, Kevin. "Greece: When Populism Fails." *LSE European Politics and Policy Blog* (blog). London School of Economics and Political Science, June 25, 2015. http://eprints.lse.ac.uk/71152/.

Featherstone, Kevin. "The Greek Sovereign Debt Crisis and EMU: A Failing State in a Skewed Regime." *JCMS: Journal of Common Market Studies* 49, no. 2 (2011): 193–217.

Featherstone, Kevin, and Dimitris Papadimitriou. "Greece: A Crisis in Two-Level Governance." In *The European Union in Crisis*, edited by Desmond Dinan, Neill Nugent, and William E Patterson, 233–52. London: Palgrave MacMillan, 2017.

Feeny, Simon, Sasi Iamsiraroj, and Mark McGillivray. "Remittances and Economic Growth: Larger Impacts in Smaller Countries?" *Journal of Development Studies* 50, no. 8 (2014): 1055–66.

Ferdinand, Peter. "Westward Ho—The China Dream and 'One Belt, One Road': Chinese Foreign Policy under Xi Jinping." *International Affairs* 92, no. 4 (2016): 941–57.

Fernandes, Jorge M., Pedro C. Magalhães, and José Santana-Pereira. "Portugal's Leftist Government: From Sick Man to Poster Boy?" *South European Society and Politics* 23, no. 4 (October 2, 2018): 503–24. https://doi.org/10.1080/13608746.2018.1525914.

Fink, Christina. "Myanmar in 2018: The Rohingya Crisis Continues." *Asian Survey* 59, no. 1 (2019): 177–84.

Folch, Christine. *Hydropolitics: The Itaipu Dam, Sovereignty, and the Engineering of Modern South America*. Princeton, N.J.: Princeton University Press, 2019.

Fonseca, Pedro, and Maria João Ferreira. "Through 'Seas Never before Sailed': Portuguese Government Discursive Legitimation Strategies in a Context of Financial Crisis." *Discourse & Society* 26, no. 6 (2015): 682–711.

Fook, Lye Liang. "China-Malaysia Relations Back on Track?" *Perspective*. Singapore: ISEAS Yusof Ishak Institute, May 15, 2019. http://hdl.handle.net/11540/10256.

Fox, Annette Baker. *The Power of Small States: Diplomacy in World War II*. Chicago: University of Chicago Press, 1959.

Fraser, Alastair. "Zambia: Back to the Future." In *The Politics of Aid: African Strategies for Dealing with Donors*, edited by Lindsay Whitfield, 299–328. Oxford: Oxford University Press, 2008.

Freedman, Lawrence. "The Rise and Fall of Great Power Wars." *International Affairs* 95, no. 1 (January 1, 2019): 101–17. https://doi.org/10.1093/ia/iiy239.

Fridell, Gavin. "The Case against Cheap Bananas: Lessons from the EU-Caribbean Banana Agreement." *Critical Sociology* 37, no. 3 (2011): 285–307.

Friedman, Max Paul, and Tom Long. "Soft Balancing in the Americas: Latin American Opposition to U.S. Intervention, 1898–1936." *International Security* 40, no. 1 (2015): 120–56. https://doi.org/10.1162/ISEC_a_00212.

Fuchs, Andreas, and Nils-Hendrik Klann. "Paying a Visit: The Dalai Lama Effect on International Trade." *Journal of International Economics* 91, no. 1 (2013): 164–77.

Fuentes-Julio, Claudia. "Norm Entrepreneurs in Foreign Policy: How Chile Became an International Human Rights Promoter." *Journal of Human Rights* 19, no. 2 (2020): 256–74.

Fuser, Igor. "Conflitos e Contratos: A Petrobras, o Nacionalismo Boliviano e a Interdepedência Do Gás Natural (2002–2010)." PhD diss., Universidade de São Paulo, 2011.

Fuser, Igor. "O Mito Da 'generosidade' No Contencioso Brasil-Bolívia Do Gás Natural." *Tensões Mundiais* 10, nos. 18–19 (2014): 231–54.

Gaddis, John Lewis. "History, Grand Strategy and NATO Enlargement." *Survival* 40, no. 1 (1998): 145–51.

Gaddis, John Lewis. "The Long Peace: Elements of Stability in the Postwar International System." *International Security* 10, no. 4 (1986): 99–142.

Galbraith, Jean. "Trump Administration Takes Domestic and International Measures to Restrict Asylum." *American Journal of International Law* 113, no. 4 (2019): 833–42.

Ganguly, Sumit, and Andrew Scobell. "The Himalayan Impasse: Sino-Indian Rivalry in the Wake of Doklam." *Washington Quarterly* 41, no. 3 (2018): 177–90.

Ganguly, Sumit, and Brian Shoup. "Nepal: Between Dictatorship and Anarchy." *Journal of Democracy* 16, no. 4 (2005): 129–43.

Gardini, Gian Luca., and Maria Hermínia Tavares de Almeida, eds. *Foreign Policy Responses to the Rise of Brazil: Balancing Power in Emerging States*. New York: Palgrave Macmillan, 2016.

Gardinier, David E. "France and Gabon since 1993: The Reshaping of a Neo-Colonial Relationship." *Journal of Contemporary African Studies* 18, no. 2 (2000): 225–42.

Garrison, Jean A. "Framing Foreign Policy Alternatives in the Inner Circle: President Carter, His Advisors, and the Struggle for the Arms Control Agenda." *Political Psychology* 22, no. 4 (2001): 775–807.

Garrison, Jean A., and Ahad Abdurahmonov. "Explaining the Central Asian Energy Game: Complex Interdependence and How Small States Influence Their Big Neighbors." *Asian Perspective* 35, no. 3 (2011): 381–405.

Garver, John W. "China-India Rivalry in Nepal: The Clash over Chinese Arms Sales." *Asian Survey* 31, no. 10 (1991): 956–75.

Garzón, Jorge F. "Multipolarity and the Future of Economic Regionalism." *International Theory* 9, no. 1 (2016): 101–35. https://doi.org/10.1017/S1752971916000191.

George, Alexander L., and Andrew Bennett. *Case Studies and Theory Development in the Social Sciences*. Cambridge, MA: MIT Press, 2005.

Gerring, John. "What Is a Case Study and What Is It Good For?" *American Political Science Review* 98, no. 2 (2004): 341–54.

Gigleux, Victor. "Explaining the Diversity of Small States' Foreign Policies through Role Theory." *Third World Thematics: A TWQ Journal* 1, no. 1 (January 2, 2016): 27–45. https://doi.org/10.1080/23802014.2016.1184585.

Gissel, Line Engbo. "A Different Kind of Court: Africa's Support for the International Criminal Court, 1993–2003." *European Journal of International Law* 29, no. 3 (2018): 725–48.

Gleijeses, Piero. "The View from Havana: Lessons from Cuba's African Journey, 1959–1976." In *In from the Cold: Latin America's New Encounter with the Cold War*, edited by Gilbert M. Joseph and Daniela Spenser, 112–33. Durham, NC: Duke University Press, 2008.

Goddard, Stacie E. "Embedded Revisionism: Networks, Institutions, and Challenges to World Order." *International Organization* 72, no. 4 (2018): 763–97.

Goddard, Stacie E., Paul K. MacDonald, and Daniel H. Nexon. "Repertoires of Statecraft: Instruments and Logics of Power Politics." *International Relations* 33, no. 2 (March 17, 2019): 304–21. https://doi.org/10.1177/0047117819834625.

Goertz, Gary, Paul Francis Diehl, and Alexandru Balas. *The Puzzle of Peace: The Evolution of Peace in the International System*. New York: Oxford University Press, 2016.

Goetschel, Laurent. "The Foreign and Security Policy Interests of Small States in Today's Europe." In *Small States Inside and Outside the European Union*, edited by Laurent Goetschel, 13–31. Springer US, 1998. https://doi.org/10.1007/978-1-4757-2832-3_2.

Goetschel, Laurent, ed. *Small States inside and Outside the European Union: Interests and Policies*. Boston: Kluwer Academic Publishers, 1998.

Goh, Evelyn. "Great Powers and Hierarchical Order in Southeast Asia: Analyzing Regional Security Strategies." *International Security* 32, no. 3 (January 1, 2008): 113–57. https://doi.org/10.1162/isec.2008.32.3.113.

Goldgeier, James M. "NATO Expansion: The Anatomy of a Decision." *Washington Quarterly* 21, no. 1 (1998): 83–102.

Goldstein, Joshua S. *Winning the War on War: The Decline of Armed Conflict Worldwide*. Penguin, 2011.

Gómez-Mera, Laura, and Andrea Molinari. "Overlapping Institutions, Learning, and Dispute Initiation in Regional Trade Agreements: Evidence from South America." *International Studies Quarterly* 58, no. 2 (2014): 269–81.

Gong, Xue. "The Belt & Road Initiative and China's Influence in Southeast Asia." *Pacific Review* 32, no. 4 (July 4, 2019): 635–65. https://doi.org/10.1080/09512 748.2018.1513950.

González, Germán H., and Mariano F. Cabrera Romero. "El MERCOSUR y la Inserción Externa de Uruguay y Paraguay, 1994–2015." *Revista Aportes Para La Integración Latinoamericana*, no. 40 (2019): 1–26.

Gordon, Gretchen, and Aaron Luoma. "Oil and Gas: The Elusive Wealth beneath Their Feet." In *Dignity and Defiance: Stories from Bolivia's Challenge to Globalization*, edited by James Schultz and Melissa Draper, 46–116. Berkeley: University of California Press, 2008.

Græger, Nina. "From 'Forces for Good' to 'Forces for Status'? Small State Military Status Seeking." In *Small State Status Seeking: Norway's Quest for International Standing*, edited by Benjamin De Carvalho and Iver B. Neumann, 102–23. Abingdon: Routledge, 2014.

Grigas, Agnia Baranauskaite. "Explaining the Policies of the Baltic States towards Russia, 1994–2010," PhD diss., University of Oxford, 2011.

Grimm, Sven. "Aid Dependency as a Limitation to National Development Policy? The Case of Rwanda." In *African Agency in International Politics*, edited by William Brown and Sophie Harman, 81–96. Abingdon: Routledge, 2013.

Grobe, Christian. "The Power of Words: Argumentative Persuasion in International Negotiations." *European Journal of International Relations* 16, no. 1 (2010): 5–29.

Grynberg, Roman. *WTO at the Margins: Small States and the Multilateral Trading System*. New York: Cambridge University Press, 2006.

Grynberg, Roman, and Sacha Silva. "Harmonization without Representation: Small States, the Basel Committee, and the WTO." *World Development* 34, no. 7 (2006): 1223–36.

Guimarães, Feliciano de Sá. *A Theory of Master Role Transition: Small Powers and Regional Powers Dominant Roles*. Abingdon: Routledge, 2020.

Guimarães, Feliciano de Sá, and Martin Egon Maitino. "Socializing Brazil into Regional Leadership: The 2006 Bolivian Gas Crisis and the Role of Small Powers in Promoting Master Roles Transitions." *Foreign Policy Analysis* 15, no. 1: (2017): 1–20. https://doi.org/10.1093/fpa/orx010.

Gunn, Geoffrey C. "China's Globalization and the Belt and Road Project: The Case of Indonesia and Malaysia." In *China's Globalization and the Belt and Road Initiative*, edited by Jean A. Berlie, 123–38. Cham: Springer, 2020. https://doi.org/10.1007/978-3-030-22289-5_7.

Gutelius, David. "Islam in Northern Mali and the War on Terror." *Journal of Contemporary African Studies* 25, no. 1 (2007): 59–76.

Guzzini, Stefano. "The Concept of Power: A Constructivist Analysis." *Millennium-Journal of International Studies* 33, no. 3 (2005): 495–521.

Gvalia, Giorgi, David Siroky, Bidzina Lebanidze, and Zurab Iashvili. "Thinking Outside the Bloc: Explaining the Foreign Policies of Small States." *Security Studies* 22, no. 1 (January 1, 2013): 98–131. https://doi.org/10.1080/09636412.2013.757463.

Habeeb, William Mark. *Power and Tactics in International Negotiation: How Weak Nations Bargain with Strong Nations*. Baltimore, MD: Johns Hopkins University Press, 1988.

Hafner-Burton, Emilie M., Miles Kahler, and Alexander H. Montgomery. "Network Analysis for International Relations." *International Organization* 63, no. 3 (2009): 559–92. https://doi.org/10.1017/S0020818309090195.

Hafner-Burton, Emilie M., Edward D. Mansfield, and Jon C. W. Pevehouse. "Human Rights Institutions, Sovereignty Costs and Democratization." *British Journal of Political Science* 45, no. 1 (2015): 1–27.

Hall, Peter A. "Policy Paradigms, Social Learning, and the State: The Case of Economic Policymaking in Britain." *Comparative Politics* 25, no. 3 (1993), 275–96.

Hambleton, Ian R., Selvi M. Jeyaseelan, and Madhuvanti M. Murphy. "COVID-19 in the Caribbean Small Island Developing States: Lessons Learnt from Extreme Weather Events." *Lancet Global Health* 8, no. 9 (2020): e1114–15.

Hamilton, Daniel S. "The Baltics: Still Punching Above Their Weight." *Current History* 107, no. 707 (2008): 119–25.

Han, Enze. "Myanmar's Internal Ethnic Conflicts and Their Implications for China's Regional Grand Strategy." *Asian Survey* 60, no. 3 (June 1, 2020): 466–89. https://doi.org/10.1525/as.2020.60.3.466.

Handel, Michael I. *Weak States in the International System*. London; Totowa, NJ: F. Cass, 1981.

Hanrieder, Tine. *International Organization in Time: Fragmentation and Reform*. Oxford: Oxford University Press, 2015.

Hanson, Victor Davis. *The Landmark Thucydides: A Comprehensive Guide to the Peloponnesian War*. New York: Simon and Schuster, 1998.

Hardiman, Niamh, Calliope Spanou, Joaquim Filipe Araújo, and Muiris MacCarthaigh. "Tangling with the Troika: Domestic Ownership's Political and Administrative Engagement in Greece, Ireland, and Portugal." *Public Management Review* 21, no. 9 (2019): 1265–86.

Harding, Alan. "The Origins of the Concept of the State." *History of Political Thought* 15, no. 1 (1994): 57–72.

Harmer, Tanya. "The 'Cuban Question' and the Cold War in Latin America, 1959–1964." *Journal of Cold War Studies* 21, no. 3 (August 1, 2019): 114–51. https://doi.org/10.1162/jcws_a_00896.

Hart, Michael. *Decision at Midnight: Inside the Canada-US Free-Trade Negotiations*. Vancouver: UBC Press, 1994.

Hathaway, Oona A., and Scott J. Shapiro. *The Internationalists: How a Radical Plan to Outlaw War Remade the World*. Simon and Schuster, 2017.

Haugevik, Kristin. "Diplomacy through the Back Door: Norway and the Bilateral Route to EU Decision-Making." *Global Affairs* 3, no. 3 (May 27, 2017): 277–91. https://doi.org/10.1080/23340460.2017.1378586.

Haugevik, Kristin. *Special Relationships in World Politics: Inter-State Friendship and Diplomacy After the Second World War*. Abingdon: Routledge, 2018.

Haugevik, Kristin, and Pernille Rieker. "Autonomy or Integration? Small-State Responses to a Changing European Security Landscape." *Global Affairs* 3, no. 3 (2017): 211–21.

Haugevik, Kristin, and Ole Jacob Sending. "The Nordic Balance Revisited: Differentiation and the Foreign Policy Repertoires of the Nordic States." *Politics and Governance* 8, no. 4 (2020): 441–50.

Hayman, Rachel. "Rwanda: Milking the Cow: Creating Policy Space in Spite of Aid Dependence." In *The Politics of Aid: African Strategies for Dealing with Donors*, edited by Lindsay Whitfield, 156–84. Oxford: Oxford University Press, 2009.

Henke, Marina E. "Why Did France Intervene in Mali in 2013? Examining the Role of Intervention Entrepreneurs." *Canadian Foreign Policy Journal* 23, no. 3 (2017): 307–23.

Hennessy, Alexandra. "Good Samaritans vs. Hardliners: The Role of Credible Signalling in Greek Bailout Negotiations." *JCMS: Journal of Common Market Studies* 55, no. 4 (2017): 744–61.

Hey, Jeanne A. K. "Luxembourg: Where Small Works (and Wealthy Doesn't Hurt)." In *Small States in World Politics: Explaining Foreign Policy Behavior*, edited by Jeanne A. K. Hey, 75–94. Boulder: Lynne Rienner Publishers, 2003.

Hey, Jeanne A. K., ed. *Small States in World Politics: Explaining Foreign Policy Behavior*. Boulder, CO: Lynne Rienner Publishers, 2003.

Hiemstra, Nancy. "Pushing the US-Mexico Border South: United States' Immigration Policing throughout the Americas." *International Journal of Migration and Border Studies* 5, nos. 1–2 (2019): 44–63.

Hinnebusch, Raymond. "The Iraq War and International Relations: Implications for Small States." *Cambridge Review of International Affairs* 19, no. 3 (2006): 451–63.

Hirschman, Albert O. *National Power and the Structure of Foreign Trade*. Berkeley: University of California Press, 1980.

Hobson, John M., and Jason C. Sharman. "The Enduring Place of Hierarchy in World Politics: Tracing the Social Logics of Hierarchy and Political Change." *European Journal of International Relations* 11, no. 1 (2005): 63–98.

Högenauer, Anna-Lena, Külli Sarapuu, and Nicos Trimikliniotis. "Small States and the 'Corona Crisis.'" *Small States & Territories* 4, no. 1 (2021): 3–12.

Hopewell, Kristen. "The BRICS—Merely a Fable? Emerging Power Alliances in Global Trade Governance." *International Affairs* 93, no. 6 (2017): 1377–96.

Hopmann, P. Terrence. "Asymmetrical Bargaining in the Conference on Security and Cooperation in Europe." *International Organization* 32, no. 1 (2009): 141–77. https://doi.org/10.1017/S0020818300003891.

Hopmann, P. Terrence. "Two Paradigms of Negotiation: Bargaining and Problem Solving." *Annals of the American Academy of Political and Social Science* 542, no. 1 (1995): 24–47.

Hurrell, Andrew. *On Global Order: Power, Values, and the Constitution of International Society*. Oxford; New York: Oxford University Press, 2007.

Hurrell, Andrew. "One World? Many Worlds? The Place of Regions in the Study of International Society." *International Affairs* 83, no. 1 (2007): 127–46.

Ikenberry, G. John. *Liberal Leviathan: The Origins, Crisis, and Transformation of the American World Order*. Princeton, NJ: Princeton University Press, 2012.

Ikenberry, G. John, and Charles A. Kupchan. "Socialization and Hegemonic Power." *International Organization* 44, no. 3 (1990): 283–315.

Ikenberry, G. John, Michael Mastanduno, and William C. Wohlforth. "Unipolarity, State Behavior, and Systemic Consequences." *World Politics* 61, no. 1 (2009): 1–27.

Ingebritsen, Christine. "Norm Entrepreneurs: Scandinavia's Role in World Politics." *Cooperation and Conflict* 37, no. 1 (2002): 11–23.

Ingebritsen, Christine. *Scandinavia in World Politics*. Rowman & Littlefield, 2006.

Ingebritsen, Christine, Iver Neumann, Sieglinde Gstöhl, and Jessica Beyer, eds. *Small States in International Relations*. Seattle: University of Washington Press, 2006.

Iommi, Lucrecia García. "Al-Bashir Didn't Start the Fire: Diversity, Low Contestedness, and the Adoption of the Rome Statute of the International Criminal Court." *Cambridge Review of International Affairs* 34, no. 1 (2020): 105–36. https://doi.org/10.1080/09557 571.2020.1751070.

Istomin, Igor, and Irina Bolgova. "Transnistrian Strategy in the Context of Russian–Ukrainian Relations: The Rise and Failure of 'Dual Alignment.'" *Southeast European and Black Sea Studies* 16, no. 1 (2016): 169–94.

Jackson, Patrick Thaddeus, and Daniel H. Nexon. "Reclaiming the Social: Relationalism in Anglophone International Studies." *Cambridge Review of International Affairs* 32, no. 5 (2019): 582–600.

Jackson, Robert H. *Quasi-States: Sovereignty, International Relations and the Third World.* New York: Cambridge University Press, 1993.

Jackson, Sarita. "Small States and Compliance Bargaining in the WTO: An Analysis of the Antigua–US Gambling Services Case." *Cambridge Review of International Affairs* 25, no. 3 (2012): 367–85.

Jácome, Ana Isabel, and Carla Alvarez Velasco. "Ecuador: The Evolution of Drug Policies in the Middle of the World." In *Drug Policies and the Politics of Drugs in the Americas,* edited by Beatriz Caiuby Labate, Clancy Cavnar, and Thiago Rodrigues, 71–86. Cham: Springer, 2016.

Jakobsen, Peter Viggo. *Nordic Approaches to Peace Operations: A New Model in the Making.* Abingdon: Routledge, 2005.

Jakobsen, Peter Viggo. "Small States, Big Influence: The Overlooked Nordic Influence on the Civilian ESDP." *JCMS: Journal of Common Market Studies* 47, no. 1 (2009): 81–102.

Jakobsen, Peter Viggo. "Still Punching Above Their Weight? Nordic Cooperation in Peace Operations after the Cold War." *International Peacekeeping* 14, no. 4 (August 1, 2007): 458–75. https://doi.org/10.1080/13533310701427751.

Jakobsen, Peter Viggo. "The United Nations and the Nordic Four: Cautious Sceptics, Committed Believers, Cost-Benefit Calculators." In *The Routledge Handbook of Scandinavian Politics,* edited by Peter Nedergaard and Anders Wivel, 281–93. London: Routledge, 2018.

Jakobsen, Peter Viggo, Jens Ringsmose, and Håkon Lunde Saxi. "Prestige-Seeking Small States: Danish and Norwegian Military Contributions to US-Led Operations." *European Journal of International Security* 3, no. 2 (2018): 256–77.

Janis, Irving L. *Victims of Groupthink: A Psychological Study of Foreign-Policy Decisions and Fiascoes.* Boston: Houghton Mifflin, 1972.

Jargalsaikhan, Enkhsaikhan. "The Role of Small States in Promoting International Security: The Case of Mongolia." *Journal for Peace and Nuclear Disarmament* 1, no. 2 (July 3, 2018): 404–35. https://doi.org/10.1080/25751654.2018.1526628.

Jaschik, Kevin. "Small States and International Politics: Climate Change, the Maldives and Tuvalu." *International Politics* 51, no. 2 (2014): 272–93.

Jenne, Nicole. "Peacekeeping, Latin America and the UN Charter's Chapter VIII: Past Initiatives and Future Prospects." *International Peacekeeping* 26, no. 3 (2019): 327–53.

Jervis, Robert. "Hypotheses on Misperception." *World Politics* 20, no. 3 (1968): 454–79.

Jervis, Robert. "Unipolarity: A Structural Perspective." *World Politics* 61, no. 1 (2009): 188–213.

Jervis, Robert, Francis J. Gavin, Joshua Rovner, and Diane N. Labrosse, eds. *Chaos in the Liberal Order: The Trump Presidency and International Politics in the Twenty-First Century.* New York: Columbia University Press, 2018.

Jesse, Neal G., and John R. Dreyer. *Small States in the International System: At Peace and at War*. Lanham: Lexington Books, 2016.

Jetschke, Anja, Sören Münch, Adriana Rocío Cardozo-Silva, and Patrick Theiner. "Patterns of (Dis)Similarity in the Design of Regional Organizations: The Regional Organizations Similarity Index (ROSI)." *International Studies Perspectives* 22, no. 2 (2021): 181–200. https://doi.org/10.1093/isp/ekaa006.

Joachim, Jutta, and Natalia Dalmer. "The United Nations and Agenda Setting." In *Handbook of Public Policy Agenda Setting*, edited by Nikolaos Zahariadis, 367–87. Cheltenham: Edward Elgar Publishing, 2016.

Johnsen, Ingvild. "Gifts Favour the Giver: Norway, Status and the Nobel Peace Prize." In *Small State Status Seeking: Norway's Quest for International Standing*, edited by Benjamin De Carvalho and Iver Neumann, 124–41. Abingdon: Routledge, 2014.

Jones, David Martin, and Nicole Jenne. "Weak States' Regionalism: ASEAN and the Limits of Security Cooperation in Pacific Asia." *International Relations of the Asia-Pacific* 16, no. 2 (2016): 209–40.

Joseph, Callixtus. "Reflections from the Arms Trade Treaty: CARICOM Punching and Succeeding Above Its Weight." *Caribbean Journal of International Relations and Diplomacy* 1, no. 1 (2013): 93–109.

Joshi, Manoj. *Doklam: To Start at the Very Beginning*. ORF Special Report 40, New Delhi: Observer Research Foundation, (2017). https://www.orfonline.org/research/doklam-start-very-beginning/

Jourde, Cédric. "The International Relations of Small Neoauthoritarian States: Islamism, Warlordism, and the Framing of Stability." *International Studies Quarterly* 51, no. 2 (2007): 481–503.

Jupille, Joseph Henri, Joseph Jupille, Walter Mattli, and Duncan Snidal. *Institutional Choice and Global Commerce*. New York: Cambridge University Press, 2013.

Jurkynas, Mindaugas. "Security Concerns of the Baltic States in the Twenty-First Century." In *Small States and International Security*, edited by Clive Archer, Alyson J. K. Bailes, and Anders Wivel, 139–55. Abingdon: Routledge, 2014.

Kaarbo, Juliet. "A Foreign Policy Analysis Perspective on the Domestic Politics Turn in IR Theory." *International Studies Review* 17, no. 2 (2015): 189–216.

Kagan, Robert. "End of Dreams, Return of History." *Policy Review*, no. 144 (2007): 17.

Kamrava, Mehran. *Qatar: Small State, Big Politics*. Ithaca, NY: Cornell University Press, 2013.

Kang, David C. "Getting Asia Wrong: The Need for New Analytical Frameworks." *International Security* 27, no. 4 (2003): 57–85.

Kang, David C. "Hierarchy, Balancing, and Empirical Puzzles in Asian International Relations." *International Security* 28, no. 3 (2003): 165–80.

Kat, Quintijn B. "Subordinate-State Agency and US Hegemony: Colombian Consent versus Bolivian Dissent." *International Studies Review*, no. viaa025 (April 21, 2020). https://doi.org/10.1093/isr/viaa025.

Katzenstein, Peter J. *Small States in World Markets*. Ithaca, NY: Cornell University Press, 1985.

Kaufman, Stuart J., Richard Little, and William Curti Wohlforth. *The Balance of Power in World History*. Palgrave Macmillan, 2007.

Kaul, Nitasha. "Beyond India and China: Bhutan as a Small State in International Relations." *International Relations of the Asia-Pacific*, no. lcab010 (July 23, 2021). https://doi.org/10.1093/irap/lcab010.

Keene, Edward. "The Standard of 'Civilisation', the Expansion Thesis and the 19th-Century International Social Space." *Millennium* 42, no. 3 (2014): 651–73.

Kelly, Patrick William. *Sovereign Emergencies: Latin America and the Making of Global Human Rights Politics*. New York: Cambridge University Press, 2018.

Kennedy, Ryan. "The Limits of Soft Balancing: The Frozen Conflict in Transnistria and the Challenge to EU and NATO Strategy." *Small Wars & Insurgencies* 27, no. 3 (2016): 512–37.

Keohane, Robert O. "The Big Influence of Small Allies." *Foreign Policy*, no. 2 (1971): 161–82.

Keohane, Robert O. "Lilliputians' Dilemmas: Small States in International Politics." *International Organization* 23, no. 02 (1969): 291–310. https://doi.org/10.1017/S00208 1830003160X.

Keohane, Robert O., and Joseph S. Nye. *Power and Interdependence: World Politics in Transition*. Boston: Little, Brown, 1977.

Kharat, Rajesh S., and Chunku Bhutia. "Changing Dynamics of India–Bhutan Relations." In *India in South Asia: Challenges and Management*, edited by Amit Ranjan, 35–55. Singapore: Springer, 2019.

Kingdon, John W. *Agendas, Alternatives, and Public Policies*. Boston: Little, Brown, 1984.

Kirby, Jen. "How Chile Built One of the World's Most Successful Vaccination Campaigns." Vox, March 10, 2021. https://www.vox.com/22309620/chile-covid-19-vaccination-campaign.

Kirk, John M. "Cuban Medical Internationalism and Its Role in Cuban Foreign Policy." *Diplomacy & Statecraft* 20, no. 2 (2009): 275–90.

Knight, W. Andy, and K. Srikanth Reddy. "Caribbean Response to COVID-19: A Regional Approach to Pandemic Preparedness and Resilience." *Round Table* 109, no. 4 (2020): 164–65.

Knoerich, Jan, and Francisco Urdinez. "Contesting Contested Multilateralism: Why the West Joined the Rest in Founding the Asian Infrastructure Investment Bank." *Chinese Journal of International Politics* 12, no. 3 (Autumn 2019): 333–70. https://doi.org/10.1093/cjip/poz007.

Kong, Tat Yan. "China's Engagement-Oriented Strategy towards North Korea: Achievements and Limitations." *Pacific Review* 31, no. 1 (January 2, 2018): 76–95. https://doi.org/10.1080/09512748.2017.1316301.

Kragelund, Peter. "'Donors Go Home': Non-Traditional State Actors and the Creation of Development Space in Zambia." *Third World Quarterly* 35, no. 1 (2014): 145–62.

Krasner, Stephen D. *Sovereignty: Organized Hypocrisy*. Princeton, NJ: Princeton University Press, 1999.

Kuik, Cheng-Chwee. "Connectivity and Gaps: The Bridging Links and Missed Links of China's BRI in Southeast Asia." In *The Belt and Road Initiative and Global Governance*, edited by Maria A. Carrai, Jean-Christophe Defraigne, and Jan Wouters, 76–96. Cheltenham: Edward Elgar Publishing, 2020.

Kuik, Cheng-Chwee. "How Do Weaker States Hedge? Unpacking ASEAN States' Alignment Behavior towards China." *Journal of Contemporary China* 25, no. 100 (2016): 500–14.

Kuik, Cheng-Chwee. "Making Sense of Malaysia's China Policy: Asymmetry, Proximity, and Elite's Domestic Authority." *Chinese Journal of International Politics* 6, no. 4 (April 25, 2013): 429–67. https://doi.org/10.1093/cjip/pot006.

Kumar, Pranav. "Sino-Bhutanese Relations: Under the Shadow of India–Bhutan Friendship." *China Report* 46, no. 3 (2010): 243–52.

Kumar Sahu, Arun. "Future of India–Nepal Relations: Is China a Factor?" *Strategic Analysis* 39, no. 2 (2015): 197–204.

Kupchan, Charles. *No One's World: The West, the Rising Rest, and the Coming Global Turn.* New York: Oxford University Press, 2012.

Kuus, Merje. "European Integration in Identity Narratives in Estonia: A Quest for Security." *Journal of Peace Research* 39, no. 1 (2002): 91–108.

Kuzio, Taras. "NATO Enlargement: The View from the East." *European Security* 6, no. 1 (1997): 48–62.

Kyaw, Nyi Nyi. "Sinophobia in Myanmar and the Belt and Road Initiative." *Perspective.* Singapore: ISEAS Yusof Ishak Institute, February 13, 2020. https://www.iseas.edu.sg/images/pdf/ISEAS_Perspective_2020_9.pdf.

Lake, David A. *Hierarchy in International Relations.* Cornell University Press, 2009.

Lake, David A., and Angela O'Mahony. "The Incredible Shrinking State: Explaining Change in the Territorial Size of Countries." *Journal of Conflict Resolution* 48, no. 5 (2004): 699–722.

Lambert, Peter. "The Myth of the Good Neighbour: Paraguay's Uneasy Relationship with Brazil." *Bulletin of Latin American Research* 35, no. 1 (2016): 34–48.

Lanko, Dmitry. "The Regional Approach in the Policy of the Russian Federation towards the Republic of Estonia." *Baltic Region* 3, no. 17 (2013): 37–45. https://doi.org/10.5922/2079-8555-2013-3-4.

Lanteigne, Marc. "'The Rock That Can't Be Moved': China's Revised Geostrategies in Myanmar." *Pacific Review* 32, no. 1 (2019): 37–55.

Lauristin, Marju, and Peeter Vihalemm. "The Political Agenda during Different Periods of Estonian Transformation: External and Internal Factors." *Journal of Baltic Studies* 40, no. 1 (2009): 1–28.

Layne, Christopher. "This Time It's Real: The End of Unipolarity and the Pax Americana." *International Studies Quarterly* 56, no. 1 (2012): 203–13.

Le Gouriellec, Sonia. "Djibouti's Foreign Policy in International Institutions: The Big Diplomacy of a Small State." In *African Foreign Policies in International Institutions*, edited by Jason Warner and Timothy Shaw, 389–402. New York: Palgrave Macmillan, 2018.

Lebovic, James H., and Erik Voeten. "The Cost of Shame: International Organizations and Foreign Aid in the Punishing of Human Rights Violators." *Journal of Peace Research* 46, no. 1 (2009): 79–97.

Lecocq, Baz, and Paul Schrijver. "The War on Terror in a Haze of Dust: Potholes and Pitfalls on the Saharan Front." *Journal of Contemporary African Studies* 25, no. 1 (2007): 141–66.

Lee, Donna, and Nicola J. Smith. "The Political Economy of Small African States in the WTO." *Round Table* 97, no. 395 (2008): 259–71.

LeoGrande, William M. *Our Own Backyard: The United States in Central America, 1977–1992.* Chapel Hill: University of North Carolina Press, 1998.

Levy, Adam. "The European Union Border Assistance Mission (EUBAM) and the Remote Control Border: Managing Moldova." In *Europe in the World*, edited by Luiza Bialasiewicz, 153–83. Abingdon: Routledge, 2016.

Libman, Alexander, and Anastassia V. Obydenkova. "Regional International Organizations as a Strategy of Autocracy: The Eurasian Economic Union and Russian Foreign Policy." *International Affairs* 94, no. 5 (2018): 1037–58.

Lim, Darren J., Michalis Moutselos, and Michael McKenna. "Puzzled Out? The Unsurprising Outcomes of the Greek Bailout Negotiations." *Journal of European Public Policy* 26, no. 3 (2019): 325–43.

Lindsay-Poland, John. "US Military Bases in Latin America and the Caribbean." In *The Bases of Empire: The Global Struggle against US Military Posts*, edited by Catherine Lutz, 71–96. New York: NYU Press, 2009.

Lisi, Marco, and Vera Ramalhete. "Challenges and Opportunities Under Conditionality: Portugal." In *The Politics of the Eurozone Crisis in Southern Europe*, edited by Leonardo Morlino and Cecilia Emma Sottilotta, 173–201. Cham: Springer, 2020.

Little, Richard. *The Balance of Power in International Relations: Metaphors, Myths and Models*. New York: Cambridge University Press, 2007.

Liu, Hong, and Guanie Lim. "The Political Economy of a Rising China in Southeast Asia: Malaysia's Response to the Belt and Road Initiative." *Journal of Contemporary China* 28, no. 116 (2019): 216–31.

Livingston, Steven G. "The Politics of International Agenda-Setting: Reagan and North-South Relations." *International Studies Quarterly* 36, no. 3 (1992): 313–29.

Long, Tom. "Coloso Fragmentado: La Agenda 'Interméstica' y La Política Exterior Latinoamericana." *Foro Internacional* 57, no. 227 (January 2017): 5–54.

Long, Tom. "Historical Antecedents and Post-World War II Regionalism in the Americas." *World Politics* 72, no. 2 (2020): 214–53. https://doi.org/10.1017/S0043887119000194.

Long, Tom. "It's Not the Size, It's the Relationship: From 'Small States' to Asymmetry." *International Politics* 54, no. 2 (March 2017): 144–60. https://doi.org/10.1057/s41 311-017-0028-x.

Long, Tom. "Latin America and the Liberal International Order: An Agenda for Research." *International Affairs* 94, no. 6 (2018): 1371–90.

Long, Tom. *Latin America Confronts the United States: Asymmetry and Influence.* New York: Cambridge University Press, 2015.

Long, Tom. "Putting the Canal on the Map: Panamanian Agenda-Setting and the 1973 Security Council Meetings." *Diplomatic History* 38, no. 2 (2014): 431–55.

Long, Tom. "Small States, Great Power? Gaining Influence through Intrinsic, Derivative, and Collective Power." *International Studies Review* 19, no. 2 (2017): 185–205.

Long, Tom. "Small States in Central America." In *Handbook on the Politics of Small States*, edited by Godfrey Baldacchino and Anders Wivel, 242–58. Cheltenham: Edward Elgar Publishing, 2020.

Long, Tom, and Francisco Urdinez. "Status at the Margins: Why Paraguay Recognizes Taiwan and Shuns China." *Foreign Policy Analysis* 17, no. 1 (2021): oraa002, 1–22. https://doi.org/10.1093/fpa/oraa002.

Longley, Kyle. *The Sparrow and the Hawk: Costa Rica and the United States during the Rise of José Figueres*. Tuscaloosa: University of Alabama Press, 1997.

Lorca, Arnulf Becker. *Mestizo International Law*. Cambridge: Cambridge University Press, 2014.

Loveman, Brian. *Addicted to Failure: U.S. Security Policy in Latin America and the Andean Region*. Latin American Silhouettes. Lanham, MD: Rowman & Littlefield Publishers, 2006.

Luik, Juri, and Henrik Praks. "Boosting the Deterrent Effect of Allied Enhanced Forward Presence." Tallinn, Estonia: International Centre for Defence and Security, 2017. https://icds.ee/wp-content/uploads/2017/ICDS_Policy_Paper_Boosting_the_Deterre nt_Effect_of_Allied_eFP.pdf.

Lukes, Steven. *Power: A Radical View*. Vol. 1. London Macmillan, 1974.

Lupel, Adam, and Lauri Mälksoo. "Necessary Voice: Small States, International Law, and the UN Security Council." International Peace Institute, 2019.

Lupu Dinesen, Ruxandra, and Anders Wivel. "Georgia and Moldova: Caught in the Outskirts of Europe?" In *Small States and International Security: Europe and Beyond*, edited by Clive Archer, Alyson J. K. Bailes, and Anders Wivel, 149–66. Abingdon: Routledge, 2014.

Maass, Matthias. "The Elusive Definition of the Small State." *International Politics* 46, no. 1 (2009): 65–83.

Maass, Matthias. *Small States in World Politics: The Story of Small State Survival, 1648–2016*. Manchester: Manchester University Press, 2017.

Maass, Matthias. "Small States: Survival and Proliferation." *International Politics* 51, no. 6 (2014): 709–28.

Magalhães, Pedro C. "The Elections of the Great Recession in Portugal: Performance Voting under a Blurred Responsibility for the Economy." *Journal of Elections, Public Opinion & Parties* 24, no. 2 (2014): 180–202.

Magnúsdóttir, Gunnhildur Lily, and Baldur Thorhallsson. "The Nordic States and Agenda-Setting in the European Union: How Do Small States Score?" *Icelandic Review of Politics and Administration/Stjornmal Og Stjornsysla* 1, no. 7 (2011): 205–25.

Maipose, Gervase. "Botswana: The African Success Story." In *The Politics of Aid: African Strategies for Dealing with Donors*, edited by Lindsay Whitfield, 108–30. Oxford: Oxford University Press, 2009.

Malik, Arif Hussain, and Nazir Ahmad Sheikh. "Changing Dynamics of Indo-Bhutan Relations: Implications for India." *International Journal of Political Science and Development* 4, no. 2 (2016): 44–53.

Malik, J. Mohan. "Myanmar's Role in China's Maritime Silk Road Initiative." In *China's Maritime Silk Road Initiative and Southeast Asia Dilemmas, Doubts, and Determination*, edited by Jean-Marc F. Blanchard, 133–62. Singapore: Palgrave MacMillan, 2019.

Mälksoo, Maria. "NATO's New Strategic Concept: What Is at Stake for Estonia?" Policy Paper. Tallin, Estonia: International Centre for Defence Studies, November 2008. https://icds.ee/en/policy-paper-on-natos-new-strategic-concept/.

Männik, Erik. "Small States: Invited to NATO—Able to Contribute?" *Defense & Security Analysis* 20, no. 1 (2004): 21–37.

Mansbach, Richard W., and John A. Vasquez. *In Search of Theory: A New Paradigm for Global Politics*. New York: Columbia University Press, 1981.

Mantilla, Giovanni. "Forum Isolation: Social Opprobrium and the Origins of the International Law of Internal Conflict." *International Organization* 72, no. 2 (2018): 317–49.

Mantilla, Giovanni. "Social Pressure and the Making of Wartime Civilian Protection Rules." *European Journal of International Relations* 26, no. 2 (2020): 443–68.

Maoz, Zeev. "Framing the National Interest: The Manipulation of Foreign Policy Decisions in Group Settings." *World Politics* 43, no. 1 (1990): 77–110.

Marchal, Roland. "Briefing: Military (Mis)Adventures in Mali." *African Affairs* 112, no. 448 (2013): 486–97.

Maris, Georgios, and Pantelis Sklias. "European Integration and Asymmetric Power: Dynamics and Change in the EMU." *European Politics and Society* 21, no. 5 (2020): 634–39.

Marriage, Zoë. "Aid to Rwanda: Unstoppable Rock, Immovable Post." In *Aid and Authoritarianism in Africa: Development without Democracy*, edited by Tobias Hagmann and Filip Reyntjens, 44–66. London: Zed Books, 2016.

Martin, Lisa L. "International Institutions: Weak Commitments and Costly Signals." *International Theory* 9, no. 3 (2017): 353–80. https://doi.org/10.1017/S175297191 7000082.

Mason, Ra. "Djibouti and Beyond: Japan's First Post-War Overseas Base and the Recalibration of Risk in Securing Enhanced Military Capabilities." *Asian Security* 14, no. 3 (2018): 339–57.

Mattern, Janice Bially, and Ayşe Zarakol. "Hierarchies in World Politics." *International Organization* 70, no. 3 (2016): 623–54. https://doi.org/10.1017/S0020818316000126.

Mazumdar, Arijit. "Bhutan's Military Action against Indian Insurgents." *Asian Survey* 45, no. 4 (2005): 566–80.

Mazumdar, Arijit. *Indian Foreign Policy in Transition: Relations with South Asia*. Abingdon: Routledge, 2014.

Mazumdar, Arijit. "India's South Asia Policy in the Twenty-First Century: New Approach, Old Strategy." *Contemporary Politics* 18, no. 3 (2012): 286–302.

Mcconaughey, Meghan, Paul Musgrave, and Daniel H. Nexon. "Beyond Anarchy: Logics of Political Organization, Hierarchy, and International Structure." *International Theory* 10, no. 2 (2018): 181–218. https://doi.org/10.1017/S1752971918000040.

McDougall, Derek, and Suan Ee Ong. "Introduction: COVID-19 and Commonwealth Countries." *Round Table* 110, no. 1 (January 2, 2021): 10–15. https://doi.org/10.1080/00358533.2021.1875663.

McGregor, Ian, and Hilary Yerbury. "Politics of Rising Tides: Governments and Nongovernmental Organizations in Small-Island Developing States." In *Climate Change and Ocean Governance: Politics and Policy for Threatened Seas*, edited by Paul G. Harris, 118–32. Cambridge: Cambridge University Press, 2019. https://doi.org/10.1017/9781108502238.008.

Mearsheimer, John J. "Back to the Future: Instability in Europe after the Cold War." *International Security* 15, no. 1 (1990): 5–56.

Mearsheimer, John J. "Bound to Fail: The Rise and Fall of the Liberal International Order." *International Security* 43, no. 4 (2019): 7–50.

Mearsheimer, John J. "The False Promise of International Institutions." *International Security* 19, no. 3 (1994): 5–49.

Mesfin, Berouk. "The Eritrea-Djibouti Border Dispute." Pretoria, South Africa: Institute for Security Studies, 2009. https://www.africaportal.org/publications/the-eritrea-djibouti-border-dispute/.

Meyer, Peter J. "Honduras: Background and U.S. Relations." Washington, DC: Congressional Research Service, July 22, 2019. https://fas.org/sgp/crs/row/RL34027.pdf.

Mezhevich, Nikolai M. "Russia and the Baltic States: Some Results and a Few Perspectives." *Baltic Region* 2, no. 24 (2015): 4–12.

Miklian, Jason. "International Media's Role on U.S.–Small State Relations: The Case of Nepal." *Foreign Policy Analysis* 4, no. 4 (2008): 399–418. https://doi.org/10.1111/j.1743-8594.2008.00077.x.

Mills, Kurt, and Alan Bloomfield. "African Resistance to the International Criminal Court: Halting the Advance of the Anti-Impunity Norm." *Review of International Studies* 44, no. 1 (2018): 101–27.

Milner, Helen. "The Assumption of Anarchy in International Relations Theory: A Critique." *Review of International Studies* 17, no. 1 (1991): 67–85.

Milton-Edwards, Beverley. "The Blockade on Qatar: Conflict Management Failings." *International Spectator* 55, no. 2 (2020): 34–48.

Mintz, Alex, and Steven B. Redd. "Framing Effects in International Relations." *Synthese* 135, no. 2 (2003): 193–213.

Mohammadzadeh, Babak. "Status and Foreign Policy Change in Small States: Qatar's Emergence in Perspective." *International Spectator* 52, no. 2 (2017): 19–36.

Momodu, Raheemat. "Nationalism Underpinned by Pan-Regionalism: African Foreign Policies in ECOWAS in an Era of Anti-Globalization." In *African Foreign Policies in International Institutions*, edited by Jason Warner and Timothy M. Shaw, 95–112. New York: Palgrave Macmillan, 2018.

Moncrieff, Richard. "French Relations with Sub Saharan Africa under President Sarkozy," Occasional Paper No. 107, Johannesburg: South African Institute of International Affairs, 2012.

Moon, Bruce E. "The Foreign Policy of the Dependent State." *International Studies Quarterly* 27, no. 3 (1983): 315–40. https://doi.org/10.2307/2600686.

Moon, Chung-in. "Complex Interdependence and Transnational Lobbying: South Korea in the United States." *International Studies Quarterly* 32, no. 1 (1988): 67–89.

Moore, Gregory J. "The Power of 'Sacred Commitments': Chinese Interests in Taiwan." *Foreign Policy Analysis* 12, no. 2 (2016): 214–35.

Moraes, Henrique Choer. "Beyond a Seat at the Table: Participation and Influence in Global Governance." *Global Governance: A Review of Multilateralism and International Organizations* 25, no. 4 (2019): 563–86.

Moravcsik, Andrew. "The Origins of Human Rights Regimes: Democratic Delegation in Postwar Europe." *International Organization* 54, no. 2 (2000): 217–52.

Morgenthau, Hans J. *Politics among Nations: The Struggle for Power and Peace.* New York: Knopf, 1968.

Mörike, Andrea. "The Military as a Political Actor in Russia: The Cases of Moldova and Georgia." *International Spectator* 33, no. 3 (1998): 119–31.

Morlino, Leonardo, and Cecilia Sottilotta, eds. *The Politics of the Eurozone Crisis in Southern Europe: A Comparative Reappraisal.* Cham: Palgrave MacMillan, 2019.

Moschella, Manuela. "When Some Are More Equal Than Others: National Parliaments and Intergovernmental Bailout Negotiations in the Eurozone." *Government and Opposition* 52, no. 2 (2017): 239–65. https://doi.org/10.1017/gov.2016.49.

Moury, Catherine, and Adam Standring. "'Going beyond the Troika': Power and Discourse in Portuguese Austerity Politics." *European Journal of Political Research* 56, no. 3 (2017): 660–79.

Müller, Harald. "Arguing, Bargaining and All That: Communicative Action, Rationalist Theory and the Logic of Appropriateness in International Relations." *European Journal of International Relations* 10, no. 3 (2004): 395–435.

Murton, Galen, and Austin Lord. "Trans-Himalayan Power Corridors: Infrastructural Politics and China's Belt and Road Initiative in Nepal." *Political Geography* 77 (2020): 102100.

Musgrave, Paul. "Asymmetry, Hierarchy, and the Ecclesiastes Trap." *International Studies Review* 21, no. 2 (2019): 284–300.

Myint, U. "'Thinking, Fast and Slow' on the Belt and Road: Myanmar's Experience with China." *Perspective.* Singapore: ISEAS Yusof Ishak Institute, October 29, 2019. https://www.iseas.edu.sg/images/pdf/ISEAS_Perspective_2019_90.pdf.

Nantulya, Paul. "Chinese Hard Power Supports Its Growing Strategic Interests in Africa." *Africa Center for Strategic Studies* (blog), January 2019. https://africacenter.org/spotli ght/chinese-hard-power-supports-its-growing-strategic-interests-in-africa/.

Neumann, I. B., S. Gstöhl, C. Ingebritsen, I. Neumann, and J. Beyer. *Small States in International Relations*, Seattle: University of Washington Press, 2006.

Neumann, Iver, and Sieglinde Gstöhl. "Lilliputians in Gulliver's World?" In *Small States in International Relations*, edited by Christine Ingebritsen, Iver Neumann, Sieglinde Gstöhl, and Jessica Beyer, 3–36. Seattle: University of Washington Press, 2006.

Neustadt, Richard E. *Presidential Power: The Politics of Leadership from F.D.R. to Carter.* New York: Wiley, 1980.

Newhouse, John. "Diplomacy, Inc.: The Influence of Lobbies on U.S. Foreign Policy." *Foreign Affairs* 88, no. 3 (May/June 2009): 73–92.

Nexon, Daniel H. "Relationalism and New Systems Theory." In *New Systems Theories of World Politics*, edited by Mathias Albert, Lars-Erik Cederman, and Alexander Wendt, 99–126. New York: Palgrave Macmillan.

Nga, Le Thi Hang, Tran Xuan Hiep, Dang Thu Thuy, and Ha Le Huyen. "India–Bhutan Treaties of 1949 and 2007: A Retrospect." *India Quarterly* 75, no. 4 (2019): 441–55.

Nickson, R. Andrew. "The Itaipu Hydro-Electric Project: The Paraguayan Perspective." *Bulletin of Latin American Research* 2, no. 1 (1982): 1–20.

Nordin, Astrid H. M., and Mikael Weissmann. "Will Trump Make China Great Again? The Belt and Road Initiative and International Order." *International Affairs* 94, no. 2 (2018): 231–49.

Noyes, Alexander. "The Role of African Regional Organizations in Post-Election Governments of National Unity." In *African Foreign Policies in International Institutions*, edited by Jason Warner and Timothy M. Shaw, 79–93. New York: Palgrave Macmillan, 2018.

Nurse, Leonard. A., Roger F. McLean, John Agard, Lino Briguglio, Virginie Duvat-Magnan, Netatua Pelesikoti, Emma Tompkins, and Arthur Webb. "Small Islands." In *Climate Change 2014: Impacts, Adaptation, and Vulnerability, Part B, Regional Aspects*, 1613–54. Contribution of Working Group II to the Fifth Assessment Report of the Intergovernmental Panel on Climate Change. Cambridge: Cambridge University Press, 2014. https://www.um.edu.mt/library/oar/bitstream/123456789/42142/1/Sma ll_islands_2014.pdf.

O'Driscoll, Mervyn, and Jamie Walsh. "Ireland and the 1975 NPT Review Conference: Norm-Building and the Role of Small States." *Irish Studies in International Affairs* 25 (2014): 101–16.

Oh, Yoon Ah. "Power Asymmetry and Threat Points: Negotiating China's Infrastructure Development in Southeast Asia." *Review of International Political Economy* 25, no. 4 (2018): 530–52.

Onuf, Nicholas Greenwood. *The Republican Legacy in International Thought.* Cambridge: Cambridge University Press, 1998.

Oomen, Barbara. *Rights for Others: The Slow Home-Coming of Human Rights in the Netherlands.* Cambridge: Cambridge University Press, 2014.

Öövel, Andrus. "Estonian Defence Policy, NATO and the European Union." *Security Dialogue* 27, no. 1 (1996): 65–68.

Osiander, Andreas. "Sovereignty, International Relations, and the Westphalian Myth." *International Organization* 55, no. 2 (2001): 251–87.

Oskanian, Kevork. "The Balance Strikes Back: Power, Perceptions, and Ideology in Georgian Foreign Policy, 1992–2014." *Foreign Policy Analysis* 12, no. 4 (2016): 628–52.

O'Sullivan, Kevin. "Between Internationalism and Empire: Ireland, the 'Like-Minded' Group, and the Search for a New International Order, 1974–82." *International History Review* 37, no. 5 (2015): 1083–1101.

Ourbak, Timothée, and Alexandre K. Magnan. "The Paris Agreement and Climate Change Negotiations: Small Islands, Big Players." *Regional Environmental Change* 18, no. 8 (2018): 2201–7.

Pace, Roderick. "Malta and EU Membership: Overcoming 'Vulnerabilities', Strengthening 'Resilience.'" *European Integration* 28, no. 1 (2006): 33–49.

Pakiam, Geoffrey K. "Malaysia in 2018: The Year of Voting Dangerously." *Southeast Asian Affairs* 2019, no. 1 (2019): 194–210.

Panke, Diana. "Dwarfs in International Negotiations: How Small States Make Their Voices Heard." *Cambridge Review of International Affairs* 25, no. 3 (2012): 313–28.

Panke, Diana. "Regional Cooperation through the Lenses of States: Why Do States Nurture Regional Integration?" *Review of International Organizations* 15, no. 2 (2020): 475–504.

Panke, Diana. "Small States in EU Decision-Making: How Can They Be Effective?" In *Small States in the Modern World*, edited by Harald Baldersheim and Michael Keating, 59–72. Cheltenham: Edward Elgar Publishing, 2015.

Panke, Diana. "Small States in EU Negotiations: Political Dwarfs or Power-Brokers?" *Cooperation and Conflict* 46, no. 2 (2011): 123–43.

Panke, Diana. "Small States in Multilateral Negotiations: What Have We Learned?" *Cambridge Review of International Affairs* 25, no. 3 (2012): 387–98.

Panke, Diana. *Small States in the European Union: Coping with Structural Disadvantages.* Farnham: Ashgate Publishing, 2010.

Panke, Diana. "Studying Small States in International Security Affairs: A Quantitative Analysis." *Cambridge Review of International Affairs* 30, nos. 2–3 (2017): 235–55.

Panke, Diana, and Julia Gurol. "Small States as Agenda-setters? The Council Presidencies of Malta and Estonia." *Journal of Common Market Studies* 56, no. S1 (2018): 142–51.

Panke, Diana, and Julia Gurol. "Small States: Challenges and Coping Strategies in the UN General Assembly." In *Handbook on the Politics of Small States*, edited by Godfrey Baldacchino and Anders Wivel, 83–97. Cheltenham: Edward Elgar Publishing, 2020.

Pant, Harsh V. "Delhi Needs to Up Its Game with Smaller Neighbours." DNA, February 5, 2013. https://www.dnaindia.com/analysis/report-delhi-needs-to-up-its-game-with-smaller-neighbours-1796350.

Parmar, Inderjeet. "The US-Led Liberal Order: Imperialism by Another Name?" *International Affairs* 94, no. 1 (2018): 151–72. https://doi.org/10.1093/ia/iix240.

Parthenay, Kevin. "Uniting (regionally) against Covid-19: Sica and Caricom." *Foro Internacional* 61, no. 2 (2021): 387–425.

Pastor, Robert A. *Exiting the Whirlpool: U.S. Foreign Policy toward Latin America and the Caribbean.* Boulder, CO: Westview Press, 2001.

Pastor, Robert A. *Not Condemned to Repetition: The United States and Nicaragua.* Boulder, CO: Westview Press, 2002.

Paul, T. V. "When Balance of Power Meets Globalization: China, India and the Small States of South Asia." *Politics* 39, no. 1 (2019): 50–63.

Paul, T. V., Deborah Welch Larson, and William C. Wohlforth, eds. *Status in World Politics.* New York: Cambridge University Press, 2014.

Pedersen, Rasmus Brun. "Bandwagon for Status: Changing Patterns in the Nordic States Status-Seeking Strategies?" *International Peacekeeping* 25, no. 2 (2018): 217–41.

Pedi, Revecca, and Katerina Sarri. "From the 'Small but Smart State' to the 'Small and Entrepreneurial State': Introducing a Framework for Effective Small State Strategies within the EU and Beyond." *Baltic Journal of European Studies* 9, no. 1 (2019): 3–19.

Pedi, Revecca, and Anders Wivel. "Small State Diplomacy after the Corona Crisis." *Hague Journal of Diplomacy* 15, no. 4 (October 12, 2020): 611–23. https://doi.org/10.1163/1871191X-BJA10044.

Pegg, Scott. *International Society and the De Facto State*. Aldershot: Ashgate, 1998.

Pelling, Mark, and Juha I. Uitto. "Small Island Developing States: Natural Disaster Vulnerability and Global Change." *Global Environmental Change Part B: Environmental Hazards* 3, no. 2 (2001): 49–62.

Penjore, Dorji. "Security of Bhutan: Walking between the Giants." *Journal of Bhutan Studies* 10, (Summer 2004): 108–31.

Pereira, Paulo T., and Lara Wemans. "Portugal and the Global Financial Crisis: Short-Sighted Politics, Deteriorating Public Finances and the Bailout Imperative." In *The Global Financial Crisis and Its Budget Impacts in OECD Nations*, edited by John Wanna, Evert A. Lindquist, and Jouke de Vries, 231–54. Cheltenham: Edward Elgar Publishing, 2015.

Perju, Diana, and Rodica Crudu. "The Evolution of Economic Relations between the Republic of Moldova and the European Union in the Period of 2007–2018." *CSIE Working Papers*, no. 12 (2019): 67–83.

Perreault, Thomas. "From the *Guerra del Agua* to the *Guerra del Gas*: Resource Governance, Neoliberalism and Popular Protest in Bolivia." *Antipode* 38, no. 1 (2006): 150–72.

Persaud, Randolph B. *Counter-Hegemony and Foreign Policy: The Dialectics of Marginalized and Global Forces in Jamaica*. Albany: State University of New York Press, 2001.

Philpott, Daniel. *Revolutions in Sovereignty: How Ideas Shaped Modern International Relations*. Princeton, NJ: Princeton University Press, 2001.

Pi Ferrer, Laia, and Hanna Rautajoki. "Navigating Coercion in Political Rhetoric: Shifting Strategies to Cope with Intervention by the Troika in Portugal." *Contemporary Politics* 26, no. 2 (2020): 206–25. https://doi.org/10.1080/13569775.2019.1663394.

Pierson, P. "Increasing Returns, Path Dependence, and the Study of Politics." *American Political Science Review* 94 (2000): 251–68.

Pierson, Paul. "When Effect Becomes Cause: Policy Feedback and Political Change." *World Politics* 45, no. 4 (1993): 595–628.

Popescu, Nicu. "The EU in Moldova: Settling Conflicts in the Neighbourhood." Occasional Paper No. 60, Paris: European Institute for Security Studies, 2005.

Porter, Patrick. *The False Promise of Liberal Order: Nostalgia, Delusion and the Rise of Trump*. New York: John Wiley & Sons, 2020.

Powell, Robert. "Bargaining Theory and International Conflict." *Annual Review of Political Science* 5, no. 1 (2002): 1–30.

Praks, Henrik. "Estonia's First Steps in the Direction of NATO and National Defence." *Eesti Sõjaajaloo Aastaraamat* 4, no. 1 (2014): 113–41.

Rabe, Stephen G. *The Killing Zone: The United States Wages Cold War in Latin America*. New York: Oxford University Press, 2011.

Rakner, Lise. *Political and Economic Liberalisation in Zambia 1991–2001*. Nordic Africa Institute, 2003.

Rakner, Lise, Nicolas van de Walle, and Dominic Mulaisho. "Zambia." In *Aid and Reform in Africa: Lessons from Ten Case Studies*, edited by Shantayanan Devarajan, David R. Dollar, and Torgny Holmgren, 533–623. Washington, DC: World Bank, 2001. https://openknowledge.worldbank.org/handle/10986/13894.

Ramachandran, Sudha. "India, Bhutan: No More Unequal Treaties." *Asia Times*, 2007. https://www.worldsecuritynetwork.com/India/Ramachandran-Sudha/India-Bhutan-No-more-unequal-treaties.

Ranjan, Amit. *India in South Asia: Challenges and Management*. Singapore: Springer, 2019.

Rasheed, Athaulla A. "Role of Small Islands in UN Climate Negotiations: A Constructivist Viewpoint." *International Studies* 56, no. 4 (2019): 215–35.

Ratuva, Steven. "Aid and Foreign Policy: New Zealand Development Assistance in the Pacific." In *Small States and the Changing Global Order: New Zealand Faces the Future*, edited by Anne-Marie Brady, 55–73. Cham: Springer, 2019. https://doi.org/10.1007/978-3-030-18803-0_4.

Read, Robert. "The Implications of Increasing Globalization and Regionalism for the Economic Growth of Small Island States." *World Development* 32, no. 2 (2004): 365–78.

Reich, Simon, and Peter Dombrowski. "The Consequence of COVID-19: How the United States Moved from Security Provider to Security Consumer." *International Affairs* 96, no. 5 (September 1, 2020): 1253–79. https://doi.org/10.1093/ia/iiaa136.

Renwick, Neil. "Global Society's Response to HIV/AIDS: Botswana's Experience." *Global Society* 21, no. 2 (2007): 133–53.

Resnick, Evan N. *Allies of Convenience: A Theory of Bargaining in U.S. Foreign Policy*. New York: Columbia University Press, 2019. https://doi.org/10.7312/resn19058.

Reyntjens, Filip. "Constructing the Truth, Dealing with Dissent, Domesticating the World: Governance in Post-Genocide Rwanda." *African Affairs* 110, no. 438 (2011): 1–34.

Reyntjens, Filip. "Understanding Rwandan Politics through the Longue Durée: From the Precolonial to the Post-Genocide Era." *Journal of Eastern African Studies* 12, no. 3 (2018): 514–32. https://doi.org/10.1080/17531055.2018.1462985.

Rickli, Jean-Marc. "European Small States' Military Policies after the Cold War: From Territorial to Niche Strategies." *Cambridge Review of International Affairs* 21, no. 3 (2008): 307–25.

Riim, Toomas. "Estonia and NATO: A Constructivist View on a National Interest and Alliance Behaviour." *Baltic Security & Defence Review* 8 (2006): 34–52.

Riquelme, Marcial Antonio. "Toward a Weberian Characterization of the Stroessner Regime in Paraguay (1954–1989)." *Revista Europea de Estudios Latinoamericanos y Del Caribe/European Review of Latin American and Caribbean Studies* 57 (1994): 29–51.

Risse-Kappen, Thomas. *Cooperation among Democracies: The European Influence on U.S. Foreign Policy*. Princeton Studies in International History and Politics. Princeton, NJ: Princeton University Press, 1995.

Rivera, Luis Guillermo Solís, and Francisco Rojas Aravena. "Central America and the United States." In *Latin American Nations in World Politics*, edited by Heraldo Muñoz and Joseph S. Tulchin, 105–28. New York: Routledge, 2018 [1996].

Rizal, Dhurba. "Bhutan–India Relations: The Shifting Bhutanese Perceptions and Geopolitical Gambit." In *India in South Asia: Challenges and Management*, edited by Amit Ranjan, 153–72. Singapore: Springer, 2019.

Rocha, Fernando, and Alan Stoleroff. "The Challenges of the Crisis and the External Intervention in Portugal." In *The New EU Economic Governance and Its Impact on the National Collective Bargaining Systems*, edited by Fernando Rocha, 150–73. Madrid: Fundación 1º de Mayo, 2014.

Rojas, Gustavo, and Lucas Arce. "La Renegociación de Itaipú: Una Nueva Oportunidad Para El Paraguay." *Meridiano 47-Boletim de Análise de Conjuntura Em Relações Internacionais*, no. 110 (2009): 19–21.

Rolls, Mark G. "Like-Minded States: New Zealand–ASEAN Relations in the Changing Asia-Pacific Strategic Environment." In *Small States and the Changing Global Order: New Zealand Faces the Future*, edited by Anne-Marie Brady, 165–77. Cheltenham: Springer, 2019. https://doi.org/10.1007/978-3-030-18803-0_10.

Rosenberg, Mark B., and Luis G. Solís. *The United States and Central America: Geopolitical Realities and Regional Fragility*. New York: Routledge, 2007.

Rosenthal, Gert. *Inside the United Nations: Multilateral Diplomacy Up Close.* Routledge, 2017.

Ross, Robert S. "On the Fungibility of Economic Power: China's Economic Rise and the East Asian Security Order." *European Journal of International Relations* 25, no. 1 (2019): 302–27.

Rothstein, Robert L. *Alliances and Small Powers*. New York: Columbia University Press, 1968.

Russell, Roberto, and Juan Gabriel Tokatlian. "From Antagonistic Autonomy to Relational Autonomy: A Theoretical Reflection from the Southern Cone." *Latin American Politics and Society* 45, no. 1 (2003): 1–24. https://doi.org/10.2307/3177061.

Sabato, Hilda. *Republics of the New World: The Revolutionary Political Experiment in Nineteenth-Century Latin America*. Princeton, NJ: Princeton University Press, 2018.

Saltalamacchia Ziccardi, Natalia. "Regional Multilateralism in Latin America: UNASUR, ALBA and CELAC." In *Routledge Handbook of Latin America in the World*, edited by Jorge I. Domínguez and Ana Covarrubias Velasco, 310–22. New York: Routledge, 2014.

Sanchez, W. Alejandro. "The 'Frozen' Southeast: How the Moldova-Transnistria Question Has Become a European Geo-Security Issue." *Journal of Slavic Military Studies* 22, no. 2 (2009): 153–76.

Sanders, James E. *The Vanguard of the Atlantic World: Creating Modernity, Nation, and Democracy in Nineteenth-Century Latin America*. Durham, NC: Duke University Press, 2014.

Sandler, Todd. "Regional Public Goods and International Organizations." *Review of International Organizations* 1, no. 1 (2006): 5–25.

Santa-Cruz, Arturo. *US Hegemony and the Americas: Power and Economic Statecraft in International Relations*. Abingdon: Routledge, 2019.

Santos, Sergio Caballero. "Brasil y La Región: Una Potencia Emergente y La Integración Regional Sudamericana." *Revista Brasileira de Política Internacional* 54, no. 2 (2011): 158–72.

Saraiva, Miriam Gomes. "Brazil's Rise and Its Soft Power Strategy in South America." In *Foreign Policy Responses to the Rise of Brazil: Balancing Power in Emerging States*, edited by Gian Luca Gardini and Tavares de Almeida Maria Herminia, 46–61. New York: Palgrave Macmillan, 2016.

Sarapuu, Külli, and Tiina Randma-Liiv. "Small States: Public Management and Policy-Making." In *Handbook on the Politics of Small States*, edited by Godfrey Baldacchino and Anders Wivel, 55–69. Cheltenham: Edward Elgar Publishing, 2020.

Schelling, Thomas C. *The Strategy of Conflict*. Cambridge, MA: Harvard University Press, 1980.

Schenoni, Luis Leandro. "The Argentina-Brazil Regional Power Transition." *Foreign Policy Analysis* 14, no. 4 (2018): 469–89. https://doi.org/10.1093/fpa/orx008.

Scheufele, Dietram A., and David Tewksbury. "Framing, Agenda Setting, and Priming: The Evolution of Three Media Effects Models." *Journal of Communication* 57, no. 1 (2006): 9–20.

Schiff, Maurice. *Regional Integration and Development in Small States*. Washington, DC: World Bank, 2002.

Schimmelfennig, Frank. "NATO Enlargement: A Constructivist Explanation." *Security Studies* 8, nos. 2–3 (1998): 198–234.

Schirm, Stefan A. "Leaders in Need of Followers: Emerging Powers in Global Governance." *European Journal of International Relations* 16, no. 2 (2010): 197–221.

Schmidtke, Oliver, and Constantin Chira-Pascanut. "The Promise of Europe: Moldova and the Process of Europeanization." In *Europe's Last Frontier? Belarus, Moldova, and Ukraine between Russia and the European Union*, edited by Oliver Schmidtke and Serhy Yekelchyk, 133–56. New York: Palgrave Macmillan, 2008.

Schmitz, David F. *Thank God They're on Our Side: The United States and Right-Wing Dictatorships, 1921–1965*. Chapel Hill: University of North Carolina Press, 1999.

Schneider, Christina J. "Weak States and Institutionalized Bargaining Power in International Organizations." *International Studies Quarterly* 55, no. 2 (June 7, 2011): 331–55. https://doi.org/10.1111/j.1468-2478.2011.00651.x.

Schraeder, Peter J. "Ethnic Politics in Djibouti: From 'Eye of the Hurricane' to 'Boiling Cauldron.'" *African Affairs* 92, no. 367 (1993): 203–21.

Schulz, Carsten-Andreas. "Civilisation, Barbarism and the Making of Latin America's Place in 19th-Century International Society." *Millennium-Journal of International Studies* 42, no. 3 (2014): 837–59.

Schulz, Carsten-Andreas. "Territorial Sovereignty and the End of Inter-Cultural Diplomacy along the 'Southern Frontier.'" *European Journal of International Relations* 25, no. 3 (2018): 878–903.

Schulz, Carsten-Andreas, and Federico Rojas-De-Galarreta. "Chile as a Transpacific Bridge: Brokerage and Social Capital in the Pacific Basin." *Geopolitics*, 2020, 1–24. https://doi.org/10.1080/14650045.2020.1754196

Schweller, Randall L. "Bandwagoning for Profit: Bringing the Revisionist State Back In." *International Security* 19, no. 1 (1994): 72–107.

Scotland, Patricia. "COVID-19 Debt Relief Must Consider the Vulnerabilities of Small States." *The Commonwealth* (blog), July 27, 2020. https://thecommonwealth.org/media/news/opinion-covid-19-debt-relief-must-consider-vulnerabilities-small-states.

Sealey-Huggins, Leon. "'1.5° C to Stay Alive': Climate Change, Imperialism and Justice for the Caribbean." *Third World Quarterly* 38, no. 11 (2017): 2444–63.

Seawright, Jason, and John Gerring. "Case Selection Techniques in Case Study Research: A Menu of Qualitative and Quantitative Options." *Political Research Quarterly* 61, no. 2 (2008): 294–308.

Serbin, Andrés. "Onstage or Backstage? Latin America and US-Cuban Relations." In *A New Chapter in US-Cuba Relations: Social, Political, and Economic Implications*, edited by Eric Hershberg and William M. LeoGrande, 179–89. Cham: Springer International Publishing, 2016. https://doi.org/10.1007/978-3-319-29595-4_13.

Sharman, Jason. *Empires of the Weak: The Real Story of European Expansion and the Creation of the New World Order*. Princeton, NJ: Princeton University Press, 2019.

Sharman, Jason C. "Power and Discourse in Policy Diffusion: Anti-Money Laundering in Developing States." *International Studies Quarterly* 52, no. 3 (2008): 635–56.

Sharman, Jason C. "Sovereignty at the Extremes: Micro-States in World Politics." *Political Studies* 65, no. 3 (2017): 559–75.

Sharman, Jason C. "War, Selection, and Micro-States: Economic and Sociological Perspectives on the International System." *European Journal of International Relations* 21, no. 1 (2015): 194–214.

Sheller, Mimi. "Reconstructing Tourism in the Caribbean: Connecting Pandemic Recovery, Climate Resilience and Sustainable Tourism through Mobility Justice." *Journal of Sustainable Tourism* 29, no. 9 (2020): 1436–49.

Shifrinson, Joshua R. "NATO Enlargement and US Foreign Policy: The Origins, Durability, and Impact of an Idea." *International Politics* 57, no. 3 (2020): 342–70.

Shin, Gi-Wook, Hilary Izatt, and Rennie J. Moon. "Asymmetry of Power and Attention in Alliance Politics: The US–Republic of Korea Case." *Australian Journal of International Affairs* 70, no. 3 (2016): 235–55.

Shoemaker, Christopher C., and John W. Spanier. *Patron-Client State Relationships: Multilateral Crises in the Nuclear Age*. New York: Praeger, 1984.

Sikkink, Kathryn. *Evidence for Hope: Making Human Rights Work in the 21st Century*. Princeton, NJ: Princeton University Press, 2019.

Silva, Ronaldo Alexandre do Amaral. "Brasil-Paraguai: Marcos Da Política Pragmática Na Reaproximação Bilateral, 1954–1973," MA thesis, Universidade de Brasília, 2006.

Simon, Eszter. "When David Fights Goliath: A Two-Level Explanation of Small-State Role-Taking." *Foreign Policy Analysis* 15, no. 1 (2019): 118–35.

Singer, Marshall R. *Weak States in a World of Power: The Dynamics of International Relationships*, New York: Free Press, 1972.

Skidmore, David. "Explaining State Responses to International Change: The Structural Sources of Foreign Policy Rigidity and Change." In *Foreign Policy Restructuring*, edited by Jerel A. Rosati, Joe D. Hagan, and Martin W. Sampson III, 43–64. Columbia: University of South Carolina Press, 1994.

Sloan, Stanley R. "Donald Trump and NATO." In *Chaos in the Liberal Order: The Trump Presidency and International Politics in the Twenty-First Century*, edited by Robert Jervis, Francis J. Gavin, Joshua Rovner, and Diane N. Labrosse, 221–34. New York: Columbia University Press, 2018.

Soares de Lima, Maria Regina. "Political Economy of Brazilian Foreign Policy: Nuclear Energy, Trade, and Itaipu." PhD diss., Vanderbilt, 1986.

Sousa, Teresa de, and Carlos Gaspar. "Portugal, a União Europeia e a Crise." *Relações Internacionais*, no. 48 (December 2018): 99–114.

Steinmetz, Robert, and Anders Wivel, eds. *Small States in Europe: Challenges and Opportunities*. Farnham, UK: Ashgate Publishing, 2010.

Stobdan, P. *India and Bhutan: The Strategic Imperative*. Institute for Defence Studies & Analyses, 2014.

Strange, Susan. "The Persistent Myth of Lost Hegemony." *International Organization* 41, no. 4 (1987): 551–74.

Strating, Rebecca. "Small Power Hedging in an Era of Great-Power Politics: Southeast Asian Responses to China's Pursuit of Energy Security." *Asian Studies Review* 44, no. 1 (2020): 97–116.

Stuenkel, Oliver. "The Financial Crisis, Contested Legitimacy, and the Genesis of Intra-BRICS Cooperation." *Global Governance* 19, no. 4 (2013): 611–30.

Stuenkel, Oliver. *Post-Western World: How Emerging Powers Are Remaking Global Order.* Boston: Polity, 2016.

Styan, David. "China's Maritime Silk Road and Small States: Lessons from the Case of Djibouti." *Journal of Contemporary China* 29, no. 122 (2020): 191–206. https://doi.org/ 10.1080/10670564.2019.1637567.

Styan, David. "Djibouti: Changing Influence in the Horn's Strategic Hub." Briefing paper. Chatham House Africa Programme. London: Royal Institute of International Affairs, 2013.

Styan, David. "Djibouti: Small State Strategy at a Crossroads." *Third World Thematics: A TWQ Journal* 1, no. 1 (2016): 79–91.

Subedi, Surya P. "India-Nepal Security Relations and the 1950 Treaty: Time for New Perspectives." *Asian Survey* 34, no. 3 (1994): 273–84.

Suri, Jeremi. "The Cold War, Decolonization, and Global Social Awakenings: Historical Intersections." *Cold War History* 6, no. 3 (2006): 353–63.

Sutton, Paul Payne Anthony. "Lilliput under Threat: The Security Problems of Small Island and Enclave Developing States." *Political Studies* 41, no. 4 (1993): 579–93.

Suzana, Mariyam, Helen Walls, Richard Smith, and Johanna Hanefeld. "Achieving Universal Health Coverage in Small Island States: Could Importing Health Services Provide a Solution?" *BMJ Global Health* 3, (2018): 1–12.

Swedlund, Haley J. *The Development Dance: How Donors and Recipients Negotiate the Delivery of Foreign Aid.* Ithaca, NY: Cornell University Press, 2017.

Swedlund, Haley J. "Narratives and Negotiations in Foreign Aid: How Post-Genocide Rwanda Uses Narratives to Influence Perceptions of Power." In *International Negotiation and Political Narratives: A Case Study*, edited by Hampson Fen Osler and Amrita Narlikar, Chapter 11, 2022. Szalai, Máté. "Small Regimes in the Middle East: A Conceptual and Theoretical Alternative to Small States in a Non-Western Region." *International Politics*, 2020, 1–20. https://doi.org/10.1057/ s41311-020-00266-0

Taneja, Nisha, Samridhi Bimal, Taher Nadeem, and Riya Roy. "India-Bhutan Economic Relations." Working paper. New Delhi: Indian Council for Research on International Economic Relations, August 2019.

Tang, Chih-Mao. *Small States and Hegemonic Competition in Southeast Asia: Pursuing Autonomy, Security and Development amid Great Power Politics.* Routledge, 2018.

Taylor, Luke. "Uruguay Is Winning against Covid-19. This Is How." *British Medical Journal* 370 (2020): m3693. https://doi.org/10.1136/bmj.m3693.

Taylor, Richard. "The Tyranny of Size: Challenges of Health Administration in Pacific Island States." *Asia Pacific Journal of Health Management* 11, no. 3 (2016): 65.

Telias, Diego, and Francisco Urdinez. "China's Foreign Aid Determinants: Lessons from a Novel Dataset of the Mask Diplomacy During the COVID-19 Pandemic." *Journal of Current Chinese Affairs*, (2021): 1–29. https://doi.org/10.1177%2F1868102621 1020763.

Tetreault, Mary Ann. "Autonomy, Necessity, and the Small State: Ruling Kuwait in the Twentieth Century." *International Organization* 45, no. 4 (1991): 565–91.

Thambipillai, Pushpa. "Brunei Darussalam and ASEAN: Regionalism for a Small State." *Asian Journal of Political Science* 6, no. 1 (1998): 80–94.

Thapliyal, Sangeeta. "India and Nepal Relations: Politics and Perceptions." In *India in South Asia*, edited by Amit Ranjan, 75–91. Singapore: Springer, 2019.

Thapliyal, Sangeeta. "India and Nepal Treaty of 1950: The Continuing Discourse." *India Quarterly* 68, no. 2 (2012): 119–33.

Thorhallsson, Baldur. "European Integration: Genuine or False Shelter." In *Small States and Shelter Theory: Iceland's External Affairs*, edited by Baldur Thorhallsson, 128–67. Abingdon: Routledge, 2018.

Thorhallsson, Baldur, ed. *Small States and Shelter Theory: Iceland's External Affairs*. Abingdon: Routledge, 2018.

Thorhallsson, Baldur. *The Role of Small States in the European Union*. Aldershot: Ashgate, 2001.

Thorhallsson, Baldur. "Small States in the UN Security Council: Means of Influence?" *Hague Journal of Diplomacy* 7, no. 2 (2012): 135–60.

Thorhallsson, Baldur. "Small States in the UNSC and the EU: Structural Weaknesses and Ability to Influence." In *Small States in a Legal World*, edited by Petra Butler and Caroline Morris, 35–64. Cheltenham: Springer, 2017.

Tickner, Arlene B., and Karen Smith. *International Relations from the Global South: Worlds of Difference*. New York: Routledge, 2020.

Tkach, Vlada. "Moldova and Transdniestria: Painful Past, Deadlocked Present, Uncertain Future." *European Security* 8, no. 2 (1999): 130–59.

Tritto, Angela. "The Belt and Road Initiative as a Catalyst for Institutional Development: Evidence from Indonesia, Malaysia, and Myanmar." Thought Leadership Brief. Hong Kong: Institute for Emerging Market Studies, September 2019. https://archives.ust.hk/dspace/bitstream/9999/47810/1/IEMS-Thought-Leadership-Brief-no30.pdf.

Tsebelis, George. "Lessons from the Greek Crisis." *Journal of European Public Policy* 23, no. 1 (2016): 25–41.

Tull, Denis M. "Rebuilding Mali's Army: The Dissonant Relationship between Mali and Its International Partners." *International Affairs* 95, no. 2 (2019): 405–22.

Tuman, John P., and Majid Shirali. "The Political Economy of Chinese Foreign Direct Investment in Developing Areas." *Foreign Policy Analysis* 13, no. 1 (2017): 154–67.

Turner, Mark, Sonam Chuki, and Jit Tshering. "Democratization by Decree: The Case of Bhutan." *Democratization* 18, no. 1 (2011): 184–210.

Tversky, A., and D. Kahneman. "The Framing of Decisions and the Psychology of Choice." *Science* 211, no. 4481 (1981): 453–58.

United States Department of State. "U.S. Relations with Mali." September 6, 2018. https://www.state.gov/u-s-relations-with-mali/.

Urdinez, Francisco, Fernando Mouron, Luis L. Schenoni, and Amâncio J. de Oliveira. "Chinese Economic Statecraft and US Hegemony in Latin America: An Empirical Analysis, 2003–2014." *Latin American Politics and Society* 58, no. 4 (2016): 3–30.

Urlacher, Brian R. *International Relations as Negotiation*. Routledge, 2015.

"US-Baltic Charter." Estonian Ministry of Foreign Affairs, January 16, 1998. https://vm.ee/en/us-baltic-charter.

Uvin, Peter. "Difficult Choices in the New Post-Conflict Agenda: The International Community in Rwanda after the Genocide." *Third World Quarterly* 22, no. 2 (2001): 177–89.

Vahl, Marius, and Michael Emerson. "Moldova and the Transnistrian Conflict." *JEMIE - Journal on Ethnopolitics and Minority Issues in Europe* 1 (2004): 1–29.

Vasquez, John A., and Richard W. Mansbach. "The Issue Cycle: Conceptualizing Long-Term Global Political Change." *International Organization* 37, no. 2 (1983): 257–79. https://doi.org/10.1017/S0020818300034378.

Verdun, Amy. "Small States and the Global Economic Crisis: An Assessment." *European Political Science* 12 (2013): 276–93.

Verma, Monica. "Rise of China and India: Nepal's Future in an Affluent Neighbourhood." In *Revisiting Nepal's Foreign Policy in Contemporary Global Power Structure*, edited by Premod Jaiswal, 166–84. G. B. Books, 2017.

Vital, D. *The Survival of Small States*, London: Oxford University Press, 1971.

Vital, David. *The Inequality of States: A Study of the Small Power in International Relations*. Oxford: Clarendon Press, 1967.

Vleck, William. "The Caribbean Confronts the OECD: Tax Competition and Diplomacy." In *The Diplomacies of Small States: Between Vulnerability and Resilience*, edited by Andrew F. Cooper and Timothy M. Shaw, 264–78. New York: Palgrave Macmillan, 2009.

Waltz, Kenneth. *Man, the State, and War: A Theoretical Analysis*. New York: Columbia University Press, 1959.

Waltz, Kenneth. *Theory of International Politics*. Reading, MA: Addison-Wesley Pub. Co., 1979.

Waltz, Susan. "Universalizing Human Rights: The Role of Small States in the Construction of the Universal Declaration of Human Rights." *Human Rights Quarterly* 23 (2001): 44.

Warner, Jason. "Beyond the Collective: The Comparative Strategic Utility of the African Union and RECs in Individual National Security Pursuits." In *African Foreign Policies in International Institutions*, edited by Jason Warner and Timothy M. Shaw, 63–77. New York: Palgrave Macmillan, 2018.

Warntjen, Andreas. "Between Bargaining and Deliberation: Decision-Making in the Council of the European Union." *Journal of European Public Policy* 17, no. 5 (2010): 665–79.

Webber, Jeffery R. "Carlos Mesa, Evo Morales, and a Divided Bolivia (2003–2005)." *Latin American Perspectives* 37, no. 3 (2010): 51–70. https://doi.org/10.1177/0094582X10364033.

Webber, Jeffery R. "From Naked Barbarism to Barbarism with Benefits: Neoliberal Capitalism, Natural Gas Policy, and the Evo Morales Government in Bolivia." In *Post-Neoliberalism in the Americas*, edited by Laura MacDonald and Arne Ruckert, 105–19. New York: Palgrave MacMillan, 2009.

Wehner, Leslie. "The Foreign Policy of South American Small Powers in Regional and International Politics." In *Handbook on the Politics of Small States*, edited by Godfrey Baldacchino and Anders Wivel, 259–77. Cheltenham: Edward Elgar Publishing, 2020.

Welch, David A. *Painful Choices: A Theory of Foreign Policy Change*. Princeton, NJ: Princeton University Press, 2005.

Wendt, Alexander, and Michael Barnett. "Dependent State Formation and Third World Militarization." *Review of International Studies* 19, no. 4 (2009): 321–47. https://doi.org/10.1017/S0260210500118248.

Westad, Odd Arne. *The Global Cold War: Third World Interventions and the Making of Our Times*. New York: Cambridge University Press, 2005.

Whitfield, Lindsay, ed. *The Politics of Aid: African Strategies for Dealing with Donors*. Oxford: Oxford University Press, 2008.

Williams, Kristen, Steven Lobell, and Neal Jesse, eds. *Beyond Great Powers and Hegemons: Why Secondary States Support, Follow, or Challenge*. Stanford University Press, 2012.

Wing, Susanna D. "Mali: Politics of a Crisis." *African Affairs* 112, no. 448 (2013): 476–85.

Wivel, Anders. "The Security Challenge of Small EU Member States: Interests, Identity and the Development of the EU as a Security Actor." *Journal of Common Market Studies* 43, no. 2 (2005): 393–412.

Wivel, Anders, and Matthew Crandall. "Punching Above Their Weight, but Why? Explaining Denmark and Estonia in the Transatlantic Relationship." *Journal of Transatlantic Studies* 17 (2019): 392–419.

Wohlforth, William C., Benjamin de Carvalho, Halvard Leira, and Iver B. Neumann. "Moral Authority and Status in International Relations: Good States and the Social Dimension of Status Seeking." *Review of International Studies* 44, no. 3 (2018): 526–46.

Wohlgemuth, Lennart, and Oliver Saasa. "Changing Aid Relations in Zambia." Policy Management Brief. Maastricht: ECDPM, 2008.

Wolf, Reinhard. "Debt, Dignity, and Defiance: Why Greece Went to the Brink." *Review of International Political Economy* 25, no. 6 (2018): 829–53.

Womack, Brantly. *Asymmetry and International Relationships*. New York: Cambridge University Press, 2016.

Womack, Brantly. "How Size Matters: The United States, China and Asymmetry." *Journal of Strategic Studies* 24, no. 4 (2001): 123–50.

Womack, Brantly, and Hao Yufan, eds. *Rethinking the Triangle: Washington-Beijing-Taipei*. Singapore: World Scientific, 2016.

Wong, Audrye. "Managing Small Allies Amidst Patron–Adversary Rapprochement: A Tale of Two Koreas." *Asian Security* 16, no. 1 (2020): 107–26.

World Health Organization. "Building Resilience: A Key Pillar of Health 2020 and the Sustainable Development Goals – Examples from the WHO Small Countries Initiative." Venice, Italy: World Health Organization, 2017. https://www.euro.who.int/__data/assets/pdf_file/0020/341075/resilience-report-050617-h1550-print.pdf.

Wu, Shang-Su. *The Defence Capabilities of Small States: Singapore and Taiwan's Responses to Strategic Desperation*. New York: Palgrave Macmillan, 2016.

Yan, Xuetong. "Chinese Values vs. Liberalism: What Ideology Will Shape the International Normative Order?" *Chinese Journal of International Politics* 11, no. 1 (2018): 1–22. https://doi.org/10.1093/cjip/poy001.

Yasin, Yasin Mohammed. "Regional Dynamics of Inter-Ethnic Conflicts in the Horn of Africa: An Analysis of the Afar-Somali Conflict in Ethiopia and Djibouti." PhD diss., University of Hamburg, 2010.

Yates, Douglas A. "France and Africa." In *Africa and the World: Bilateral and Multilateral International Diplomacy*, edited by Dawn Nagar and Charles Mutasa, 95–118. Cham: Palgrave Macmillan, 2018.

Yean, Tham Siew. "The Belt and Road Initiative in Malaysia: Case of the Kuantan Port." *Perspective*. Singapore: ISEAS Yusof Ishak Institute, 2019.

Yean, Tham Siew. "Chinese Investment in Malaysia: Five Years into the BRI." *Perspective*. Singapore: ISEAS Yusof Ishak Institute, February 27, 2018. https://www.iseas.edu.sg/images/pdf/ISEAS_Perspective_2018_11@50.pdf?

Yee-Kuang Heng. "Small States." In *Oxford Research Encyclopedia of International Studies*, July 30, 2020. https://doi.org/10.1093/acrefore/9780190846626.013.545.

Yu, Hong. "China's Belt and Road Initiative and Its Implications for Southeast Asia." *Asia Policy* 24, no. 1 (2017): 117–22.

Zahariadis, Nikolaos. "Bargaining Power and Negotiation Strategy: Examining the Greek Bailouts, 2010–2015." *Journal of European Public Policy* 24, no. 5 (2017): 675–94.

Zambon, Francesco, and Leda Nemer. "The WHO Regional Office for Europe Small Countries Initiative: An Introduction." *Public Health Panorama* 4, no. 2 (2018): 259–64.

Zarakol, Ayşe. "'Rise of the Rest': As Hype and Reality." *International Relations* 33, no. 2 (2019): 213–28.

Zartman, I. William, and Jeffrey Z. Rubin. *Power and Negotiation.* Ann Arbor: University of Michigan Press, 2002.

Zemanová, Štěpánka. "When Could New 'Potent Small States' Emerge? A Study of the Recent Metamorphosis of Czech Human Rights Foreign Policy." *Journal of International Relations and Development* 18, no. 2 (2015): 129–54.

Zin, Min. "Myanmar in 2019: Deepening International Pariah Status and Backsliding Peace Process at Home." *Asian Survey* 60, no. 1 (February 1, 2020): 140–45. https://doi.org/10.1525/as.2020.60.1.140.

Zorbas, Eugenia. "Aid Dependence and Policy Independence: Explaining the Rwandan Paradox." In *Remaking Rwanda: Statebuilding and Human Rights after Mass Violence,* edited by Scott Strauss and Lars Waldorf, 103–17. Madison: University of Wisconsin Press, 2011.

Index

For the benefit of digital users, indexed terms that span two pages (e.g., 52–53) may, on occasion, appear on only one of those pages.

Tables and figures are indicated by *t* and *f* following the page number